ames H. Gray is one of western Canada's leading popular historians. Born in Manitoba in 1906, he worked for the *Winnipeg Free Press* for many years and was editor of several other publications. He is the author of many bestselling and award-winning books on the social history of western Canada, including *Booze, Red Lights on the Prairies, The Winter Years,* and *Men Against the Desert.* Gray has received numerous honours, including the Alberta Order of Excellence in 1987, the Order of Canada in 1988, and the 1995 Pierre Berton Award for "distinguished achievement in popularizing Canadian history." He lives in Calgary.

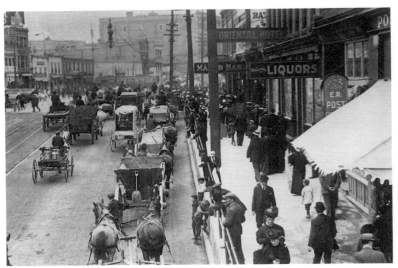

Courtesy Provincial Archives of Manitoba/N7968

The Boy from Winnipeg

JAMES H. GRAY

FIFTH
HOUSE
PUBLISHERS

SASKATOON & CALGARY

Cover and interior illustrations by Myra Lowenthal
Cover illustration hand-coloured by Laurel Wolanski
Frontispiece, "Main Street, Winnipeg, c. 1904," reproduced
courtesy Provincial Archives of Manitoba/N7968
Cover and series logo designed by Sandra Hastie
and John Luckhurst/GDL

The publisher gratefully acknowledges the support received from
The Canada Council and Heritage Canada.

Printed and bound in Canada by Friesens, Altona
96 97 98 99 00 / 5 4 3 2 1

Canadian Cataloguing in Publication Data

Gray, James, H. 1906–
The boy from Winnipeg
2nd ed.–

(Western Canadian classics)
ISBN 1-895618-71-1

1. Gray, James H., 1906 2. Journalists-
Canada–Biography 3. Winnipeg (Man.)–History.
I. Title. II. Series.

PN4913.G68A3 1995 971.27'43 C95-920079-7

FIFTH HOUSE LTD.
#201-165-3rd Avenue S
Saskatoon SK Canada
S7K 1L8

#9-6125-11 Street SE
Calgary AB Canada
T2H 2L6

CONTENTS

For Pat, for Alan, and for Linda

OTHER WESTERN CANADIAN CLASSICS

———————

Red Lights on the Prairies by James H. Gray
Booze: When Whisky Ruled the West by James H. Gray
Men Against the Desert by James H. Gray
Red Crow: Warrior Chief by Hugh A. Dempsey
The Palliser Expedition: The Dramatic Story of
Western Canadian Exploration, 1857–1860 by Irene M. Spry

t was the first city of the Prairies—Winnipeg. The Gateway to the West. The Chicago of Canada. And for one five-year-old boy from Whitemouth, Manitoba, his new home. James Gray's family had moved to Winnipeg in 1911 in search of better opportunities. And there was every reason to believe that the largest metropolis in Western Canada could fulfil these hopes. Between the turn of the century and the second year of the Great War, Winnipeg's population quadrupled in size, jumping from 45,000 to an astounding 187,000. In the process, the city emerged as the dominant wholesale, manufacturing, commercial, and financial centre for the Prairies; railway tracks entered the Manitoban capital from no less than fifteen directions in 1916, while local grain companies marketed and shipped more wheat than any other city in the world. But just as the Winnipeg boom collapsed and gave way to a long slow decline beginning in the 1920s, Harry Gray's weakness for booze and his inability to keep a steady job reduced his family to "a yo-yo existence" of ups-and-downs. Little did anyone realize at the time, perhaps most of all young James, how the story of these childhood years on the streets of Winnipeg would be transformed half a century later into an award-winning bestseller.

The Boy from Winnipeg was written by James Gray to appease an angry publisher. In 1966, some two decades after it had been prepared, Macmillan of Canada released *The Winter Years*, Gray's first-hand account of life in Winnipeg during the Great Depression. Under the terms of the contract, Gray was obligated to submit his next project to Macmillan for possible consideration. Several chapters on the agricultural crisis in the prairie dry belt, however, had been dropped from *The Winter Years* manuscript. And when Saskatoon-based *Western Producer* expressed interest in a book on the farm problems of the 1930s, Gray immediately pulled together the rejected chapters and submitted the work under the stirring title *Men Against the Desert*. This new book appeared in the late fall of 1967 under the Prairie Books imprint and, like *The Winter Years*, was favourably received across the country—by all except Macmillan. The company was furious that Gray had published with a competitor, and even though he pointed out that the agricultural material had been turned down, Macmillan continued to insist that Gray had violated his agreement. Eventually, the misunderstanding was resolved when Gray agreed to produce a new book on his early years in Winnipeg.

This new project, according to Gray, came easily—and for good reason. By the late 1960s, he had some three decades' experience behind him in journalism and public relations. In 1935, after three, long miserable years on relief, Gray literally wrote his way into a staff reporter's job with the *Winnipeg Free Press*. There, he covered all kinds of events and stories before being promoted to editorial writer in 1942 and then Ottawa correspondent four years later. These were heady days for Canadian journalism, when the very nature of the country and its government and institutions, especially in the postwar world, were hotly debated. And Gray happily waded into the discussion, drawing upon his own Depression experiences, until he lost his job in 1947 because of a bitter dispute with his editor over Canadian trade policy. He made his way back to Winnipeg and did some freelance work for a short time before relocating permanently to Calgary, where he served as editor of two journals and then public relations manager for the Home Oil Company for the next twenty years. He turned his back on this lucrative position in 1966 at the age of sixty—when most people are contemplating retirement—to embark on a new career as an historian.

The Boy from Winnipeg benefited greatly from Gray's

journalism skills, in particular his keen sense for a good anecdote and his straightforward, engaging style. He also tried to break out of the autobiographical constraints and broaden the focus of the story as much as possible to include information about places and events from Winnipeg's heyday. But what animates the book are the "do-it-yourself boyhood" joys that he experienced and retells so vividly. Here was a boy who, at his mother's urging, was forced to retrieve his drunken father from the nearest bar, who never stayed for any length of time in one neighbourhood and was constantly changing schools, and who was no better off than the unwelcome foreigners living in poverty in Winnipeg's notorious north end. And yet, instead of wallowing in his misfortune, he and the other boys of his generation "took our fun where we found it . . . This was our Winnipeg." What follows, then, is an entertaining—at times, compelling—account of the episodes that shaped and defined his childhood years: from hawking newspapers announcing the start of the Great War to supplying block ice from his wagon during the 1919 Winnipeg General Strike to getting his first pair of long pants for his new job as an office boy on the Winnipeg Grain Exchange three years later.

The Boy from Winnipeg was released in 1970 and proved a resounding success—even Gray was pleasantly surprised by the reception. There was no denying, though, that his childhood memories touched the hearts of thousands of appreciative readers. Indeed, the accolades, including the University of British Columbia medal for popular biography, were well-deserved. Gray's story may not be representative, but it certainly adds a richly human dimension to our understanding of Prairie working-class life during the second decade of this century. "They were my Huck Finn years," Gray fondly recounts today with a boyish grin on his face, "and I was Tom Sawyer."

BILL WAISER
UNIVERSITY OF SASKATCHEWAN

CHAPTER ONE

This Was the Town
And These Were the People

innipeg during the era of the First World War: what a marvelous, exciting, and wonder-filled world it was for small boys! There were things to do and places to go, and discoveries to make with automobiles, motion pictures, airplanes, and radio. Seldom have two decades been more wonder-filled for growing up in than the first twenty years of our century. Truly, we could say with Thomas Hood that no sun peeping in at morn ever brought too long a day.

The Winnipeg of my boyhood was a lusty, gutsy, bawdy frontier boom-town roaring through an unequalled economic debauch on its way to the grand-daddy of all economic hangovers. The spree lasted for thirteen years and the hangover in varying degrees of severity persisted for twenty-six. From a city of 42,000 in 1901 Winnipeg ballooned to 136,000 in 1911 and 160,000 by 1916. In a single decade more than 500,000 immigrants found their way from the four corners of Europe to Western Canada. All of them passed through Winnipeg, and a good one in ten of them went no farther. Winnipeg was not only the "Gateway to the West", as the boosters advertised, it was the tollgate to the West. Nothing—neither people, nor goods, nor chattels—moved into or out of prairie Canada save through Winnipeg. The tolls levied by Winnipeg business, industry, commerce, and labour sparked the Winnipeg

1

boom and its own population explosion. All summer long, British and European immigrants trudged back and forth between the Canadian Pacific and the Canadian Northern stations en route to their new homesteads. Carpenters, brick-layers, stonemasons, tinsmiths, plasterers, and painters worked from dawn to dark putting up new railway shops, new warehouses for wholesalers, and new homes for the thou-sands of trainmen, machinists, retail store clerks, bank clerks, and bartenders who were flocking into town on every train from the east.

Many of the railway employees and office clerks had been recruited in England, Scotland, and Ireland. Others came out to join relatives or friends who had settled earlier. But whether they were recruited or came independently, they fell into patterns that were almost inexorable. On arriving in Winnipeg they moved into districts with their own, either their own occupationally or their own ethnically. The railway shop trades established Anglo-Saxon colonies in the Weston area, hard by the C.P.R. shops on Logan Avenue; in Riverview and south Fort Rouge around the C.N.R. shops; and in Trans-cona where other C.N. and C.P. yards were established. Though no statistics were gathered, the general impression was that the Scots dominated the Canadian Pacific shops while the English tradesmen favoured the Canadian Northern Railway.

When the population influx began, Winnipeg's popula-tion was composed predominantly of Canadian-born Anglo-Saxons, something like 26,000 out of 42,000 in 1901. In the next decade they became a submerged minority. The pre-boom working class lived mainly in the downtown area in streets given over to brick row houses three storeys high with great verandahs stretching the entire length, or in single houses on the streets paralleling the C.P.R. tracks. The merchant and upper white-collar classes lived between Broadway and the Assiniboine River, but the grain brokers and economic upper crust had already begun to move across the river into Fort Rouge and Crescentwood, and along Wellington Crescent.

The city was totally unprepared for the mass influx that

hit after the turn of the century. Newcomers crowded in with relatives or friends, or into the downtown row houses, sometimes one family to a room. A typical example of settlement patterns was the experience of the small community of about 1,000 Jews who had come to Winnipeg by the turn of the century. The Jewish community was concentrated in the Point Douglas area between the C.P.R. main line, the Red River, and Main Street. In the next fifteen years almost 1,000 Jews a year moved into Winnipeg and piled into the ghetto. The earlier arrivals, as soon as they could acquire the necessary resources, moved northward on both sides of Main Street, often into still uncompleted houses. The ghetto spread until the Jewish district stretched clear down to Powers and later to Arlington Street and as far north as St. John's Avenue. There was throughout these years a steady upgrading of housing accommodation as the immigrants prospered and could afford to buy or rent houses of their own. But there was never enough low-rental accommodation because, in addition to the Jews, the Ukrainians, Germans, Russians, and Poles were flocking in by their thousands, and the great majority also went to the North End.

The Anglo-Saxon immigrants spread west from Sherbrook Street, the Icelanders and Swedes gathered into their own community along Sargent Avenue. The Anglo-Saxons who did move north usually leap-frogged over the Jewish-Ukrainian-Polish area to the old area around St. John's Cathedral and St. John's College. Gradually as the years passed the ethnic and national groups tended to collect into homogeneous communities; but in the beginning the so-called foreigners occupied one gigantic melting pot north of the C.P.R. tracks. In pre-war Winnipeg, nobody paid much attention to the racial or national origins of the foreign immigrants. The official practice was to identify them with their native regions in the Austro-Hungarian Empire. Thus the census tables listed Ruthenians, Moldavians, Bukovinians, Serbians, Slovakians, and Galicians. It was not until the mid-1920s that these designations disappeared in favour of Ukrainian, Russian, or

Polish. The attitude of the Anglo-Saxons to the Europeans was epitomized by the canvassers for *Henderson's City Directory*. When they came to a family with an unpronounceable name, or an unspellable name, they simply used the word "foreigner" which seemed to satisfy everybody. To the average Winnipegger when the need arose to recognize the existence of the new Canadians, the generic term most widely used was "Galician".

Even without the tendency of the newcomers to live with their own kind, Winnipeg, by the very nature of its geographic setting, was pre-ordained to develop into a sprawling, gap-toothed collection of ghettos. It was located on a site that would have unhinged the mind of any town planner who blundered into the job of laying out the city. Nature had crossed it with two meandering rivers and further divided it with three creeks. The course of the Red River was mainly north, when it was not veering sharply to east or west. The Assiniboine flowed mainly eastward to its confluence with the Red, except for the half-circles it cut to the south and back to the north. The streets evolved haphazardly. Mainly they followed cow paths and buffalo trails to water, with criss-crossing along what had been short-cuts between neighbours. Then along came the railway contractors to carve up the area into even more segments, like a berserk pastry cook attacking an apple pie with a meat cleaver. In this environment, Winnipeg came to life as a clutch of frame buildings around what later became Market Square where the gaudiest gingerbread city hall in all Christendom was erected. Until the turn of the century, Main Street, which curved in a flat arc between the Hudson's Bay Company store on the south and the C.P.R. tracks on the north, was the business and retail street. When Eaton's came in with the twentieth century and built the biggest store west of Toronto at Portage Avenue and Donald Street, the merchandising centre of gravity began shifting rapidly up Portage Avenue. By this time the city's street patterns were well established. In the downtown area they took off in all directions from Portage and Main and from the

City Hall square. Elsewhere the main thoroughfares tended to parallel the nearest river or railway line and the cross streets were laid out at right angles.

Even without the railway lines, Winnipeg streets would have been a maze; the railways turned it into a nightmare. The C.P.R. crossed the Red River into the city from the east and made a beeline out of it to the west. It located its main yards and station in what eventually came to be quite close to the geographic centre of the town. A quarter-mile to the south of the C.P.R. yards were the Midland Railway yards at the end of its line which entered the city from the southwest. The Canadian Northern main line crossed the Red River half a mile or so south of the C.P.R., cut sharply to the south, and then left by the southwest quadrant. One railway from the south came in on the east side of the Red River to the C.P.R. depot and another came in on the west side to Union Station. The Canadian Northern located its main assembly yards and shops in the southwest area and nestled its freight yards in behind the station on Main Street. Finally the two main railways were connected by transfer tracks along the banks of the Red River. Across the Red River to the east were the suburbs of St. Vital, Norwood, and St. Boniface.

This, then, was the chaotic hunting ground into which the hordes of real estate developers stormed with the boom. They bought up surrounding farmland and subdivided it into twenty-five-foot lots stretching far out into the country. Such new subdivisions as Kirkfield Park, Silver Heights, St. James, East Kildonan, West St. Paul, St. Charles, Tuxedo, River Heights, Fort Garry, Elm Park, Windsor Park, and Deer Lodge were promoted with specially conducted weekend tours by streetcar and automobile. The enthusiastic unwary not only bought lots on which to build houses, they bought additional adjoining lots as investments which they hoped to sell at a fat profit to pay for their lots and the houses on them. Geography, the railways, and the real estate developers combined to turn Winnipeg into a series of self-contained enclaves separated by great stretches of empty prairie, and pock-marked within by vacant lots in almost every block. No civic authority regulated the developers, so residential building crowded in on industrial areas and industries collected around the railway trackage in residential districts.

Inevitably with the massive influx of new Canadians, who were dumped and forgotten in the North End, monstrous social problems soon plagued the town. Juvenile delinquency became an increasing problem among the foreign-born. When the real estate boom collapsed in 1913, hundreds of immigrant families became so utterly destitute that the city had to establish a welfare system of sorts to provide emergency food. All the church groups became involved in welfare undertakings. After the outbreak of war, the discrimination against all aliens, particularly the Germans, made mere survival an ordeal for many. But while the patriotic pew-holders were demanding the deportation of aliens at their church and lodge meetings, their wives were down in the North End succouring the alien women and children.

Early Winnipeg was typically frontier in its ambivalent moral attitudes. It was such a Sabbatarian stronghold that milk and bread deliveries were banned and not even streetcars could operate on Sunday. But it voted joyously for segregated prostitution, and tolerated wide-open gambling and drunkenness. The mass migration that brought in the ambitious, the devout, the honest, and the skilful also included its full quota of thieves, pickpockets, card sharps, confidence men, madams, prostitutes, and pimps. Winnipeg by 1910, to paraphrase the Reverend J. G. Shearer, could have claimed the title of vice capital of the country.

The Reverend Shearer was a Presbyterian divine who visited Winnipeg in the summer of 1910 and returned to Toronto to be interviewed by the Toronto *Globe*. He said, among other things, that "Winnipeg had the rottenest condition of social vice to be found in Canada." He accused the police of conniving in the operation of a red-light district and deplored the open defiance of the liquor laws, which were scandalously lax in the first place. The accusations erupted into a shouting war in Winnipeg. The newspapers denounced Dr. Shearer and the ministerial association denounced the newspapers. To restore peace and quiet, the Roblin government named Judge H. A. Robson to investigate. His report stated:

> I have to report that a policy of toleration of the offence in question, in a limited area, with regulations as to conduct, was adopted by the Police Commissioners; that such an area was accordingly established by immoral women; that since October, 1909, there was no attempt to restrict the increase of houses of vice in the area and the number of houses of this class grew from 29 to 50; that illicit liquor dealing has been general and continuous in the houses in this area, and that, as already particularly shown, the law regarding the same has not been properly enforced; that the result of the above state of affairs has been the disturbance of peace and good order in the locality, a menace to morals and great depreciation in the value of property of neighbouring residents.

At the Robson hearings it was revealed that Winnipeg had had several segregated areas for prostitution before 1905. Then a reform wave hit the town and the houses were closed. The prostitutes scattered through the city and their soliciting on the streets soon became a common nuisance. So in 1908 the police commission decided to go back to segregation. The chief of police called in Minnie Woods, the leading madam of the day, and asked her to pass the word around among her fellow bawdy-house keepers. In looking around for a red-light area, Police Chief McRae selected one which appeared perfect for the purpose—MacFarlane and Annabella streets near the tip of Point Douglas, north of the C.P.R. tracks. These adjacent streets were bounded on the west by a huge and odoriferous artificial-gas coking plant, on the east by a lumber yard, and on the north by the Red River and an electric power

7

station. Geographically as well as sexually segregated, it was within easy walking distance of the C.P.R. station and the Main Street hotels.

When the area was selected, the fifty houses within the pocket were occupied by perfectly respectable hard-working families. That hardly concerned the chief of police. He called in a real estate agent and put him in touch with all the madams, and very soon the owners of the Annabella and MacFarlane street houses were being bought out. Nobody consulted the residents about turning their district into a red-light district. When they discovered what was going on they objected loudly but could attract no attention, not even from the patrolmen on the beat. Soon the respectable citizens were having their meals and slumbers interrupted by drunks blundering into their houses looking for sexual service stations. Residents en route back and forth to work were propositioned by girls sitting in the whore-house windows. Sometimes they had to step over and around drunks tossed into the street by the bouncers employed by the houses. Occasionally they were afflicted, they said, by the sight of the girls, naked to the waist, riding horse-back up and down Annabella Street in mid-afternoon.

For the residents it was a losing battle and in the end the bawdy-houses took over the whole district. The *Henderson's City Directory* of 1911 found both streets given over largely to such householders as Lulu Thornton, Lucy Dupont, Minnie Woods, Della Westall, Stella Wilson, Mignon Farcor, Goldie Jones, Addie Divine, Doris Venette, and forty other madams. It was conservatively estimated before the Robson Commission that two hundred prostitutes plied their trade in these two short city blocks.

The Robson report put the question of segregated prostitution squarely up to the Winnipeg citizenry, and it became the issue of the next election between the forces of righteousness and the legions of evil. E.D. Martin, with the support of most of the churches, papered the town with 100,000 leaflets detailing the Robson inquiry revelations about the segregated brothels. Martin was opposed by W. Sanford Evans, who was mayor during the whore-house takeover. Mr. Evans was vindicated by a comfortable 1,500-vote majority and the brothels on Annabella Street continued to operate openly until the trade fell victim to amateur competition, a full thirty years later. Mr. Evans, who was the editor of the *Winnipeg Telegram,* later became the Conservative Party leader in the Manitoba legislature.

Aside altogether from prostitution, pre-prohibition Winnipeg was as crime-ridden a city as there was in Canada, and liquor was at the bottom of it all. Whisky sold for a dime a shot, beer a nickel a glass. For many that was only a down payment. After a few drinks they would fail to notice the fingers extracting the final payment from their pockets. Between the C.P.R. and Union stations the concentration of hotel bars per block would have rivalled the saloon concentration in the Chicago loop. From Higgins Avenue to Portage Avenue pedestrians were never beyond the range of the aroma of booze that wafted through the windows and doors of the hotels. On several intersections there were hotels on three of the four corners. On the east side of Main Street in the six blocks between the C.P.R. and Market Street were the Alberta, Nugget, Mansion House, Albion, Occidental, Imperial, Belmont, Brunswick, Strathcona, Grand Union, Manitoba, and Iroquois hotels. On the opposite side of the street were the Manor, Maple Leaf, Oriental, Bell, Avenue, Club, Exchange, and McLaren. Off Main Street on the side streets and on King Street were the Seymour, National, Midland, Majestic, Lombard, Leland, LaClaire, King George, Jimmy's, Oxford, Queen's, Roblin, Royal Albert, Royal Oak, St. Andrews, St. Charles, Reno, Arlington, Bank, Cabinet, Corona, Grand Central, Grange, and Frontenac. South Main Street was comparatively arid. The Empire Hotel occupied a full block north of Union Station, and there were three regimental canteens on the west side together with the Winnipeg and Commercial hotels.

Many of the hotel bars had poolrooms attached, where

the players could get soused while they gambled with the pool sharks who infested the joints. Between the poolroom and the next hotel there was likely to be either a wholesale boozerie or a "Free Admission Parlour" stocked with nickelodeons and slot machines in front and a shooting gallery along the rear walls. After the customers became sated with the flicking-card movies, slot machines, and target practice, they could wind up the entertainment with a prostitute in the back room. The Free Admission Parlours operated with but a single rigid rule—they were all death on kids. Once on an excursion along Main Street bound for a Saturday movie, several of us twelve-year-olds were lured into a parlour opposite the City Hall by the open doors, the "free admission" sign, and the sight of all the machines standing along the walls. We went in and had barely started to pull the handles when a loud-voiced woman exploded through a curtained door at the back of the room and ran us off. Being chased away from the machines naturally increased our curiosity about them, particularly about what they contained that growing boys were not allowed to look at. Thereafter we seldom passed a Free Admission Parlour without stopping to case the joint from the doorway, and weigh our chances of sneaking a peek at the machines without getting caught. When we eventually worked up the nerve to try again, we discovered that none of the handles on the machines would work without inserting a nickel. We were never curious enough to risk a nickel on them and our interest gradually waned, though the parlours survived well into the 1920s.

In and around the railway stations were usually concentrated the greatest assemblage of pimps, pickpockets, confidence men, thugs, and sneak thieves in the country. The confidence men—"boosters", they were called—concentrated on immigrants and farmers. Many of them were products of the North End slums and could speak half a dozen languages which enabled them to lure the immigrants into their webs. If the newcomers got past the confidence men, they had to contend with the snatch-and-run baggage thieves who hung around watching for something to steal. Pickpockets were such a menace that the police department had a special detail which concentrated on "dips".

The only way into or out of Winnipeg was by train. Main Street between the railway stations, therefore, became the gauntlet every immigrant, every Christmas-shopping farm family, every going or coming harvester, had to run. By their sheer numbers, the bars were an impossible temptation for the bush workers and railway builders who hit the town with their season's pay cheques burning holes in their pockets. Even for the strong-willed who were full of resolve to stay sober, Main Street was hopelessly booby-trapped. Between the railway stations and the nearest bank they had to thread their way through more thieves and confidence men, masquerading as workers, but whose only work was to lure the newcomers into the bars and get them drunk enough to separate them from their summer's wages.

The Winnipeg bars were far from a Canadian version of the Englishman's pub, where a workingman could while the hours away sitting around with his cronies and a pint or two. The Winnipeg bars were for getting drunk in standing up, in an age when manhood was often measured by the amount of whisky that could be consumed standing at a bar. Bellying up to the bar and knocking back two fingers of whisky was the manly thing to do as a prelude to almost any kind of activity. For the thieves who infested the boozeries, it was a twelve-month season. They worked on the incoming harvesters in the early summer, the outgoing harvesters and the farmers coming into town with their families in the fall, the railway construction workers in the early winter, and the immigrants and bush workers in the spring. Only in the dead of winter did they fall on lean times when they had to depend on what they could steal or beat out of the permanent residents. However, over the years, the resident drinkers learned to isolate themselves from the riff-raff, and confined their drinking to bars where they were known. I can well remember my father verbally chastising his brothers for stopping off at what he called the C.P.R. hotels—those nearest the station—when they arrived in Winnipeg. He had good reason to know the danger inherent in tarrying too long in a strange bar, about which more anon.

With such a concentration of bars as Winnipeg boasted in 1913, it had to be one of the most drunken cities in the country. If this cannot be proven statistically owing to lack of data for municipal crime, it can at least be indicated by provincial reports on drunkenness. Manitoba's rate for drinking convictions in 1913 was double that of Ontario and almost three times that of Quebec. In addition to drunkenness *per se,* there were a dozen other crimes and misdemeanours associated with booze that contributed to Manitoba's pre-eminence in petty crime. There were 16,513 summary convictions in 1913, almost double the *per capita* figure for Ontario and well over double that of Quebec. But the conviction statistics could hardly begin to tell the story. Only the thoroughly obnoxious drunks would ever be taken to jail, and then only that small portion of the obnoxious which came to police notice. Drunkenness clearly was a Winnipeg problem that extended very far beyond the realm of statistics. If it had not, it is inconceivable that the liquor trade could have become the issue around which all reform groups in Winnipeg united for twenty-five years. Temperance missionaries were everywhere—in the churches, in the schools, in the trade unions, in the legislature, and at public meetings, rallies, and petition gatherings beyond number.

This, then, was the Winnipeg in which I grew up and these were the forces which shaped my boyhood environment; yet we were mainly unaware of them, except when they affected us or our families directly. Economists could drool over the causes and consequences of the "boom and bust" that ended the era of Winnipeg's growth. The social scientists could mesmerize themselves with the effects produced by mixing poverty, lawlessness, booze, mass immigration, the First World War, and the 1919 General Strike in the Winnipeg melting pot. But we who grew up in the teen years of the century experienced life within a different frame of reference. The kids who grew up near the Annabella Street brothels acquired a worldly wisdom long before those in Crescentwood. But those in the North End ghetto knew no more about life among the Anglo-Saxon rich than the latter did about life among the ghetto poor.

My own experience happened to be wider than that of most boys because we never stayed long in any one neighbourhood. We moved on an average of once a year, and in one two-year period moved from William to Giroux to Mountain to Salter to Young streets. In this nomadic existence, we flitted from the North End melting pot to the fringe of Little Belgium in South St. Boniface and back again; then into the Italian district on Young Street, to the upper middle-class Westminster area and over the Anglo-Saxon heaven south of the Assiniboine. Our sojourn in North Winnipeg enabled me to become involved in the great Krafchenko manhunt, perhaps my most vivid childhood memory—playing cops and robbers with a real live escaped murderer as the quarry. The North End also taught me how to survive in a school year as a minority of one, the skinny, half-sickly kid all the tough little "hunky" kids could beat up. On Young Street we could tear up Portage Avenue to watch the wartime military parades that seemed to be forever on the march with trumpets blaring and drums pounding. In Fort Rouge we savoured the sport of hitching rides on freight trains that shunted back and forth hard by our Red River swimming hole.

Each of Winnipeg's many enclaves had its own special flavour and its own mores. In the North End we were seldom much beyond range of the odour of garlic; in Fort Rouge the smell was unknown. In Fort Rouge, most kids acquired hockey skates and baseball mitts as a matter of course; in the North End whoever had a baseball glove lent it to the catcher and the rest played bare-handed. The week seldom passed in the North End when a new immigrant pupil or two failed to show up for classes. In the South End the same children moved from grade to grade together, year after year, and foreign-born kids were unknown. In the North End, where the struggle for existence became exceedingly sharp with the collapse of the boom in 1913, the kids were physically and probably mentally tougher than they were in the Anglo-Saxon communities. Spending money and allowances were common in the south and unknown in the north, so the push-cart peddlers of ice cream and popcorn lived north of the tracks but worked south.

Until they became bicycle owners at around thirteen, most boys tended to stay fairly close to their home districts. There was usually enough going on to keep us around, and the natural barriers of rivers, railway tracks, or vacant lots helped to hive us off by ourselves. But once we got on wheels we explored the town from stem to gudgeon.

Distance was never a deterrent to desire in our bicycling days. One Hallowe'en we pedalled all the way from River Avenue clear out to Brooklands, beyond McPhillips Street, to up-end the back-yard privies, only to discover that other pranksters had beaten us to them. When we discovered the game of golf and the Bird's Hill courses, we often cycled out at dawn on Sunday morning, caddied a couple of rounds, and rode home again. All summer long the circuses followed one another into Winnipeg—Barnum and Bailey, Ringling Brothers, Sells-Floto, Johnny J. Jones. When they tented up on the Happyland grounds on Portage Avenue every boy with a bike in Winnipeg seemed to wheel onto the site. We followed the circus parades wherever they went, dodging the police to ride as close to the calliope as we could get. When a barnstorming aerial circus turned up at River Park we were there to pester the aviators, unsuccessfully, for rides in their fabric-covered machines. Compared to the thrill of catching a first glimpse of a real airplane bumping into flight, even the blasting off of a rocket to the moon would take second place. It is highly unlikely that the world will ever again produce a thrill to match the all-encompassing boyhood excitement of watching a daredevil hang from his knees from the undercarriage of an airplane, then pull himself up fighting the prop-wash and climb onto the wing and back into the open passenger seat. We saw that happen at River Park in, I think, 1920 or 1921. One of my chums was so transported with nervous tension that he wet his pants, and none of the rest of us could relax enough to laugh at him.

The frantic hammering, sawing, and nail-pounding that orchestrated the real estate boom collapsed into complete silence when the boom ended in 1913. Whatever the disasters that overtook our elders, and there were many, for the emerging generation there were innumerable dividends from that collapse. It left us, for example, with vacant lots in almost every residential block and often two or three at the corners. These we turned into baseball diamonds or, in winter, into hard-packed snow rinks on which we played hockey with frozen road apples. The sudden cessation in construction left the city with a rash of incomplete houses which we turned into forts, castles, and battlegrounds for our interminable games of cowboys and Indians, and cops and robbers. Some rather substantial construction projects came to abrupt halts half finished. At the corner of Young Street and Westminster Avenue two large apartment blocks—the Huntley and the Clayton—were three-quarters complete when work stopped. The walls were up, the roof was on, and the partitions were in for all the rooms. Throughout the war the first snowfall was a signal for all the kids in the neighbourhood to climb to the roof of the Clayton block to drop snowballs on any pedestrians who happened by. We seldom were very accurate in calculating distance and falling time so that the snowballs usually missed the target. Once, when we hit a man smack on the head with a heavy blob of wet snow, he looked up and spotted us. He tore into the building and up the front stairs. We escaped with our lives by running down the back stairs and outrunning him to the safety of the next street.

During the boom the city enforced one regulation: it insisted that all the new heavy wood-planked sidewalks be placed eighteen inches above the surrounding ground level. This created a serious hazard for drunks lurching home, but it had several advantages for everybody else. It let the citizens keep their feet dry during heavy rains, it prevented them from sinking out of sight in Winnipeg gumbo during the early spring floods, and it gave the basement diggers a place to dump the dirt from their excavations. They simply spread it around on the lots, which raised the level to that of the sidewalks. The high-level sidewalks had the final advantage of being self-cleaning in the winter, since the wind blew the snow off the surface. But for us the plank sidewalks had many other purposes. We burrowed under them and made forts. They provided us with grandstand seats when the excavators moved in with their horses and scrapers to gouge out basements. We could sit entranced at the ability of the horses to know when to pull, when to slack, when to turn, and when to stop—all without a command from the teamster. Sometimes we would even be allowed to help by lifting the scraper handles and dumping the bucket, a task that took surprisingly little strength.

Our best use of the plank sidewalks was as an instrument for practical jokes. Our favourite trick was to nail an old tin can under a sidewalk and then run a piece of string, which we had coated with beeswax, through a small hole in the can to a place under the sidewalk or behind a fence. Once the trap was set we would lie in wait for women pedestrians. As they walked over the place where the can was attached, the string would make a squeaking noise like a mouse if we pulled it through the can just right. The squeals of the girls could be heard half a block away when the trick went off as planned. Though it seldom did, the trick never lost its zest; and neither did life itself. If there were no tricks to be played there was other devilment to get into, or games of our own to organize. The fun we had was the fun we made for ourselves. There were no organized teams and leagues run by adults save those involving the Y.M.C.A., the Sunday schools, and the regular school soccer league. Ours was a playtime that was free of both regimentation and instruction, for the notion of recreational do-gooding had not yet been conceived.

Memory, of course, can play strange tricks, but it seems to me that most of us stopped relying on our parents to do things for us about as soon as we got into school. In many ways, a new world was unfolding about which our parents, Anglo-Saxon as well as immigrant, knew little more than we did. It was our generation, for example, and not the adults', that launched the radio-listening boom that swept Winnipeg in 1920 and 1921. It began with us fourteen- and fifteen-year-olds who became overnight experts in wireless telegraphy. I was infected by my friend Gordon Main, who lived across from us on Bryce Street. He had picked up the germ from a family friend. One late fall day I found him sitting in the kitchen winding copper wire onto an empty Old Dutch Cleanser can. He was, he said, building a wireless set on which he would be able to hear music being broadcast on Station KDKA in Pittsburgh, Pennsylvania. Within the hour I had absorbed all of Gordon's newly acquired expertise and we were off together on a complicated telecommunication project. In addition to listening to Pittsburgh, we decided to set up a system to send messages in Morse code to each other back and forth across the street. While Gordon got busy in his back shed, I rushed home and cleaned out an old chicken coop in our back yard for my wireless room. Then we toured the neighbourhood and gathered up all the electric wire we could find that did not seem to be in use. We burned the rubber insulation off it and made it into aerials which we strung between clothes posts above the clothes lines. We converted doorbells into telegraph sounders, made keys out of pieces from a Meccano set, powered our apparatus with a series of salvaged dry cells, and began memorizing the Morse code.

Despite our perseverance we were never able to establish wireless contact. Gordon persisted, however, and, when he got a spark-gapping coil from a Ford car and a storage battery, he actually got into communication with other set-builders in the neighbourhood. In the meantime, most of our peers were infected by the radio bug. Functioning as we did mainly from ignorance, we naturally spent more time wandering around looking for answers to problems, and giving instructions, than we did winding cans and fiddling with cat's-whisker detectors. What mainly sparked the wireless boom was the fact that we could get all the supplies we needed to buy for a few cents. Boys who lived in homes with telephones disconnected the ear pieces and attached them temporarily to their wire-wound cans behind galena crystal detectors. Those who had no telephones resorted to open theft. Winnipeg apartment blocks were equipped with telephones which connected the vestibules with the apartments. The telephone consisted of a small earpiece on a hook and a fixed mouthpiece. Almost overnight, the earpieces disappeared from all the apartment blocks, never to be replaced. With them, we got Station KDKA Pittsburgh on our crystal sets.

With our homemade crystal sets we not only astounded our parents, who discovered they had budding geniuses in the family, but we also flabbergasted the neighbours with the snatches of music coaxed from our sets. In a matter of weeks the wireless boom was on. Eaton's set up a special wireless department to dispense crystals, cat's whiskers, condensers, aerial wire, and all the advice needed for assembly. It was a boom that went on and on from there. But the credit for it belonged to my generation, and we made life miserable for science teachers with our questions, lugged home tons of

discarded dry cell batteries, fiddled endlessly with cat's whiskers, and in the process blundered into one of the most
esoteric of the sciences without ever really knowing what we
were doing.

We were leaving our boyhoods behind when our excursion into the world of radio was launched. Yet this episode
seems perfectly to typify the Winnipeg childhood of the teen
years of our century. Ours was a do-it-yourself boyhood in
which we took our fun where we found it without benefit of
adult assistance or supervision. Few of our games were ever
played to a finish. We played hockey or baseball or kick-the-
can until we lost interest or had to go home. But whatever the
game, it was such fun that we could hardly wait to get back at
it again. What follows here, then, is a boy's-eye view of life in
Winnipeg in the teen years when it was incomparable fun to
be growing up, even growing up in poverty in an environment
being rocked continually by moral, political, and economic
crises. This was our Winnipeg, and most of us lived to count
ourselves among fortune's favourites for having come upon
the scene when we did.

CHAPTER TWO

Father, Dear Father, Come Home

The family into which I was born on August 31, 1906, at Whitemouth, Manitoba, was devoid of distinction, with two very minor exceptions. My paternal grandfather was a man of super-sensitivity and my maternal grandfather was clearly born without a sense of direction. My paternal grandfather's name was John Brown, and he was forced out of England by the French revolution of 1848. His elder brother had gone up to London, from Gainsborough in Lincolnshire, where he rose rapidly from clerk in a London bank to teller in the Paris branch of the bank. All Paris banks had suffered heavy losses from looters in the revolution of 1789. When trouble threatened in 1848 they were determined not to be caught a second time. The bank loaded all its spare cash into a couple of suitcases and piled them, along with my granduncle, into a coach for Calais. He was never heard of again. When news of his disappearance reached London fear was expressed that he had fallen victim of foul play. That suspicion was not shared by the neighbours back in Gainsborough. They taunted my grandfather with snide suggestions that his brother had made off with the money. When he went shopping he was chided with questions about whether the money he was spending had come from his brother; and did he expect his brother to send for him when the absconder was safely settled in Australia. After several years of needling, my grandfather decided he could stand the jibes no longer. He changed his name from Brown to Gray and fled to the backwoods hamlet of Holland Landing, north of Toronto. There he married and raised a family of two daughters and six sons, of whom my father was the second youngest.

My maternal grandfather's name was John Sargent and he came from an Irish Protestant family that settled in West Virginia after the American Revolution. Following the outbreak of the Civil War he enlisted in the Confederate army while still in his teens and saw service in the midwestern border states. Toward the end of the war his unit seems to have been reduced mainly to guerrilla activities because, in a skirmish with Northern troops, he lost both contact with his outfit and his bearings. When he managed to get himself orientated he discovered he was fifty miles farther north than it was safe for any Southern soldier to be. So he threw away his uniform and gun, stole some clothes, and kept on going until he reached the Dakota Territory. Eventually he drifted into Manitoba where he met and married my grandmother, who had come west as a girl with her family on a wagon train from Guelph, Ontario, in 1870.

Following their marriage my maternal grandparents settled in Winnipeg on a river lot farm on the Red River near where the Provencher bridge now stands. Soon after my mother was born in 1879, my grandfather decided Winnipeg would never amount to much so he sold out and moved back to Carman where my grandmother's relatives lived. My father's path crossed my mother's in Boissevain in the fall of 1904. My father had lost his right arm in a train accident in Buffalo, New York, a couple of years previously and was still trying to get his life re-sorted. At the time he met my mother, he was driving a butcher's rig for his brother, and it was apparently love at first sight when he delivered a roast to the back door of the house where my mother was staying. They were married in the summer of 1905. They spent the better part of the next six years in the bush of eastern Manitoba where my father worked as a timekeeper and storekeeper for the National Transcontinental Railway, and where my brother Walter and I were born.

My earliest memory, etched by terror, is of a summer's day in 1910 when my mother and I and my younger brother were picking berries along the railway tracks near our railway-siding home outside Rennie, Ontario. A black bear with a cub sauntered out of the bush a hundred feet away from us. My mother let out a scream and grabbed Walter in her arms and me by the hand, and we fled in panic up the path to our house. The bear, fortunately, chose to ignore us, but for the next several weeks our fear of bears kept us all very close to our front yard.

My first memory of Winnipeg is of standing on the back fence at 606 William Avenue watching a couple of roosters fighting in the yard next door. They flew at each other with claws churning, pecked at each other's head, and chased each other around and around the yard until there were feathers everywhere and both birds were streaked with blood. Meanwhile all the hens were cackling and flying about and the noise brought the lady of the house running into the yard. She quickly drove the roosters apart into opposite ends of the yard and then used her apron to shoo them into separate pens. What probably fixed the episode firmly in my mind was the shock I felt when the woman turned angrily on me and chewed me out for not calling her when the roosters started to fight.

My second Winnipeg memory is one of my shortest—walking down William Avenue with the boy next door to enrol at either Victoria or Albert school, which then shared a common yard in a large city block west of the Normal School. I could hardly have attended this school for very long because I have no recollection of anything that happened to me after we got there. Its only importance was that it let me into the Winnipeg school system. It was the first of a dozen schools I attended in the course of the next nine years. It was followed in quick order by Norwood, Strathcona, Machray, Isbister, John M. King, Isbister again, Mulvey, Fort Rouge, Gladstone, Alexandra, La Vérendrye, and Kelvin schools. I was into and out of three of the schools quickly as the School Board did some frantic switching of its overflow school population from over-populated to under-populated schools. When we were living at the corner of Young Street and Ellice Avenue I first checked into Isbister, was transferred to John M. King, and was sent back again to Isbister within a matter of a few months. This sort of shuffling went on all over the city. It was accompanied by having pupils in a general area all take their carpenter shop training at a central school. Thus all the boys going to Fort Rouge, Gladstone, and Alexandra schools attended La Vérendrye school for shop classes.

My own erratic course through the Winnipeg schools was the result of two special circumstances. My father had only one arm, so that the clerical jobs he could get were limited in number; and he had developed an addiction for alcohol that prevented him from keeping the jobs he did get. So our first years were spent in circumstances bordering on destitution. We moved frequently, sometimes from one house to another, sometimes into and out of unfurnished rooms. The year war broke out our living habits were stabilized when my parents discovered that they could live rent-free as apartment block janitors. They first got a small block, the Richmond Apartments, at the corner of Young Street and Ellice Avenue. After a year they moved to the Harald Apartments on Westminster Avenue which paid a small stipend in addition to free rent. A year and a half later they moved to the Rozell Apartments on Clark Street in Fort Rouge where the pay was better.

It was my father's alcoholism that led to my involvement in one of the greatest political movements of all time—the struggle for prohibition. Admittedly, the winds of change blew like gales through the "Gateway to the West" when I was a boy growing up in Winnipeg. In the period between the outbreak of the Great War and the opening of the Manitoba legislature in 1921 by a brand-new Farmers Government in a brand-new scandal-ridden building, an era died and another struggled to be born. The first hesitant step was taken toward the welfare state with the passage of the Manitoba compulsory school attendance act of 1916. Political parties were being torn apart by the forces of internal dissension and external economic pressures. The trade union movement was caught up in an ideological struggle that culminated in the 1919 General Strike, which all but destroyed it. The European immigrants, who had stormed into the West in the previous decade, were discovering the hard way that they had come to no promised land. Far off on the prairies an agitation was beginning which would revolutionize grain marketing and destroy the wheat futures market. These were the issues which have attracted historians; yet it has always seemed to me that they have consistently ignored the most abrasive, longest-enduring gut issue of the times—the great issue that affected every community, erupted in every election between 1892 and 1916, and touched more people in their daily lives than any of the others. That issue was booze. It was at once a burning local issue and a national issue, from one end of Canada to the other, except for Quebec. It gave rise, over the years, to endless temperance organizations—Women's Christian Temperance Union, Royal Templars of Temperance, Loyal Temperance Legion, the Moral and Social Reform Council. It united the Protestant churches, the trade unions, and women's organizations into one long, embittered, and in the end successful campaign for prohibition. Yet where Canadian historians deal with the booze problem at all, it is given the most casual treatment, confined mainly to references to rum-running and bootlegging. Indeed, some of our prestigious pedagogues have managed to write histories of Manitoba that ignore the subject; some notice it only in passing and even get their facts awry.

The hindsight verdict of politicians and social scientists alike is that prohibition was a ghastly failure because it was an impossible attempt to remake human nature and enforce morality by law. It led to contempt for the law, which led to gangsterism, which led to international tension abroad and social chaos at home. Yet it has also seemed to me that prohibition was in part the victim of the give-a-dog-a-bad-name syndrome.

My father and mother were both deeply involved in the prohibition crusade. Curiously enough, despite my father's addiction to alcohol, he supported the "banish-the-bars" crusade just as enthusiastically as did my mother. Like her, he was convinced that if the temptation were removed he would have no more trouble with demon rum. So in the election campaign in the summer of 1915 he worked actively for the Liberals, who promised to bring in prohibition, and against the Conservative administration of Sir Rodmond Roblin, which supported temperance in principle and the booze business in practice. After supper that summer I used to go with my father to a temperance rallying point in the St. Stephen's Church Hall on Portage Avenue and we would each take an armload of literature to distribute along pre-selected routes. I enjoyed this immensely and even volunteered to help with the deliveries during the day. But such was the bitterness of the feelings aroused in Winnipeg that the people in charge thought it unsafe for a nine-year-old to go out on his own. I remember being completely baffled by the decision, for it was rare indeed that any householder objected to our leaving the material. Perhaps that was an augury of the vote to come because the Liberals led by T.C. Norris went in by a landslide, aided mainly by the Legislature Building scandal which all but destroyed the Roblin regime.

Instead of enacting a prohibition law of his own, Premier Norris announced that he would re-enact the law drafted by Sir Hugh John Macdonald in 1900 but never proclaimed. First, however, there would have to be a plebiscite. That set the wets and drys off on another six-month battle during which there seemed to be some sort of public meeting every night. If the meeting was close by, my mother and father would often decide to attend and leave me to look after my younger brothers, much to my chagrin. I can remember becoming apprehensive when my father was reading the paper aloud after supper and discussing attending a meeting that was announced. I always felt completely comfortable, and safe without question, on the streets, in daylight or after dark. But

I was fearful of staying home alone at night with my brothers, even in an apartment block full of people. No matter how late it got, or how tired I got, I can never remember going to sleep before their return.

Often, after my parents had come home, they would sit for an hour hashing over what they had heard. It was an age of oratory in religion, law, and politics, and every Winnipeg preacher who was at all prominent took to the sawdust trail that winter to crusade for prohibition. Such noted clergymen as the Reverend Salem Bland, the Reverend C.W. Gordon (Ralph Connor, the most famous author Winnipeg had produced), and the Reverend J.S. Woodsworth, were among the divines who were supported by social workers, business leaders, and trade unionists galore. Periodically, for special rallies, they would bring in Nellie McClung, the famous Edmonton author and temperance lecturer. The wets, of course, were equally active. They once imported Clarence Darrow, the Chicago criminal lawyer, in an effort to swing labour against the temperance cause. Darrow had recently defended Eugene Debs, the American labour leader, and the MacNamara brothers in the *Los Angeles Times* dynamiting case, and was the best-known labour lawyer on the continent. My parents never even considered going to *his* meeting.

In addition to promising the electors prohibition, the Liberal Party had also pledged itself to compulsory school attendance and to bring in woman suffrage. While the plebiscite campaign was at its height, the votes-for-women issue threatened to divide the temperance legions. People such as Nellie McClung were all for granting women the vote before the plebiscite. They reasoned that this would assure a whopping majority, even if the wets went on the ballot-stuffing blitzes they had used to defeat previous votes on the question. The Norris administration decided against granting the women the vote before the plebiscite, on the grounds that it would be impractical to put a new voters' list together in time. On March 13, 1916, the adult males of Manitoba went to the polls and voted in prohibition by a count of 50,484 to 26,502.

When the liquor licences came up for renewal in May the government stopped issuing them and the prohibition era arrived in Winnipeg.

But I needed neither the temperance lecturers nor the prohibition campaign to inform me about the ramifications of the liquor problem in Winnipeg. By the time I was ten I knew more about the devastating effect of booze on family life than a beer truck filled with Nellie McClungs and Ralph Connors.

On a payday night in the winter of 1913, my father was waylaid behind a bar, beaten to a pulp, robbed of what was left of his pay, and left to die in the snow. He was found some hours later and hospitalized for five weeks with pleurisy that turned into double pneumonia. Yet, curiously enough, this experience had less permanent effect on my father than it did on my mother, or on me. Once back on his feet, he was quickly able to erase the beating from his mind. When he got another job and collected another pay he resumed where he had left off the night of the attack, but with one small change. He did his drinking as far away as possible from the North Main bars. Although my father was able to forget his experience my mother never could. Thenceforth on paydays she would begin to get edgy if my father was not home when she started to make supper. By the time the meal was cooked, she was beside herself with anxiety.

"Jimmie," she'd say, after the umpteenth trip to the window, "you'd better get on your things and run down to the corner and see if you can see Daddy. He may have fallen and hurt himself."

Only she didn't mean the corner. We had been through this so often that she no longer had to spell out what had to be done. She wanted me to backtrack along my father's route home from the Clarendon Hotel opposite Eaton's to the Queen's Hotel at the corner of Notre Dame and Portage Avenue. I was about eight at this time and my mother knew that I'd walk as far as the Queen's Hotel, sneak a peek into the "longest bar in the West", and if my father was inside I'd go in and try to talk him into coming home. This was illegal, of course, since children, women, and Indians were all forbidden by law to enter bars. If the Queen's bartender spotted me he'd bang on the counter with his fist and shout at my father, "Harry, get that goddamn kid the hell out of here! You want to get me fired and lose the hotel its licence?"

I have a memory of once running out the door when the bartender shouted, and sitting on a big leather-bottomed chair in the Queen's Hotel lobby until my father came out. On another occasion, I stood my ground, and my father swung his arm at me and almost fell over. Then he left and we went home, with him leaning on my shoulder for support most of the way.

The kids who lived with liquor problems of varying severity could be quite casual about it, and we used to compare notes on parental behaviour quite objectively. When a chum turned up unexpectedly at our house after supper it often meant that he was taking shelter until a family row subsided, and he would say so. Yet, though we went through these experiences often enough so that we learned to live with them, few of us ever became completely desensitized. In the winter, when it all happened after dark, I thought little of these adventures. They were somewhat akin, I suppose, to taking out the garbage. In the summer, when the other kids were all out playing on the street, it could be a tormenting experience to hear some boy shout as we passed: "Hey, there's Jimmie Gray taking his old man home again." I would hide my face and pretend I didn't hear and try to hurry my father along. But like as not another shout would take the edge off the first.

"Hey Jimmie, hurry back 'cause we're choosing up sides for Relievoh and you can be on our side if you get back before Gimpy gets here."

Drunkenness on the streets where we lived was such a common sight that the kids accepted it as a normal manifestation of life, like dogs that barked at bicycles. Riding herd on drunken fathers was an obvious minus for a lot of boys, but there were some pluses, too, in having an alcoholic father. For example, it enabled me to set some kind of record for school transfers. Unlike most kids of my age I was able to savour most of Winnipeg's most interesting environments. I lived in the slums on the near north side; on the outer fringe of the immigrant area in North Winnipeg with the Jews, Ukrainians, and Poles; in Little Italy on Young Street; then within a stone's throw of the garden of the wealthy lieutenant-governor of the province; and I went to school with rich kids from the Roslyn Road mansions. With a non-alcoholic father we would probably have missed both sides of the tracks, taken root on a respectable street in St. James, and missed all the fun.

In addition to circulating through the school districts, we moved frequently in the early years within the districts. As our economic position worsened, we sought cheaper housing. Then as it recovered and we could pay the rent we climbed back to better-quality shelter. It was a yo-yo existence, but I cannot recall ever thinking my life was much different from that of the other boys of my age. If no one seemed much worse off than we were, none of them seemed to be much better off either. Whether we were going up or down we didn't really go far in either direction. In any event our economic condition had little effect on our enjoyment of life and most of the memories we accumulated were happy ones of exciting adventure that could be relived with relish for the rest of our lives.

My father was what was known then as a periodic drunk. There would be long dry spells stretching into months when he would not take a drink. He would get a job, work hard, save his money, and get caught up on back bills. During these arid stretches he came close to being a perfect father. He was patient, generous, and considerate, and could charm a scowl off a wooden Indian. Certainly he recognized his weakness and struggled against it as best he could. He encouraged my mother to pick up his pay, or to meet him on payday. As I learned later, a lot of effort on the part of both employers and employees went into preventing the Winnipeg bars from gobbling up workers' pay. My father once had a night watchman's job where he got paid coming off shift three hours before the bars opened, and then there was no place to go but home. When he was timekeeper during the construction of the General Hospital, the foreman used to come around with the pay envelopes just before lunch so the workers could turn their money over to their wives who came to pick it up. Sometimes there were some almighty rows around the contractor's office between husband and wife over how much the former would keep out of his pay.

Even when my father was on the wagon the whole family was nervously resigned to the fact that sooner or later he would fall from grace, and my mother carefully hoarded her resources against that day. I have a suspicion that he went along willingly with my mother's little schemes to improve the odds, for he seldom objected to them. She never could be sure which of my father's offhand reasons for getting away from the house were real and which were merely excuses to escape to the bar. So her favourite counter-move was to suggest to him that he take me along. It was this dodge that provided me with some of the most vivid memories of my Winnipeg boyhood. My father once took me along to a meeting that turned into the anti-conscription riot in the Grand Theatre in 1917. We were sitting near the door when the soldiers invaded the hall and broke up the meeting and smashed things up. He took me with him to the mass meetings at Victoria Park during the 1919 strike. And I got taken to a lot of baseball games that otherwise I never would have seen, and neither would he, I suspect, if I had not been along.

As I have said, drunkenness was so much a part of ordinary life in Winnipeg that even the kids I played with took it mostly in their stride. But there was certainly nothing normal by ordinary sober standards about the lives that were lived inside the homes of drunken fathers. Instead there was frequently hatred begotten of violence, poverty, privation, and actual hunger. Yet as often as not, the outraged anger of battered wives and children was directed more toward the source of their tribulation—the bars—than toward the cause—

their drinking husbands and fathers. I have a feeling that my mother spoke for all womankind when she used to cry out tearfully, "Oh God, if only we could get rid of those accursed bars!"

Certainly she was echoing the sentiments of thousands of farm wives who came to Winnipeg in joyous expectation of a shopping splurge at Jerry Robinson's, or the Hudson's Bay Company, or Eaton's, and went home with half their needs unfilled because their husbands had tarried too long at the bar, or had disappeared with their shopping money into the red-light district with new-found "friends" from the bar.

The bar had become the focal point for the attack on the evils of booze long before I was born. A prohibition law was passed in Manitoba as early as 1900 but was declared *ultra vires*. Then a law was passed setting up a system of local option which was largely ineffectual. The licensing of saloons was ended in 1904 and bars were confined to hotels thereafter. But the changes were more apparent than real. The closing of the saloons was followed by the opening of licensed private clubs, which stayed open all night for gambling as well as drinking.

The campaigns against the bars and clubs took many forms. One of the most popular was song. Many of these songs were sung in the schools as well as at churches and temperance meetings. There were several groups organized in the schools. One was the Band of Hope. Another was the Loyal Temperance Legion, which gave us lapel buttons engraved with L.T.L. The meetings consisted mainly of short talks by lady visitors, followed by the singing of several songs and then a treat of candy or cookies. Our songs included: "Drink, drink, drink drink; drink, drink, drink drink; I'll drink cold water pure!" and "Lips that touch liquor will never touch mine!"

The greatest temperance anthem ever written was "Father, Dear Father", by H. C. Work, who also wrote "Marching Through Georgia" and "Grandfather's Clock".

"Father, Dear Father" was his battle hymn of temperance and it was as popular in Canada as it was in the United States.

By the time I was ten years old I could recite it in my sleep and it had a place on every school entertainment I can remember. When a travelling Chautauqua elocutionist got through with it, there was seldom a dry eye in the house. Certainly my own never were, for I was well into my teens before I could keep from bawling unashamedly as the reciter or singer worked toward the denouement. For kids like me that song struck as close to home as any ever written. Reading it over all these years later it comes out as the gushiest kind of sentimentality. In a word, pure corn. Yet in the great temperance crusade before the First World War, it was capable of moving millions. Here it is in its entirety!

> Father, dear father, come home with me now!
> The clock in the steeple strikes one;
> You said you were coming right home from the shop,
> As soon as your day's work was done.
> Our fire has gone out—our house is all dark—
> And mother's been watching since tea,
> With poor brother Benny so sick in her arms,
> And no one to help her but me.
> Come home! come home! come home.
> Please, father, dear father, come home.

Chorus
Hear the sweet voice of the child,
Which the night winds repeat as they roam!
Oh, who could resist this most pleading of prayers?
"Please, father, dear father, come home!"

Father, dear father, come home with me now!
The clock in the steeple strikes two;
The night has grown colder, and Benny is worse,
But he has been calling for you.
Indeed he is worse—Ma says he will die,
Perhaps before morning shall dawn;
And this is the message she sent me to bring—
"Come quickly or he will be gone."
Come home! come home! come home!
Please, father, dear father, come home.

Father, dear father, come home with me now!
The clock in the steeple strikes three;
The house is so lonely—the hours are so long
For poor weeping mother and me.
Yes, we are alone—poor Benny is dead
And gone with the angels of light;
And these were the very last words that he said
"I want to kiss papa good night."
Come home! come home! come home!
Please, father, dear father, come home.

By the time my family arrived in Winnipeg, the liquor problem had already reached the explosive stage. Among the women, as exemplified by my mother, the burning faith that the "liquor problem" could be solved once and for all by removing the cause of temptation was a conviction based on fact. When liquor was not available, their husbands did not drink. In the dry towns husbands and wives could go to town every week for a year without liquor becoming a problem. But let them come into Winnipeg, as many farm families did in the fall, and the curse of strong drink laid a heavy hand on the husband's shoulder.

For my mother in particular, the logic of the prohibition-ist position was utterly unassailable. She had met and married my father, and had borne him two children, without ever discovering that he had a liquor problem. They had met in a Manitoba country town where there was no booze to be had. Then they had lived for six years in a remote area where there was no liquor. So she had incontrovertible evidence that if liquor was not available my father did not drink. My mother was not alone in her belief; in every small town in Manitoba the women had first-hand knowledge of the disasters that occurred when husbands got loose in areas where liquor was being sold.

To the thousands of women who shared my mother's conviction the solution was simple—get rid of the bars and the problem would cease to exist. And she saw her judgment in the matter completely vindicated when prohibition came in in 1916 and the bars were closed.

Had my mother cared to consult the record in later years she could have proved her point statistically. In 1913, the province of Manitoba recorded no less than 7,493 convictions for drunkenness. In 1917, the first year of prohibition, the figures dropped to 1,085 and only once in the next twenty years, despite the growth of bootlegging and a gradual return to legalized booze, did convictions again get above 2,000. The figures for the other western provinces were equally striking. In Alberta the convictions dropped from 7,283 in 1913 to 391 in 1917. In Saskatchewan the decline was from 2,970 to 770 and in British Columbia from 8,316 in 1913 to 778 in 1918.

In any event my father got a minor clerical job in the comptroller's department at the City Hall in 1917 and held it through two strikes until 1921. It enabled us to move from the Rozell Apartments to a semi-modern house on Bryce Street, where we survived quite well on his small salary and what my brother Walter and I earned with our paper routes. In the end my father resumed his bout with John Barleycorn and lost his job. This, too, reinforced my mother's insistence that there was a direct relationship between availability of booze and alcoholism. De facto prohibition began to disappear soon after the war, though repeal did not come until 1923. Enforcement, meanwhile, became exceedingly lax as the hotels reopened their bars for the sale of beer. Prior to prohibition, my father had never cared much for beer, so in the early years he never bothered with the beer joints. But as the beer bars increased in number he couldn't resist temptation and the end was predictable.

If my father had wanted to look for excuses for getting drunk they would not have been hard to come by. After a short exposure to schooling at Holland Landing he had migrated to Toronto and drifted from one job to another until he was approaching thirty. Then he moved to Buffalo, New York, and fell into a type of employment for which he had a decided aptitude. He became a combination salesman and window-display arranger in a large shoe store. His window displays brought in the customers and he built up a growing clientele that waited for him to serve them. When the World's Fair came to Buffalo in 1901, his firm entered one of my father's shoe displays in a competition, and he won a bronze medal and a certificate with his name in gold lettering. He also got a raise in pay and offers of better jobs began to reach him from Chicago and New York.

Arranging women's shoes in a display window may fall far short of being the ultimate in artistic expression. To the rest of the world it might not even have seemed like much of a job. But it was a new trade: both a way of self-expression and a way to make a living, and my father was becoming recognized as being good at his trade, an artisan no less. One day a representative of a large manufacturing company approached him with an offer to set him up in his own shoe store. They shook hands on the deal and adjourned to an adjacent bar to seal it with several rounds of whisky. A telegraph messenger caught up with him there, with the news that his mother had just died in Holland Landing. There was barely time for him to rush home to his room, pack a bag, and catch the night train to Toronto. En route to the station he stopped to buy a bouquet of flowers and the conductor was calling "all aboard" as he came through the gate. He sprinted after the moving train with his bag in one hand and his flowers in the other. He caught up with the train, but as he was about to scramble aboard he missed his footing and fell. His right arm went under the train and was amputated at the shoulder.

By the time he got out of the hospital months later both the shoe company's offer and his old job were gone. Fitting shoes to the feet of women customers was no job for a one-armed man, even if he could have written well enough to make out the bills. And window dressing had not yet progressed to the point where shoe stores or department stores were hiring full-time display arrangers, even with two arms. The only job he could get was with the railway, which, on compassionate grounds, hired him as a watchman at a level crossing. The job did not last and my father drifted back to Canada and eventually to Manitoba, where one brother farmed at Cartwright and another ran a butcher shop in Boissevain. While he was courting my mother he applied for and got a job with the National Transcontinental Railway, which was soon to start building east from Winnipeg and west from Quebec. They spent the first six years of their married life at the railway cache between Whitemouth and Rennie.

The 225-mile stretch of the Transcontinental line between Winnipeg and Superior Junction was the only really snake-bitten section of this great project. The contractors managed to get the right-of-way cleared and the steel laid in two years. Ballasting it, however, and bringing it up to standard took another four years. The Government of Canada and the Grand Trunk Railway were engaged in some bitter financial in-fighting at the time and there were rumours that completion of the section east of Winnipeg was being retarded by the government to tighten the pressure on the railway. The result, for our family, was to lengthen our stay in the woods from two years to six. By the time we moved into Winnipeg in the spring of 1911, my brother Walter had been added to our family and my brother Robert was on the way. My parents rented a house at 606 William Avenue near Sherbrook and settled down to await the opening of a job that had been offered my father in the new National Transcontinental shops at Transcona. The construction of the shops got bogged down in politics and the promised job failed to materialize.

My father never earned more than $60 a month during the six years they lived in the bush. But it was "all found", so they saved most of his salary and had better than $2,000 in W. F. Alloway's bank when they arrived in the city. If my father had no drinking problem before, he made up for lost time when he hit the Winnipeg bars. He never stopped drinking until most of their nest egg was gone, much of it unquestionably into the pockets of the vermin that infested the bars. My father often used the expression "being driven to drink". Whether he was driven by his lack of qualification for any special kind of work, or whether his addiction to booze made it increasingly difficult for him to get or hold a job, can be left to the psychiatrists. A thin little fellow of 5′6″, he would have been a manual-labour reject even with two good arms. For most work he would have rated below the most recently arrived alien immigrant. With only one arm he had to do a super sales job to get any kind of employment, particularly when he lacked recommendations from his last employer. So he lost the jobs he got and in little over a year their savings had been dissipated and we were only saved from being thrown onto the street when relatives of my mother took us in.

No one had to document for my father how stupid his drinking was. Whisky depressed rather than lifted him and his bouts were followed by monstrous hangovers which, strangely enough, were shared by my mother, a lifelong teetotaller who suffered frightfully from migraine.

My father's brothers blamed his liquor problem on the loss of his arm, and they worried a good deal about him. Whenever any of them came to Winnipeg, they'd quickly get into *sotto voce* confabs with my mother over "Harry's drinking".

"Why?" they would ask him over and over. "Harry, why can't you be like the rest of us? Go into a bar on your way home and have a drink or glass of beer or two and then leave! Why can't you bring a bottle home and take a drink and put it away when you've had enough? Why do you always have to make a pig of yourself and not stop till you've drunk yourself out of house and home?"

My father would sit and take his verbal lumps, saying nothing, for he accepted everything that was said as being fully justified. He knew he had a problem, but it was one that baffled him even more than it did his brothers.

"I don't know," he would say. "I just don't know. I try. God knows I try. But I don't know what happens to me. I just don't know."

My uncles could get pretty impatient, perhaps because he wouldn't fight back at them. As we grew older, my brother and I would watch for a chance to slip away from the house when any of our uncles came to visit. There was always a family row that we never understood and it always seemed to end with my mother in tears.

"Harry, for God's sake listen to reason," they'd say. "You've got to quit this feeling sorry for yourself. All right, you've lost your arm and you can't do the things you used to. But that was years ago. You've learned to write again. You have had good jobs. You can get others. But you've got to make up your mind that you have to work twice as hard to overcome your handicap. My God, Harry, lots of men have lost arms and legs without letting it ruin their lives."

Along about here my mother would chip in.

"If you ask me the arm has nothing to do with it. He doesn't need two arms for the work he does. And look at Uncle Finlay. He had *both* his hands and *both* his feet frozen off and that hasn't driven him to drink and he's a better man than many I know who have all their limbs. Anyway," she'd say, "talking does no good. Nothing does any good."

By the age of eight I became deeply involved in this controversy as a by-product of my father's handicap. When we lived at Rennie he whiled away the evenings reading aloud to my mother. He had a curious interest in poetry, or perhaps it was only that the packing case full of books he sent away for contained mainly books of verse. After the loss of his arm he had to teach himself to write all over again with his left hand. It was a long and tedious process that went on for years. For practice he used to copy out passages from Gray, Byron, and Keats, and from the *Rubáiyát*. He began teaching me to write as he practised his penmanship. Reading went along with it, so I could read and write long before I went to school. My mother, as part of the practice process, would get me to write letters for her. Gradually she fell into the habit of having me write most of her letters. As often as not, I wrote the appeals she sent out to my uncles for financial help when we were faced with eviction for non-payment of rent.

I remember only vaguely moving in with the relatives, and it was probably during the weeks my father was hospitalized after the assault and robbery. But I have a very vivid recollection of moving to a house on Giroux Street in St. Boniface. The house had been vacant for some time and the rent was cheap. We discovered why after we moved in. A large stain covered a good segment of one corner of the front room and resisted my mother's best efforts with scrubbing brush and soap. She wondered and wondered what could have caused such a stain. A neighbour boy supplied me with the answer, which I rushed home to pass on to my horrified family. The previous tenant had committed suicide behind the door in the front room. For the next few days I was the celebrity of the neighbourhood. I was the new kid who lived in the house "where the man cut his throat". It was not long until the kids beat a path to our door, to call on me and then ask in loud whispers if I'd let them see where the guy killed himself. I was delighted to oblige, until my mother discovered the ploy and angrily put an end to the curiosity-seeking.

It was while we were living on Giroux Street and I was going to Norwood school that I came down with St. Vitus's dance. The disease was discovered when my nervous twitching disrupted the rest of the Grade One class. After a long siege in bed I was kept out of school for the better part of a year. In the interval we moved a couple of times and wound up in a small cottage on Salter Street near Mountain Avenue. During my illness I collected one dividend that ceased with my recovery. Because my thrashing around kept my brothers awake, I got to sleep by myself on a couch in the parlour instead of three in a bed as we had done before and did after I got better. It was while I was sleeping on the couch that I awakened one night as the doctor was telling my mother that I had outgrown my affliction and could return to school. It was a conversation that did more to shape my character, distort it even, than anything that ever happened to me. I blame whatever aggressive tendencies I have developed in life to eavesdropping on that conversation.

The doctor was warning that there were after-effects of St. Vitus's dance that would take time to clear up. He said I would tend to be excessively timid, would cry easily, and would probably be picked on by the other children at school. For years after, whenever I became involved in a schoolyard argument and was getting pushed around, the doctor's words would come thundering back to me and I'd lash out with my fists, as if to repudiate his judgment of me. Then I'd land flat on my back, to be pummelled roughly by a kid half my size. I was a year older and considerably taller than boys in my class, but the hard-muscled little Jewish, Ukrainian, and Italian kids out-weighed me by ten or fifteen pounds and could outfight me by a country mile. And I, who never won a schoolyard fight, somehow acquired a reputation of being a bully because I was always taller than my opponent, and was roundly abused for "picking on the little kids". There was no other kind, and I was always the one who emerged from the fight bruised and bawling. I was some bully!

CHAPTER THREE

The Saga of the Fine-toothed Comb

Machray school where I was enrolled in 1913 was far from being a slum district school, yet its population was almost as cosmopolitan as any. Mountain Avenue was a sort of borderland between the congested new Canadian settlements to the south and the predominantly Anglo-Saxon district to the north. But the former was steadily expanding northward by sheer force of numbers. Thus many families that had moved out of the ghetto to more comfortable quarters often gave shelter to relatives or friends newly arrived from the old country. So there was a steady infusion of immigrant children into Machray school. My own experience illustrates the situation. My transfer from Norwood school was issued with the space for the name of the new school left blank. I took it to Strathcona school near Stella and Salter and was accommodated there for a couple of months. But so great was the crush of new immigrant pupils into Strathcona that I was shifted to Machray, which was somewhat closer to our home on Salter Street.

The Strathcona school year was a towerless Babel and during my short attendance I often felt completely out of place because I spoke no language but English. It was different, and a lot more comfortable, at Machray, where English predominated. Both schools, however, wrestled with the problem of beginning children who came into class without a word of English to their names. By this time the teachers had worked out a rough-and-ready system of handling the problem.

They would seat the children who could speak some English next to those who could speak none so that work could proceed with one translating for the other. Within a matter of weeks, even days sometimes, the children caught on so quickly that translation could be dispensed with. Once compulsory school attendance became law in 1916, however, it brought such an influx into the school system of pupils who could speak no English that this method would no longer work. There were rooms in Strathcona school, for example, where scarcely a child understood more than a dozen or so words of English. The teachers there solved their instructional dilemma by a combination of signs, sounds, and gestures. The day might begin with three words, "take out book", repeated slowly by the teacher several times. Then the class would repeat each word with pantomimic action. Then the sounds went onto the blackboard and letters were made in scribblers.

In the schoolyards the kids tended at first to cluster together in national groups and to use their native languages. That once led to an agitation by the super patriots that a regulation be enforced requiring only English to be spoken on the schoolyards. However, some sort of centrifugal force operated to spin the children out of their national groups into conglomerates. The most potent force was the playing of schoolyard games. A couple of Polish girls might have some qualms about inviting a Jewish girl into their skipping game. But rope-turners were always needed, so they handed her one end of the rope and she was in. With the boys, who tended more toward team sports, rounding up a couple of soccer teams or baseball teams required the participation of every boy in the room. Left to their own devices, the small fry tended to use their own languages at the games. But there were usually enough English-speaking children around to dominate the shouting. While all the other children learned English, the only foreign words we ever learned were the swear words.

Of all the immigrant groups the swear words of the

Ukrainians were probably the most earthy. For years and years a Ukrainian bookstore on North Main Street exhibited a huge print in its window of a famous painting by a Russian master. It was entitled "The Cossacks' Reply to the Czar". It showed a group of rowdy Cossack soldiers gathered around a table at which one of their number was writing down insults dictated by the others. The soldiers were laughing uproariously at their epistle, which ran to several pages. A Ukrainian acquaintance once said that many of the insults were readable, upside down, in the original, but the print maker had opaqued the writing to make it indecipherable to the more prudish eyes of modern Ukrainians. When the small fry got angry at their games, which was frequently, most of them turned to their homey native oaths to express their displeasure. The English language was vastly inferior when it came to name-calling, so we all picked up their oaths and added them to our vocabulary.

Once, when we lived on Mountain Avenue, I had gotten into a row with a couple of Ukrainian kids who chased me home crying. When I reached the safety of my yard I turned and let fly a string of swear words I had accumulated. My mother heard the ruckus and came out to investigate just as a Ukrainian woman was passing.

"Missus," she said, "Missus know what boy say?"

My mother shook her head. "He say so bad words." She held her hand over her mouth. "Oh so bad words." Then she beckoned to my mother and whispered a rough translation of what I had said. My horrified mother caught me by the back of the neck and lathered me up the steps and into the house. All the time she was threatening to tell my father when he came home. She never did, largely, I suspect, because she couldn't bring herself to repeat the translation even in a whisper to my father. It was, as I later discovered, an all-encompassing, mouth-filling oath that ran the gamut from bestiality through incest to rape and was usually the last insult hurled before the fight started.

Every nationality delighted in the ancient game of teaching

the *auslander* swear words for articles of common usage. In this game we came out far ahead because the foreign kids were much more eager to learn our language than we were to learn theirs. Eventually they learned the danger of asking any of us Anglo-Saxons, "Please, how do you say 'drink'?"

It was a common occurrence for a shy little immigrant child to raise her hand in school to ask to leave the room and use one of our four-letter words for something entirely different. That set off a storm of laughter which made the day for the Anglo-Saxons in the room. I have always suspected that the practice of identifying desired purposes by holding up one, two, or three fingers derived from such earthy language difficulties.

The language problem was by no means as acute at Machray school as it was at Norquay and Strathcona. If I had been in Grade Three or Four when I came to Winnipeg I might never have known it existed. By that time English was the language of communication among the various ethnic groupings. But I started school in Grade One, which was where all the new immigrants in the neighbourhood started regardless of age unless they could speak English. Naturally, as quickly as they picked up the language they moved into the appropriate peer group. But in the beginning our Grade One at Machray struggled with the same problems that occurred in Strathcona and the other melting-pot schools.

Winnipeg, no less than Canada itself, owes its existence in large measure to Sir Clifford Sifton's immigration policies. No Canadian history ignores this policy or fails to mention the hundreds of thousands of settlers who came to Canada as the direct result of it. But my generation knew nothing of Sifton or policies of immigration. We knew only the end result of his policy as it was personified by a funny-looking little immigrant boy standing by the edge of the Norquay schoolyard watching the rest of us play soccer, and wanting passionately to participate. Or as it was illustrated by the little immigrant girl in the beginners' class at Machray school, reaching up to scratch her head and triggering a class uproar.

"Anna," the teacher would call sharply, putting her work to one side and reaching into the middle drawer of her desk, "come up here, please."

There was always a short pause while the teacher zeroed in on which of the half-dozen Annas in the class she wanted. When that was sorted out the little girl would usually burst into tears before getting to her feet. Sometimes the teacher had to come and take her by the arm. There were even times when more physical force than a girl teacher could muster was needed to move the pupil out of her seat. Then the teacher would appeal to one of the other children to explain to the little girl in her own language what was involved and what had to be done. For some reason or other, it always seemed to take two other little girls, both talking at once in Ukrainian, Polish, German, or Yiddish, to quiet the object of the teacher's attention and get her to co-operate.

What was involved was a hair-combing with a fine-toothed comb, in search of lice in the hair of the pupil. The teacher knew from experience that when any pupil started scratching at a real insect it would not be long before half the room would be scratching away at imaginary itches. So Anna took her place beside the teacher's desk while the teacher ran her comb through the pupil's hair in long, slow strokes. At Machray school our teacher was Miss Horn, who kept a newspaper in a bottom drawer. This she spread out over the desk, and leaned the pupil's head over the centre of the sheet so that the lice that failed to adhere to the comb dropped onto the paper, to be squashed with an inkwell. When the combing was finished the pupil returned to her seat and the room went back to work. Our first brush with public school delousing at the beginning of the term was an exciting event and we all watched goggle-eyed. A girl in the front row near the teacher's desk squealed excitedly, "There it is, Miss Horn! There it is! I saw it drop on the paper, right there."

So there was a lot of neck-craning and some of us even left our seats. As the weeks passed the lice hunt eventually lost its zest and we ignored it and went on with whatever we were doing while the operation was being performed. Or perhaps the homes of the immigrant children became less infested, and less public combing was needed. Certainly a fine-toothed comb was standard equipment in all the North End homes, for lice were no less endemic in the over-crowded immigrant homes than they were in the schools.

The regular North End school teachers quickly learned to cope with the scratching problem. There were other problems that took longer. The worst thing that could happen to a little immigrant boy was to make a winter entry into the public school system and bump into a substitute teacher with unrealistic ideas about neatness. Our standard winter footwear was a pair of moccasins or shoepacks with two or three pairs of socks. Immigrant children, however, often wore knee-length heavy felt mukluks to which rubbers were permanently attached at the bottom. Some of them kept slippers in their pockets and in school they'd take off the mukluks and wear the slippers. But many of the newcomers had the tops of their mukluks stitched to the bottoms of their pant legs just below the knees. When these kids started clumping around the room, a new teacher would instruct them to go into the clothes lobby and take off their rubbers. Impossible. If the rubbers came off, so did the mukluks and so did the pants! Most regular teachers understood all this and learned to survive in rooms reeking with the smell of mukluks drying out. But every now and then a teacher from south Winnipeg would turn up. It would take the class half the morning to get her straightened out about the facts of daily life in the North End of Winnipeg.

Teachers were easily shaken down, but I have often wondered since what effect the first few months in Canadian schools had on the personalities of the immigrant children. It was hard enough for an Anglo-Saxon like me, who knew the language, to move only from one school to another. Each move always entailed a couple of split lips and bloody noses before I settled into my place in the schoolyard pecking order. How much more painful, terrifying even, it must have been for the newcomers to be pitchforked into such an environment, where the natives were unfriendly and the language was impossible. It must have been humiliating in the extreme for a shy and sensitive seven-year-old to be summoned forward, by a teacher she feared, to have her hair combed, often ungently, by a sharp-toothed instrument that dug at the scalp or got snagged on knots. And it must have been cold comfort to discover later that the combing ordeal was one that everyone in the room would undergo eventually, for such was the way of the migrant lice in the cloakrooms of the North End schools. But painful though the experiences were at the time, I doubt that they did much permanent harm to the psyches of the new Canadians. For one thing, they were a lot stronger and tougher physically than we were. For another, they had already come halfway round the world and survived a hundred shocks and surprises, not the least of which was an interminable ocean voyage followed by an interminable railway journey. Mere teachers they could take in their stride, and if not, they could work off their frustrations beating up the Anglo-Saxon kids in the neighbourhood. They did.

I have often wondered how much of the prejudice that developed in Winnipeg against the whole immigrant population germinated in what could be called the fine-toothed-comb syndrome. For many Anglo-Saxon families, it was the first intimate contact they had with the immigrant world, and to use my mother's word, a "disgusting" one it was. It was not that the average Anglo-Saxon was any more fastidious than the average Ukrainian or Jewish family. Nor did the immigrant kids have a monopoly on transporting lice to school. At this stage, however, the Anglo-Saxons were firmly established several rungs further up the economic ladder than the immigrants. Hence they were not hived off in enclaves crowded with lice-infested rooming houses in the older parts of the city. The English, Scottish, and Irish immigrants, moreover, were not driven to congregate together because they could not speak the language of the country. They were thus able to spread out a little more, in cottages clustering around the

C.P.R. shops in Weston, for example. If they lived in North Winnipeg, however, there was no way in which they could isolate themselves from the lice if they had children in school.

Even in the best homes in North Winnipeg, as in the district's better schools, the scratching of a young head evoked an automatic response. Out came the fine-toothed comb. When the lice were extracted they were dispatched simply by squashing between thumb nails or, for the more squeamish, by drowning in coal oil or by burning.

"There! That must be all of them," an impatient mother would sigh. "Now for goodness' sake stay away from those hunky kids because I am sick and tired of combing bugs out of your hair!"

Where parents harboured no original prejudices against the immigrants, the repetition of hair-combing incidents was well designed to create them. They were certainly prejudiced against lice; "hunky" kids and lice went together. The fact that there were immigrant families who were as finicky about bugs as they were probably never occurred to them. Their responses were as automatic as those of Pavlov's dogs. Scratching signified lice, which produced the fine-toothed comb and the combination spelled hunky.

It would, however, be unwise to blame too much of the prejudice on lice. Adult Winnipeg of the era was as race-proud, bigoted, and prejudice-driven as any city on earth. The Ukrainians, Poles, and Jews who had come to Canada to escape from the Czar's military conscription did not rush madly to join the Canadian army when war broke out. Indeed, the only big rush was by the recently arrived British immigrants, many of whom saw the war as a free ride home for a visit, as something that would be over long before it involved them. When that illusion was shattered, and recruiting fell off, the aliens became a target for everyone. If an Anglo-Saxon wanted a job that some immigrant had, he thought nothing of demanding it as his right and insisting that the immigrant be fired. When labour troubles developed, they were blamed on alien agitators. The deportation of aliens was demanded by newspapers, labour leaders, preachers, and politicians with varying degrees of intensity.

Winnipeg prejudice, moreover, was not something about which simple generalizations were possible. Within the prejudices of each of the general categories of people were a lot of subsidiary ones. My father, for example, thoroughly disliked all Englishmen. How much of this went back to his days in anti-British Buffalo, and how much was new growth from the fact that the English dominated the civil service in Manitoba, is problematic. Whenever he failed in an attempt for some sort of clerical job in the civil service, his explanation was always the same: "They gave it to a bloody Englishman!"

There may have been a shadow of substance to his reasoning. All the immigrant groups quickly developed mutual aid associations, formal or informal. Getting a start in the new world was hard enough for any of the newcomers. When one got a job, he naturally looked around for a job for his wife's brother or the cousin of a Liverpool, Manchester, or London neighbour. There were not only English, Irish, and Scottish fraternal societies running full blast, there were secret societies and trade unions in which they could work for mutual advancement. A circumspect immigrant from Glasgow could certainly improve his chances if he were a Royal Arch Mason of the Scottish Rite, a member of the Sons of Scotland or the Knights of Pythias, a Knight Templar, and a supporter of the Dunfermline, Dundee, and Strathroy Association. Even the religious denominations tended to become mutual assistance societies, functioning to exclude those they disliked from gainful employment. It was curious how one catch-phrase was used by so many diverse groups: "Let one of them in and they'll take over the place."

The Presbyterians used it against the Catholics, the Catholics used it against the Jews. The Irish and English used it against the Scots and all the Anglo-Saxons used it against all the aliens.

But this was in the adult world. In ours, we also chose up sides racially and nationally, perhaps with the herd instinct operating in the interest of self-preservation. If a couple of Irish, English, Jewish, or Polish kids got into a fight with each other, the rest of us tended to stand back and let them go at it. We confined our participation to shouting encouragement to the one we favoured. But if a Jewish kid tangled with a Polish kid, it was not long before several other Jewish-Polish fights were going on, or two or three of one group would gang up on one of the other. We learned quickly, in the North End, always to make a quick nose count of the odds before letting the first fist fly. But in our vocal world, as distinct from our physical world, we tended to use all the labels without cluttering them with odious connotations. "Hunky" was a generic term that included all aliens of whatever national origin or religious persuasion. If we didn't know the name of a boy we were trying to identify we would refer to him as "the hunky kid who lives down the lane in that brown house".

Whether the process was helped by referring to him as a "hunky kid" never caused us any concern. It was a word we used when a better one did not come readily to mind. When we wanted to differentiate more sharply, we might refer to him as the "Polack kid", or the "Uke kid", or the "Jew kid". It was only when we got mad and started bandying insults that we used words that were intended to cut and slice—words like "bohunk" or "kike" or "wop"—and these usually were coupled with "dirty" for better effect. All these words, it should be emphasized, were words that got into our vocabulary in the schoolyards and were not consciously selected to define social attitudes. What the foreign kids called us we never really knew, because, as I have said, they reached into the language underground of their own tongue for suitable epithets.

The plain truth was that many an Anglo-Saxon kid spent much of his life envying the foreign kids. The Jews, for example, always seemed to be getting off on special holidays of their own while we had to stay in school and work. Not only did the Ukrainian kids have our Christmas holidays, they had a week in January when they had Christmas all over again. Even the Catholics who were not foreigners got away with murder, in our judgment. They had saints' days and feast days which gave them extra time away from school. There was even a custom then of honouring St. Patrick's Day, St. George's Day, and Burns' Day with special entertainment in the schools. Except for Victoria Day, the only day Canadian kids had anything to celebrate was the First of July and that was a holiday anyway.

There was undoubtedly a great deal of anti-Semitism in the North End of Winnipeg, and some of the parental attitudes must have filtered down to the children. Certainly the Poles and the Jews kept their distance from each other and the Ukrainians brought their prejudice against both with them when they came. For us, however, "Jew" was just another generic word that often included the peddlers who were Italian or Greek. When we scrounged bottles and scrap metal it was to sell to "the Jew", who was anybody that came along buying junk. The word "Jew" was also a verb that was synonymous for "bargain vigorously". If we haggled successfully over something we would say, "I Jewed him down."

I was well on in school, indeed, before I discovered that the Jews did not celebrate Christmas like the rest of us. We were living in the Rozell Apartments on Clark Street by then. A Jewish family lived on the third floor and their boy Izzy was in my brother's room at school. On Christmas morning I was overjoyed with my present—a pair of C.C.M. Automobile D skates which were screwed to my summer boots. My brothers each got a sleigh and my father bought a table gramophone for my mother. It came with half a dozen records. Four of them were Christmas hymns; one was "Carry Me Back to Blighty" and the other was a comic recitation entitled "The Preacher and the Bear".

After we had taken turns winding the gramophone and had squeezed as much laughter as possible out of it, I wanted to try out my skates. So I went to see if Izzy wanted to go skating with me. He had also got some new skates and I brought him down to see our new gramophone and listen to "The Preacher and the Bear". He wanted to listen to our other records so I put them on one after the other. He liked "Hark! the Herald Angels Sing" and "Adeste, Fideles". He kept time with those by pretending he was playing the piano and whistling. We played them a couple of times. Then he asked my mother if he could borrow the two records to play on his gramophone and see if he could follow them on the piano. It didn't come off. He would get going nicely and then hit a couple of wrong keys while the gramophone music got away and he could never catch up. It never occurred to me then, or even much later, that his was the only kosher household in Winnipeg from which Christmas carols could be heard emanating that morning. After a while I got tired winding the gramophone and jockeying around with the needle so we went down to the Kennedy rink and tried out our new skates.

CHAPTER FOUR

A Sporting Life, and a Good One

On all Winnipeg there is not a single statue, plaque, or illuminated address to the worth of the Wilkinson brothers. Nobody has even nominated them for the Hockey Hall of Fame, which must be the ultimate in over-sights, for without them many of the men who made the Hall of Fame later would never have learned to skate. During the first two decades of the century, the Wilkinsons operated a winter sports centre on the Assiniboine River at the foot of Kennedy Street. Each year in late November when the river froze over they would descend onto the ice, build a large warming shack, erect two toboggan slides, smooth off and flood about five acres of ice surface for public skating, and erect a couple of hockey rinks. Ultimately, the Wilkinsons were done in by too much sewage in the river and the construction of neighbourhood playground rinks by the Parks Board. But at its peak of popularity at the end of the Great War, the Kennedy rink was jammed every week night and all weekend with winter sports enthusiasts.

In Winnipeg most kids learned to skate in back-yard rinks flooded by the weaker-minded neighbourhood fathers. To flood a back yard was to bid good-bye to privacy, and peace and quiet for the winter. Many Winnipeg houses in those years had attached but unfinished back sheds in which wood was stored for the kitchen range; usually the back entrance to the house was via the shed into the kitchen. In later years, after electric stoves were invented, the woodsheds were converted into sun rooms or dens. In our day they served as ideal dressing-rooms in which to put on our skates, and of course we were in and out all the time getting warm. No eight- or ten-year-old ever closed a door, so on cold days the mother of the house was forever shouting at us to close the outer door and keep the draft out of the kitchen. There was at least one back-yard rink in every other residential block and most householders learned very early in the game that banning the playing of hockey was the course of wisdom. The inexpert stick wielding of beginning skaters always resulted in an outbreak of minor injuries serious enough for the recipient to howl with pain. The congestion was usually so great that a slight movement of a stick would thump, upset, or skewer someone. If the uproar grew too horrendous, an adult would emerge from the house, chase half the kids home, and warn the other half they too would go the next time anybody was heard crying. In retrospect the parents of that day were a long-suffering and patient lot who never learned from experience. They would flood the back-yard rinks year after year, despite the annual harvest of trouble.

Our first skates were always the type that were attached to our boots by an ankle strap at the back and a clamp on the front. The front clamp was tightened against the shoe sole by turning a screw with a key. Those of us with weak ankles bought supports that were laced tight over our socks before we put on our boots. A sudden stop or sharp turn would cause the skates to fly off the boots. We all wore boots that had several holes for laces at the bottom and a series of hooks at the top. When we got them laced tightly enough around the ankles the laces were sure to break with the first bit of extra pressure. So we spent more time going into and coming out of the back sheds than we did on the ice. This was just as well since there was seldom room on the ice at one time for all the kids who flocked to the rink from all over the neighbourhood. How we ever learned to skate under these conditions I'll never know. But we did. As we improved we progressed to skates that were screwed on to a pair of street boots, usually after the boots were worn out or almost outgrown. It was dubious progress at best. The screws tended to work loose and sometimes the entire front part of the skate would come away from the sole. When that happened junior-sized stove bolts were worked down from the inside of the shoe through the hole left by the loosened screw.

The screw-on skates were also used with the special skating boots which were then coming into vogue for children. When the skating season was over, the skates were removed and the boots were worn like regular footwear. By the time we moved within "sneaking-in" distance of the Kennedy rink I was eleven and had progressed to the point where I was using screw-on skates. It wasn't until I was fourteen and trying out with the Canadian midgets that I became the owner of a pair of hockey skates riveted to regular hockey boots. The skates most desired then were C.C.M. Automobile D's, which were replacing the tube type of skates for the hockey players. The Automobile D's were regular blade skates but the part next to the boot was made of aluminum. The Automobile D was much lighter and stronger than either tube or regular skates. When the first boy in a neighbourhood was given an Automobile D outfit, every other boy wanted a similar pair, and lack of proper skates became an explanation for a poor showing on the ice. My brother Walter, who grew into the things I grew out of, inherited my screw-on skates, and my brother Bob came into his clamp-ons.

Ours was a hand-me-down family, as indeed was every other family I knew with growing boys. Our winter overcoats—"reefers" we called them—lasted so well that one might serve as many as three boys before being discarded. Where there were no second and third sons to hand on outgrown things to, neighbour boys often fell heir to them. I don't remember any stigma being attached to giving or getting used clothing as far as boys were concerned, but I know nothing of the feminine reactions. There were no girls in our family. My mother, however, did quite a bit of sewing, making over dresses and coats for the girls of the neighbourhood.

Clothing wore out, of course, but skates never seemed to. So there was seldom a time when even the poorest kids could not scrounge a pair of second- or third-hand skates for attachment to their shoes. The first halting step toward adulthood was taken when they were allowed to leave the back-yard rinks and try their blades and legs at the Kennedy rink.

As free-enterprisers, the Wilkinsons struggled with an insurmountable problem: they had to earn enough in the four good months of winter operation to keep them for the year; but there was no practical way to fence off their enterprise or to keep out the youngsters of the neighbourhood who invaded it from all directions, intent on slipping in without paying. The only tollgate the Wilkinsons had was their warming shack, where the adults checked in to put on skates and hang their shoes, or to pay for the rental of a toboggan. They charged adults twenty-five cents and children ten cents for skating and, I think, twenty-five cents an hour per person for use of the toboggans. Or perhaps they rented toboggans by the length, for it was common for eight or ten young people to crowd together on a single long toboggan.

The war that the Wilkinsons waged against the young dead-beats was a losing one, but they gave it the old college try. Those of us who lived fairly close to the rink, say within a half-mile, would put on their skates at home and skate over on the packed sidewalk snow and through the River Avenue Park. Those who lived farther away changed into their skates on the river bank and left their street boots or moccasins in the snow while they skated. On quiet days, the Wilkinsons would keep pretty close watch on the rink from the windows in their office. When they saw a pack of freeloaders arriving they'd send an employee after us with a hockey stick. To be cornered by surprise in a hockey rink could result in a larruping of such painful intensity that further skating was out of the question for the rest of the day. They laid on the wood with an enthusiasm that raised king-sized welts on legs and lumps on heads.

On weekends the Wilkinsons depended more on stealth and guile than on frontal assault. Not only did we sneak onto the rink without paying, our gall was such that we even sneaked into their shack and soaked up the Wilkinsons' heat. The brothers divided their work between inside and outside. One looked after flooding the ice, cleaning snow, and policing the toboggan slides. The other stayed inside and collected admissions, sold soft drinks, laces, and such, and kept watch over the rink from the windows. He, we soon discovered, had a photographic memory for faces. He would wait until half a dozen of us were congregated in a corner getting warm. Then he would sneak up on us with an employee and seize our hockey sticks. When we went home and brought back the dime for our admission, we got our sticks back. Meanwhile, the outside brother would do a swing around the river banks and gather up all the boots and moccasins he found there. These too could be reclaimed by the payment of the admission charge. I took particular interest in the outside brother who, like my father, had one hand missing. Unlike my father, whose amputation was at the shoulder, this Wilkinson had lost his hand at the wrist. He never seemed to miss it, and he could do almost everything with the stump that any other man could do with a whole hand. He chopped and carried wood, manhandled the twenty-foot brooms they used to sweep the ice, fixed toboggans, and did most of the carpentry.

Every year the Wilkinson brothers became embroiled in a struggle with the forces of righteousness who invoked the Lord's Day Act against them. Soon after the season got under way, the police would turn up on Sunday afternoon, buy a ticket, and then issue a summons to the Wilkinsons for charging admissions on Sunday. Thereafter, the brothers would operate on a silver collection basis. Naturally, many of the customers would try and get by with a ten-cent donation instead of twenty-five cents. The Wilkinsons were imaginative enough, however, to restrict the activities and comforts of those who tried to beat the tariff. Over the long haul, they did not suffer much financial loss from their collisions with the Blue Laws.

As we grew older most of us made our peace with the Wilkinsons and each year acquired season tickets which gave us unlimited use of the facilities. These tickets sold for $2.50, and we borrowed and loaned them back and forth quite freely, until the inside brother got to know each of us by name. Then he seldom asked to see our tickets, but if he found one in the possession of a non-regular, he would confiscate it and give the real owner fits before returning it to him. With a season ticket, the Kennedy rink became the second home for the boyhood population of the areas bounded by Portage Avenue on the north, Main Street on the east, Sherbrook Street on the west, and the C.N.R. main line on the south. On any Sunday afternoon there would be a hundred boys playing hockey in each of the hockey rinks. And not only young boys. Most of the members of the senior and junior teams who played at the Amphitheatre and the Auditorium would be on hand, practising stickhandling in end-to-end rushes at top speed through scores of ten- to fifteen-year-olds who were all determined to trip them up, or at least to check them. Mostly we got knocked flying, because it was almost impossible to knock Ching or Ade Johnson, Ken Finkelstein, Sammie McVey, Konnie Johannson, Wally Fridfinnson, or Joe Simpson off their feet. But we tried and there was something more delicious than painful in the bruises or bumps we got from the adult stars who invaded our world.

"Boy, look at the lump I got!" "See, right there! That's what I got when I checked Ching Johnson into the boards!" For the next week we bragged about our injury to anyone in the schoolyard who would listen.

Hockey was the *big* deal at the Kennedy rink for us. But it was not the only attraction. The Wilkinsons arranged things so that speed skaters could train at the rink. They confined hockey within the fenced areas, and pleasure skating within a marked area in the centre of the open expanse. Speed skating was allowed around the outside of the pleasure-skating area. Occasionally during Sunday afternoons the big unfenced area

would be cleared of skaters to let the barrel jumpers take over. Then such stars as Jack Stack or Mike Goodman, who went to the 1920 Olympics as a speed skater, would put on barrel-jumping displays. They would circle the rink as fast as they could skate and then come down the centre and hurtle over eight or ten apple barrels laid on their sides. They would keep adding barrels until they could no longer leap them. Then their skates would hit the last barrel and they would sprawl headlong and slide for forty or fifty feet along the ice. Or they would land on top of the barrels with such force that a couple of apple barrels might be shattered and the ice would be littered with broken barrel staves. Naturally all the kids tried to emulate them, but few of us could leap a single barrel and maintain our balance when we came down on the other side.

In this era, before "Little Leagues" were invented, organized hockey began with the midget leagues for boys up to fifteen. The midget leagues played on the old Auditorium rink on York Avenue on Saturday mornings and on several public outdoor rinks throughout the city. I cannot recall any midget league team ever having uniforms except for the hockey stockings which came almost to our hips and were fastened, fore and aft, with safety pins. Our only protective devices were the shin pads made of thick felt that covered our knees as well. Ultimately most of us had at least one hockey glove but few even of the senior players bothered with shoulder pads, hip pads, or elbow protectors. The St. Boniface Canadians supplied their players with red, white, and blue hockey stockings. I played one season with them as a defenceman and wore my stockings in the Sunday-school league and the scrub team we put together at the Kennedy rink. The latter had the improbable name of the Gertrudes because half the kids on the team lived on Gertrude Avenue. Our Sunday-school team represented Augustine Church, and we had a league of sorts going with the other churches in Fort Rouge. There was always talk of a city championship when the season opened but the weather usually put an end to hockey before the schedule of games could be concluded. Except for the midget league games, all our hockey was played on outdoor rinks, and the weather had to be particularly frightful to cause a game to be postponed. Mostly, however, we played pick-up or scrub hockey at the Kennedy rink. Two Fort Rouge schoolboys from the Kennedy rink rats eventually made good as professionals—forwards Bill Alsip and Johnny McVicar. I think Jack Brockest, our goalie, may also have played pro. For every one of my former teammates who became a professional, there were dozens of others who went on to pro hockey from the Kennedy rink. In fact, unless he had served time there, it would have been difficult for any boy from the south end of Winnipeg to graduate to the indoor leagues.

Situated as it was on the edge rather than in the centre of a residential area, the Fort Rouge school had an environment quite different from that of other Winnipeg schools. In a way it was more like a country school than a city school. It contained only four rooms for the six grades. In each room there were not only separate learning classes within a grade, but two and sometimes three grades. Thus, Room One would be mostly beginners and a dozen in Low Grade Two. Room Two could have Low Grade Two, High Grade Two, and Grade Three. Room Three could have a few Grade Three and all but a handful of the Grade Fours. Room Four was the principal's room and was composed of a few High Grade Fours, Grade Five, and Grade Six. The nature of the school population and the size of the school provided considerable mobility between grades. Thus, bright pupils in Grade Five might absorb a good deal of Grade Six work simply by being in the same room. Because arithmetic was taught mainly by rote, there was a tendency for teachers to ignore class divisions and include all pupils in the drills and memory work. An additional factor blurring the division between grades was the regular Friday afternoon spelling bees and reading bees, in which the whole room was divided into two teams, which then competed individually in oral spelling and reading. Sometimes a pupil who was a dud at Grade Five arithmetic would be a whiz at Grade Six spelling.

The blurring inside the classroom was carried over into the schoolyard. In the larger schools, the pupils tended to shake down into associations with their own age groups. At Fort Rouge that did not happen. The bigger Grade Four boys chummed around with boys of their size in Grade Five and even Grade Six if they were in the same room. The small enrolment at the school intensified this process.

In late winter many of us took time out from hockey to practise speed skating in the hope that our school would be able to put together a team for the city skating championships which were held in the Amphitheatre. But as these races were broken down into both weight and age groups within each school, we could never find enough fast skaters in any one group to field a relay team. Nor was it ever possible to field a team for any other sport from any particular peer group. Our soccer teams always drew on the Grade Fours as well as on the

Grade Sixes. We had great difficulty putting any kind of a baseball team together to challenge Gladstone school because of lack of manpower. Our outfield was always made up of little kids whose fielding ineptitude usually turned scratch singles into home runs. On the other hand, the younger boys always got to play because ball games were usually impossible without them.

The end result of all this was that the Kennedy rink provided those of us with a passion for hockey with a chance to play with boys our own size and larger. Hockey was truly the national outdoor sport in those years, on skates and off. It was played under street lights at practically every residential intersection where a dozen boys could be gathered together all winter long. Sometimes the snow on the street would be frozen hard enough to skate on, but mostly it was played without skates. The best pucks were always those supplied by passing horses, "road apples" we called them.

But hockey was not the only outdoor sport. There must have been dozens of snowshoeing clubs in Winnipeg, all with their own distinctive costumes and given to walking for miles after every snow, usually stopping for a wiener roast somewhere along the way. Mostly they wore extra-long, heavy woollen coats that came to the knees and were gaily decorated with club colours and tightly tied waist sashes. Every year when a member paid his dues he got a patch to sew on his coat, and some members displayed fifteen or twenty patches. When one coat was worn out, the patches were all removed and resewn on the new garment. It was a common sight to see fifty to seventy-five members of a snowshoeing club plodding along the river any winter evening. All the large stores and commercial enterprises sponsored athletic associations. They had track and field teams, baseball teams, swimming teams, soccer teams, and cricket teams in the summer and toboggan clubs, skating clubs, and snowshoe clubs in the winter. The T. Eaton Company even maintained its own athletic establishment on Sargent Avenue that eventually became Sargent Park.

When it came to sports Winnipeg in the Great War era was truly a boy's world, both winter and summer. Where there was any kind of activity for girls, as with snowshoeing, tobogganing, and pleasure skating, it was something they did by going around with boys.

There were athletic events for girls only at the ubiquitous summer picnics. The railways lived off the picnic excursion business all summer long. The C.N.R. had a string of beaches along the lower east side of Lake Winnipeg with a terminus at Grand Beach. The C.P.R. served an equal number of summer settlements and tent villages on the west side. Every Saturday both sides of the lake were crowded with group picnics that ranged in size from a few score to several hundred. Periodically there were king-sized outings attended by nearly a thousand people. Two organizations in Winnipeg vied with each other for the largest picnic. The Orangemen marched down Portage Avenue to the C.P.R. station and spent the "Glorious Twelfth" refighting the Battle of the Boyne at Winnipeg Beach. The Caterers' picnic in early August saw all the food stores in the city shut down for an excursion to Grand Beach. The highlights of all the big affairs were the track and field events which were run off all day. The prizes offered were well worth going after. In the senior events luggage, golf sets, and clothing were offered in the men's section. The women competed for such things as dresser sets, combs, and mirrors. The men ran and jumped in track shoes, shorts, and gym shirts. But the women wore bulky bloomers, long stockings, and shirtwaists. Few of the muscles needed for running and jumping were ever developed by the girls in their early life for the simple reason that there were no games for them to play except hide-and-seek and skip the rope.

Going to the Caterers', or the Orangemen's, or the Knights of Columbus, or the Sons of Scotland, or the Sons of England, or Eaton's, or Jerry Robinson's picnic was often the highlight of our summer. This was a time when vacations with pay were comparatively rare. The building trades, for example, worked steadily all summer long to make up for the enforced idleness caused by the severe Winnipeg winter. Some office workers, bank employees, and retail clerks were given time off in summer. After the 1918 strike the civic employees got paid vacations and the government staffs also got time off. Some families had summer cottages at the beaches where they spent the summer while the fathers "batched it" in Winnipeg. But the overwhelming majority relied on such occasional outings as the picnics to the beaches provided.

The picnics were always one-day safaris because the last train from the beaches had to be on its way before midnight on Saturday. Winnipeg was well into the twentieth century before even streetcars were permitted to operate on Sunday, and it took a long and bitter struggle against the Sabbatarians to get the Sunday observance laws amended to permit the railways to run trains to the beaches on Sundays. So it was quite natural for us to begin to get excited about the Caterer's picnic a couple of weeks in advance of the event. If we discovered that any of our chums were going we always rushed home to break the news with breathless excitement. When the great day arrived we were always in a hurry to get to the station an hour before departure, but we never got there early enough to be near the head of the queue. When the doors to the station platform opened, the strongest boys of the family rushed madly up the stairs to grab a seat by the window and hold onto it for dear life. The sorting of families into seats was quickly done and one special train followed another out of the station with black smoke belching, wheels clicking, and couplings clattering all the way to the beach.

Once at the beach it was every family for itself. The members of the Caterers' Association went off on their own and the rest of us spotted our lunch kits, towels, and swimming things at a convenient table and let the day take over. I could hardly wait for the races to begin and took off at once for the athletic grounds. The big picnic sponsors used the track and field meets as spectator sports with which to attract picnickers. Naturally they devoted most of their attention to staging the senior events, but there was nevertheless a full program of races and games for the boys and girls. While our parents visited around and talked and made lunches, we were into everything—sack races, three-legged races, and straight sprint races. While I could outrun most of the boys at Fort Rouge school, I never won a first prize at any of the big picnics.

But whether we won or not never really seemed to matter much to any of us. Perhaps one reason we didn't win was our wasteful expenditure of energy running from one amusement to another. We would rush into our bathing suits and into the water. When we tired of that we would go picking sand-cherries. Then there would be a dozen work-your-way-in baseball games in which everybody was welcome to join. Other groups broke out soccer balls, and scrub football games would go on in the middle of the baseball games. In between all this activity we would consume immense quantities of sandwiches and homemade lemonade. Naturally most of us got sick some time during the day. But we would throw up, lie down in the shade for a while, and then start in all over again. It was small wonder that we willingly piled into the trains for the return journey and slept most of the way home, even with the windows open and the air filled with smoke and cinders.

Aside from the picnics, the fun we had growing up in Winnipeg was mostly the fun we made for ourselves. Nobody organized us and nothing seemed to reach a conclusion. We could play baseball for hours without deciding the game, perhaps because we usually lost track of the score halfway through it. When darkness fell we turned to Relievoh or Kick-the-Can, which we played under the street light at Alsip's corner at River Avenue and Bricker Street. For some reason that none of us ever investigated, we always met at Alsip's corner for all our activities. It did not matter whether we were going down to the schoolyard for baseball, swimming in the Red River off the old *John A. Macdonald* (a barge hulk long sunk by the shore on the other side of the C.N.R. tracks), going out to the Alsip brickyard to swim in the clay pits or to watch the huge fires burning in the brick kilns. Even on school days we'd all meet at Alsip's corner and walk or ride the final block to school together.

If our group had a leader, I suppose Bill Alsip was it. Physically, he was the best co-ordinated kid in the school and seemed to have a natural aptitude for games. He never had to learn to skate like the rest of us. He got his first pair of skates the year I moved into Fort Rouge school, which would have made us both eleven years old. Why he had never skated before I never knew, but he dropped by my place with his new skates and we went to the Kennedy rink together. I was still using the screw-on type and his new outfit was the fanciest I had ever seen. The tube skates were riveted to the boots, which were seemingly identical to the kind that the senior players used. They had built-in, lace-up ankle supports, raw-hide outer laces, and hard toes that were guaranteed to withstand the impact of blows from a hockey stick. Bill took a long time lacing up his ankle supports and getting into his skates. On the ice he took a few tentative steps and fell down several times, but at the end of an hour he was skating almost as well, in a straight line, as kids who had been skating for years. Within a matter of months he caught up with us all.

It seemed unfair to us that anybody should be as good at games as Bill Alsip, and have a rich indulgent father to boot. Bill's father's name was Elmer and he was one of several brothers who owned the Alsip Brick, Tile and Lumber Company. The company operated a clay brickworks in Elmwood, and one of our favourite summer recreations was to ride our bikes out to the brickyard and swim in the large holes left by the excavation of the clay for the bricks. These holes were quite remote from the residential area so we never worried about bathing suits. One towel would do for half a dozen of us.

We had one problem for which we never found an adequate solution—how to get from the water to where our clothes were piled without getting covered with mud to our knees. The clay beds from which the brick material was removed were overlaid by about three feet of Manitoba black gumbo. Horse-drawn scrapers peeled off the gumbo from an area one hundred feet square and dumped it around the edge of the hole. The exposed clay was impervious to water and after heavy rains or the spring run-off the pits would fill up to become permanent water holes. To get into the water we just slid down the gently sloping sides and flopped into the pond. But to get out we had to clamber over the gumbo banks made slippery by our splashing and the dripping from our feet and legs. We would sink into the mud and then we had to stand on one foot while we tried to pull the other out of the black glue that held it tight. In the end we found the best procedure was not to fight the caked-on gumbo when we got out of the water but to walk back barefooted to the brickyard and turn a hose on our feet and legs. It was an imperfect solution. We had either to walk along a gravel road, or to pick our way through a field overgrown with nettles, Canada thistle, and burr bushes, and strewn with broken glass. Bill and the other boys overcame that problem by stuffing their stockings in their pockets and donning their boots, muddy feet and all. I couldn't afford to do that because the dirt left on my boots would be telltale evidence that I had been swimming. My mother and father were non-swimmers who feared water, a fact we discovered when a truant office caught a bunch of us jumping into the Red River from the old *John A.* On the lee side where we paddled around, the water was never over five feet deep, but my mother feared for our lives anyway. Either parent would have forbidden me to go swimming at the brickyard if I had asked permission. So I never asked. This meant that I had to be very careful not to come home with any obvious evidence of having been swimming in the clay pits. Bill's father was more tolerant; Bill could do almost anything without parental disapproval. If we became overtired from our exertions, Bill's father sometimes found an excuse to send one of his brick wagons in the general direction of Fort Rouge and we could load our bikes on the wagon and rest all the way home.

Fort Rouge school was the most peaceable school I ever attended in Winnipeg. Unlike Isbister or Machray, where there always seemed to be two or three fist fights going on at any given time, a fight at Fort Rouge was rather unusual. Perhaps eleven- and twelve-year-olds are less aggressive than the six- to nine-year-old group. Perhaps the diverse ages in our classes had a dampening effect on pugilistic tendencies. Or perhaps I had grown somewhat more able to take care of myself and hence had ceased to be the school patsy. Two years before, when we lived in the Harald Apartments and I went to Mulvey school, I got beaten up so regularly that my father decided to take a hand. He discovered that the Y.M.C.A. had a boxing instructor and he enrolled me in the boys' section. In addition to gym and basketball I had the benefit of some professional boxing coaching. The coach was a well-marked veteran of the British prize ring by the name of Seaman Smart who had the wildest cockney accent I had ever heard. He was an exponent of the counter-punching school of boxing.

"Een eenstructing you een the manly awt of salf defence, Oiy 'ave two puhposes een maund," he would say at the beginning of each lesson. "Moy first eyem is to prevent you from being 'urt. Moy second eyem is to enable you to use youh fists in such a wye as to discourage any other blightah from tryin' to 'urt you. So the first lesson you must learn is balance."

He broke out a batch of skipping ropes and we practised skipping rope while staying on the balls of our feet. To encourage us he said after the first lesson, "W'en Oiym finished wif yer, you'll all be able to move around the ring like this—". He dropped his rope, struck a boxer's pose, and began skipping and darting and twisting and turning around the gym like a shadow-boxing ballet dancer. Our class watched him goggle-eyed, for we had never even suspected that dancing and boxing had anything in common. Eventually after the fourth or fifth lesson, we were allowed to don gloves and engage in sparring matches.

"Naw Oiy wants you to remember moy basic rules at all times," he said. "First, on the balls of youh feet. Second, get that chin tucked under the left shouldah. Third, keep youh eyes on those shouldah muscles because when youh opponent moves 'is shouldahs 'is hands will follow. And always feint for the jaw and follow to the body below those ribs. They's where you pump the steam outta 'im, right at that rib line!" To emphasize his point he'd dig a fist playfully into a pupil's belly and double him up. The weekly boxing classes evolved into a series of sparring matches with Seaman standing aside and calling instructions to us. None of us ever developed much aptitude and the only dividend I got from the course was the discovery that I could take a good punch on the nose without crying. I never finished the course, however, for I went home one day with a thick ear. I regarded it as an honourable scar of battle and showed it proudly to Walter and the kids in the neighbourhood. When I made the mistake of showing it off to my mother she put the kibosh on further boxing instruction. No son of hers was going to go through life with a thick ear like a plug-ugly; why, the next thing would be a broken nose. When my mother put her foot down, it had all the force of a pile-driver.

My instruction, however, came in useful when I began my career as a newspaper carrier boy and grocery deliverer. Every neighbourhood had at least one boy who played "chicken" with all the delivery boys who came around. Having sized up the strange boy, he would nudge the boy, or his bike, and challenge him to a fight.

At Fort Rouge school the acknowledged schoolyard champion was an Italian boy named Art Courtney. He wasn't much of an athlete and seldom got into our ball games or hockey games. But he was always spoiling for a fight. Any strange telegraph boy, railway call boy, or delivery boy for the stores who came into our area had Art Courtney to contend with. However, most of these boys had already encountered other Art Courtneys in their rounds and knew how to deal with them. When Art would throw down his challenge with, "Hey, kid, you wanna fight?" the countering gambit was, "Yer dam' right I do. Do you wanna fight?" To this Courtney would of course reply that he did. So they would try staring each other down for a while. The telegraph boy would then dictate the next move in these terms:

"Look kid, I can lick you or a dozen like you with one hand. But I ain't stupid. I ain't going to get into a scrap with you and have one of your gang jump in to help you. I know you guys. You start a scrap and then when you get the worst of it you cry for help and I'll have to fight three or four of you. No siree, I ain't that stupid." This brought an automatic rejoinder from Courtney:

"Okay then, let's choose a place and I'll sure beat your head in for you. Go ahead, you name it and you bring your gang along and I'll lick them too, one at a time or in a bunch!"

Usually these exchanges never came to anything because in truth one of the disputants was usually afraid and the other was glad of it. A fight only started when somebody made the fatal blunder of reacting timidly to one of Art Courtney's challenges. Any boy who turned the other cheek was bound to get it pasted. The only fight I ever knew to develop out of a talking match was one in which I was enlisted as Art Courtney's second. He had got into a verbal row with a C.P.R. telegraph messenger and they had agreed to meet the following Saturday morning in the lane behind the C.P.R. office at Portage and Main. Courtney bragged all the way to his appointment about what a beating he would administer to the messenger. There were a couple of other boys sitting in the back doorway when we got there and Courtney asked if number 86 was around.

"Hey, 86, there's a guy here wants to see you."

The boy came out and at first he didn't recognize Courtney. Then, when he did, he asked him to wait a minute while he went in and took off his messenger coat and hat. Then he and Art picked out a level place in the lane and squared off. They circled each other feinting and shooting out jabs that fell a foot short of landing. One of the other boys baited Art.

"Come on snot-nose!" he shouted. "You come all the way

down here for a fight why don't you start one? Y're yellow, I bet."

Art turned to threaten the heckler and got a belt behind the ear for his pains. They resumed their circling, and as Art backed close to the two spectators, one of them gave him a push in the back. I pushed that boy back into the doorway and as the gladiators came around I pushed Art's opponent into him and Art punched him a couple in the mouth. At this point the clerk in charge of the boys came out with messages for them to deliver and the fight was over.

"Boy," said Art Courtney as we started to return home, "I'll bet that dumb kid will think twice before he starts picking on anybody from River Avenue again."

The other boy shouted something insultingly defiant and disappeared into the telegraph office. Like most of the schoolyard fist fights, this one ended with little damage being done. But both antagonists emerged with an imaginative eye cocked on a future career in the higher reaches of professional pugilism.

CHAPTER FIVE

The Horse-power Symphony and Ginger Snooks

*O*f I had to choose one thing that made life most worth living for the kids of my generation, it would be horses. In those years Winnipeg ran on horse-power and horses were everywhere. Winter and summer, but even more in winter, they provided us with the means of getting around the city. We never walked when we could "hitch" a ride. And we could hitch a ride from almost anywhere to almost anywhere else. The consumer was still king then and the retail establishments of the city wore paths to his door. Nobody carried parcels and all the large stores and many of the smaller ones used light horses and wagons for making their deliveries. The railway companies operated both express and baggage transfers. The bread and milk companies all had horse-drawn vehicles. So did the dairy farmers, whose sons serviced regular routes through the city. The ice companies made their daily deliveries with fleets of heavy wagons, each drawn by two horses. Coal and wood deliveries were by horses and all the trash was collected by horse-power.

It sounds like the golden age of horsedom, yet the signs were already there to indicate that the days of the horse were numbered. The Horse Show Amphitheatre on White-hall Avenue had become simply the "Amph" where all the main hockey matches were held. The last horse show was held there well before the war. The stables for the show horses on the east side of the building were long gone, and the grounds where the carriages of the upper crust had once parked eventually became the birthplace of the Winnipeg Blue Bombers football team.

But for us that time was not quite yet, though the interest of many of the boys was beginning to veer from horses to cars. Here and there, back-alley stables were being converted into garages in which young fellows with mechanical aptitude set themselves up in the business of repairing cars. In the main, however, the automobile was still a luxury and few Winnipeggers drove to work. The exceptions were the rich grain brokers who made the journey from their Wellington Crescent mansions to the Grain Exchange in chauffeur-driven Packards. Some of their cars even had California tops with glass windows which replaced the canvas top and isinglass side curtains that were standard winter equipment. Keeping the cars running almost required a full-time mechanic for most car owners.

Down Clark Street from the Rozel Apartments lived the owner of a Hupmobile, a car with a queerly shaped engine bonnet. Every Saturday afternoon he would don a pair of blue-striped carpenter's overalls and a railway cap and go to work on his car. The ground around was soon strewn with oil cans, pieces of cotton waste, cans of grease, and assorted parts and fittings. He didn't seem to mind us watching, though he was a surly fellow and it was hard to tell. He tolerated us, provided we neither touched the car nor tried to help. Most of all he didn't want us passing any tools to him. He'd rather crawl out from under the car and get what he wanted than have us touch anything.

The Hupmobile, like most other early cars, had a badly engineered rear end, though it was probably far superior to that of the old Model T Ford. If we saw a car blocked up on pieces of firewood with the two back wheels lying akimbo and asked the owner what he was doing, he would swear lustily and say he was replacing the crown gear and pinion and order us off the premises. Crown gear and pinion were the first automobile words in our vocabulary.

When the Hupmobile owner was through tinkering with his car he would hang his overalls on a nail in the garage and take the car for a spin, after listening carefully for knocks while the engine was warming up. If we saw him at work we'd hang around hoping that he might invite us to go for a ride. He never did. Our attitude, I suppose, could be summed up this way: automobiles interested us but horses were a constant source of excitement and wonder.

Most exciting of all were the fire engines, and nothing in the years that followed ever matched, for me, the exhilaration that came from the sight of a horse-drawn hook-and-ladder outfit or a pumper engine outfit galloping madly to a fire with bells clanging. When my father worked for the city, and we lived in the Harald Apartments, I often went down to meet him and walk home with him on paydays. I was eleven years old at the time and could often talk one of the neighbourhood kids into going along with me by suggesting we call in at the Fire Hall and wait for my father there. The Fire Hall was located on the V where King and Albert streets came together between Bannatyne and William avenues, on an island of its own with streets on all sides. We used to watch the firemen going endlessly through the motions of shining the brass and nickel fittings on their machines. Sometimes they would let the horses' harness down from the ceiling and polish the harness fittings as well. We used to debate what would happen if a fire alarm sounded while the harness was being cleaned and whether the horses would get all caught up in the harness. We asked the firemen but they didn't know either, so it had never happened, we supposed.

Most of Winnipeg's worst fires took place in winter. In the summer, however, there were lots of false alarms and we would sit on the curb across from the main doors of the Fire Hall waiting for the place to explode into activity with the sounding of an alarm bell. It almost never did while we were watching. Occasionally, however, the firemen would have practice runs, and these were often as exciting as the real thing. The horses were kept in box stalls behind the rigs which were all parked facing the street. When the alarm sounded, the stall doors would burst open—how, we never did understand—and the horses would charge to the front of the engine and stand on either side of the tongue. The harness would drop from ropes which held it to the ceiling and while one fireman put on the bridle, another would do up the britching. Then the main doors would be flung open and away they would go at a gallop, striking sparks from the cobblestones of the street. We used to argue about which was our favourite piece of equipment—the pump engine that was hauled down the street belching smoke and stood snorting at fires like an angry elephant, or the hook and ladder, which was so long that the fireman who steered the back wheels always seemed to whip the rear end around corners in dire risk of his life.

My father's work took him into the Fire Hall occasionally and he introduced me to the men on duty. After a while I became familiar enough to pester them into letting me slide down the pole from the upstairs rooms. They did, once. If one of them hadn't stationed himself under the pole to catch me I'd have hit the ground with a wallop that could have broken both legs. That pole was the slipperiest piece of metal I had ever encountered. How the firemen ever got down it without breaking their legs I never did discover. One trip was enough for me.

There were a dozen other fire halls scattered around the city. When one of the crews was going to a fire it created such an uproar, with its ringing bells and the clatter of galloping iron horseshoes on pavement, that it could be heard for blocks. And the sound of the alarm was a signal for all the kids within earshot to drop what they were doing and run. It never mattered much to us that it was only a false alarm. The excitement was in the chase and we never tired of it.

Only slightly less exciting, though they were not a frequent occurrence, were the runaways. Mostly it was the one-horse delivery rig that ran away, though once I was able to claim full credit for having single-handedly stopped a runaway team of heavy work horses that had taken off with a dump wagon. By the time the team came around our corner the wagon had lost a rear wheel, and the horses had pretty well run themselves into exhaustion. In any event, as they rounded the corner the protruding axle end caught a power pole, gouging a great chip of wood from it, and almost upended the horses before it slithered off. The horses came to a stop not ten feet from where I was standing. It all happened so quickly that I had not even been aware of the runaway. But I grabbed the rein that was dangling beside one of the horses and tied it onto the front fence of a near-by house, taking pains all the time to keep well away from the puffing horses which, as it turned out, were quite content to await the arrival of somebody to take them in hand. If the horses had still wanted to run, they could probably have pulled the fence out by the roots and taken off with it as well as the wagon. Unhappily for me, none of the other kids were around to witness my great feat. So all I got out of it was a pat on the head from the teamster when he arrived, and scornful disbelief from my friends when I tried to embroider the adventure to make it somewhat more heroic. All I did was convince most of the kids that I had nothing to do with it, though several neighbourhood adults had come upon the scene early enough to accept the evidence of their eyes that I had in fact tied up the horses. Indeed, the lady owner of the fence was complaining that I had no right to tie the horses to her fence, but she wouldn't get close enough to the horses to untie them.

For the peddlers and junk dealers, a runaway was a double disaster. Their wares would be strewn all over the streets, and this robbed them of their capital. Like as not, their rigs and harness would be severely damaged and the cost of repairs was an expense they could ill afford. Occasionally a horse would injure itself so badly it would have to be destroyed. However, with the number of horses on the streets, it was surprising that there were not more runaways.

None of us who ever watched the spectacle of the Eaton horses debouching from the company stables in the Mail

Order Building on Graham Avenue will ever forget that sight. The Eaton stable-master managed the dispatch of his afternoon delivery with all the showmanship of a sergeant of the Royal Horse Guards sending his charges away for the trooping of the colour. The Eaton wagons were assembled in a long line on the inside of the building. At the appointed moment a policeman would step into the Graham and Hargrave intersection and halt traffic in all directions. Then the big door would fly up and the first rig in line would lunge onto the street and head north. The first few wagons usually came out with the horses jumping and prancing, but as the parade took shape the horses from farther down the aisle settled into their trot before they emerged from the building. With the drivers holding tightly to the reins, the horses seemed always on the point of bolting out of control; but they never did. Occasionally, though, the wagons would skid dangerously rounding the corner going west. The Eaton delivery rigs were such an attraction that people who were in the vicinity regularly gathered on the corners to wait for the show. Those of us who took our lunch to school at near-by Alexandra or St. Mary's frequently joined the gathering to help send the one o'clock delivery on its way. To us, Eaton's had the finest stable of delivery horses in the whole world and we would almost have rather been Eaton's drivers than locomotive engineers.

The Eaton horses were mainly hackneys, and each driver had two horses which were spelled off, one for the morning and one for the afternoon deliveries. The wagons, like the horses, were the finest available. They were equipped with rubber-tired wheels in summer and many were converted into steel-runnered sleighs in the winter. The horses never moved at any pace except a fast trot. It was a wonderful trot to behold, with the hocks snatching the back feet sharply from the pavement and the front ankles flexing quickly in and out as the legs rose. The driver rode, in the main, standing with one foot on a round step attached to the shafts and the other on the shafts itself. One hand grasped the hand-hold on the side of the wagon and the other held the reins, which were attached to a hook on the top canopy of the wagon.

The wagon bed itself rode about shoulder height from the ground, with foot-high wooden sides surmounted by strong wire mesh rising another five feet to a solid roof. Inside the mesh were rolled fabric curtains which could be lowered to protect the goods inside. The ensemble was painted red, white, and blue. The driver made his deliveries in a way that would have got him expelled from any teamsters' union on earth. The merest pressure on the reins brought the horse to a halt in front of the house where a parcel was to be delivered. The driver would reach into the rig, grasp his parcels, trot to the front steps, and mount them two at a time. There was none of this "all deliveries at rear" nonsense with any Eaton's driver. He would place the parcels at the front door, ring the bell, and be off. The horse watched as the driver ran down the steps, and started up as he reached the sidewalk. The driver swung onto the rig on the run as the horse trotted down the street. If the driver walked down the steps to the wagon, however, the horse would not move until he got the order from the driver. He knew that the driver had another parcel in the wagon which had to be delivered before he moved. For as long as the Eaton horses were on the streets, they caught my eye and held my full attention whenever they came into sight. They did so even though they were a total frustration for me. No Eaton driver was ever allowed to give a boy a ride on his rig. And no boy ever tried harder to curry their favour, with less success, than I did.

Next to the Eaton wagons, the most exciting delivery horses were those owned by the bread and the milk companies. These horses sometimes knew the milk and bread routes better than the drivers. They would stop and start as the drivers serviced their customers and seldom needed a word or a touch on the rein. It took a little time for them to become accustomed to changes of customers, however, and they would have to be driven by the houses of departed users and taught to stop at houses added to the routes. Unlike the Eaton rigs, the milk and bakery wagons used the back lanes. And as the lanes in winter were never wide enough for two rigs to pass, they all travelled their routes in the same direction.

The mavericks in the world of household deliveries were the drivers who delivered milk directly from the dairy farms to the consumers. They carried their milk in bulk in ten-gallon cans. The liquid was poured from these containers into smaller cans that held a couple of gallons which the drivers carried from house to house. The tops of the small cans were cylindrical and held a quart when full and a pint when half full. The driver always came into the kitchen, measured out the milk, and poured it into the customer's container. My mother never believed in pasteurized milk so she always patronized the dairy farmers. She was convinced that the process of heating milk to destroy germs also destroyed its good qualities. We always saved the bread crusts that got too hard for us to eat to feed to the milkman's horse. In the summer, when the wartime gardens were ripening, we also saved the carrot tops and the pea vines we pulled up to feed them as well. The dairy drivers would occasionally take the sons of their customers around their routes with them, to play at driving the horse, which needed no driving. But the drivers of the regular creamery rigs and the bakery rigs would not tolerate passengers, though the baker hired me occasionally as a Saturday helper to run back and forth to the rig to fetch goodies the customers wanted that were not in the baskets he carried.

The teamsters who drove the dump wagons were uninhibited by "no passenger" regulations and in fact seemed to like the company of small boys. But there was nothing very glamorous about sharing a seat on a dump wagon, which was usually full of dirt from an excavation, cinders, garbage, or street refuse. But if we were bound for Happyland, or an inter-school soccer game, or just downtown, and a dump wagon was going our way, we never scorned a ride. Most of the delivery men managed to get through life without too many problems with the kids. The bakery drivers and ice wagon drivers, however, were exceptions. The former kept their bread, cakes, and other confections on trays on the inside of their wagons. They would load a large basket with a variety of baked goods before disappearing into an apartment block. Many of them had locking devices high up on the rear door that none of the small boys could reach. Those who left their doors unlocked kept the boys of our neighbourhood in doughnuts. But not for long. The baker reported the thefts to our parents and insisted on collecting from them for the stolen goods. When we lived on Clark Street, Walter and I were accused half a dozen times of pilfering cakes when we hadn't been within blocks of the rig. Our tearful denials failed to save us from whatever penalty was thought proper at the time.

There was no problem of having to pay for the ice we grabbed from the ice wagons. In fact, if we asked, the iceman would usually let us take the chips off the blocks that were melting anyway. His problem was with kids cluttering up the inside of his wagon on hot days. Not only did we track dirt into the wagons, which eagle-eyed housewives complained about when he delivered the ice, but there was considerable danger of us pulling some of the six-hundred-pound blocks of ice down on top of ourselves. So giving us chunks of ice to suck on was a small price for him to pay to be free of pestering kids. As we grew older few of us ever tasted a libation that could equal the cooling qualities of the slivers of ice we sucked after a hard game of baseball.

Horses, of course, meant barns, not only the small barns in the back lanes where the peddlers kept their horses, but the huge cartage company barns. There was such a barn on William near Princess that eventually became a garage. There was a big barn near the Midland railway yards and another in behind the C.N.R. main line off Water Street. Saturday seemed to be shoeing day in these stables and the job could never be done without an audience of a dozen boys standing open-mouthed as the blacksmith applied the red-hot shoe with a sizzle of smoke to the hoof of the big Percheron or Clyde. There seemed to be horses everywhere at the Jewish market on Derby Street, where my mother did her weekly shopping for vegetables and butter and eggs when we lived in the North End. My brother Walter was five then, and Robert was two and had almost outgrown his carriage. My mother would load him in it and on Saturday morning we'd all walk from Salter and Mountain to Derby and Dufferin where it would take her an hour to load the carriage with vegetables and groceries. My mother was a very slow shopper, which suited us fine for we would walk around and pet the horses that were tied behind the farm wagons, or were being shod in a near-by blacksmith shop. In summer some of the horses wore straw hats that were equipped with holes through which their ears poked. Some had stripped leather arrangements over their noses to keep off the flies. Some even had a sort of shawl covering from which long strings drooped, again to keep off the flies.

All the horses I knew as a boy were friendly, neither kicking, biting, nor making threatening gestures, except toward dogs that rushed at their heels without warning. By the time I was fifteen I must have been on petting terms with two hundred horses over the years. The first time I ever saw a twitch used on a horse was on the race track, where I also first got to know horses that were strikers, kickers, biters, weavers, cribbers, and stall walkers. There is no place like a race track to turn a soft-hearted horse lover into an implacable horse hater; such is the pure meanness of thoroughbred dispositions. Yet the meanest horse I ever knew was not a thoroughbred at all. He was not even a horse. He was a Shetland pony by the name of Joker. He was owned by a boy named Harold who lived over on Balmoral when we lived in the Richmond Apartments. Harold used to drive the pony around in a cart which he said was called a dog-trap. It was made entirely of wicker and had a sort of raised seat at the back and two side seats at near floor level in front. Harold sat on a front seat with his back against the side of the rig when he drove. He was twelve or thirteen when I was eight or nine. Harold would drive Joker round and round the block but he never gave any of the other kids a ride.

"Don't ask me for a ride," he would always say when he drove up and stopped where some of us were sidewalk-sitting. "My father says if I ever let anybody else in this cart I'll never get to drive him again. Joker doesn't like to pull two people and if he ever ran away somebody might get killed."

Some of the older kids argued with Harold but he never gave in. However, as a favour to us, he'd let us feed Joker sugar or carrots, or pull grass for him. Joker was the original misanthropic horse. If he was offered a carrot held in the fingers he would bite the fingers. Offered something from the palm of the hand, he would bite the hand that fed him, literally. If you got close enough to make the offer comfortably, he'd find a way of stepping on your foot and you could yowl and push but the iron-clad hoof would stay put until Joker decided to remove it. If you stood within a yard of his hind legs while someone else was feeding him he would find a way of kicking your shins. And if you leaned against the rig he would find a way of backing quickly to run the wheels over your feet. When and if we struck back at Joker, there was Harold and his whip to contend with. I learned about ponies from Joker, and owning a pony was one of the top items on my unwanted list. His owners did something to me too. For the rest of my life I was never able to become friendly with anybody named Harold, though I met several with that name who seemed like nice enough persons. They were condemned, however, through guilt by association because of a pony they never knew existed.

The most horse-fun was in hitching rides in the winter, when all traffic moved at a much slower pace. Most of the cars had long since been put up on blocks in back yards to await the return of spring. Every horse had a set of bells attached to his harness in winter so we could hear a potential lift approaching far enough away to be prepared for it. There were coal and wood rigs moving in every direction all day.

Winnipeggers used an immense volume of both fuels. The electric stove had not yet made its appearance. Gas stoves had been in use for many years but they were confined mainly to apartment buildings. My mother never really mastered the gas ranges in the various blocks we lived in. I suspect her main motivation in escaping from janitoring was not the hard work involved but the fact that the blocks all had gas ranges. She had grown up with coal and wood stoves, preferred wood to coal, and regarded gas as a most inferior type of fuel for cooking food. She feared gas, she distrusted it, and she was convinced to her dying day that not only was it unhealthy but it spoiled the taste of whatever was made on it, including the water boiled for tea. Enough other women shared her suspicions that most of the house kitchens I was ever in used wood- and coal-burning ranges which doubled as household water heaters.

Reliance on these fuels meant that every household had a storage area. There were woodsheds behind every house, save those in the wealthy districts. The kindling for the furnace and the stove-length wood for the range were chopped and stored in these sheds. Most of the fuel wood was delivered in sleigh racks. The rack was simply two pieces of eight-inch-square timber stretched along two sets of steel-tired runners. Uprights against which the four-foot lengths of wood were piled were reinforced with steel braces that ran from the ends of the timbers to the tops of the uprights. A heavy piece of supporting lumber was nailed from one timber to the other outside the uprights. The racks were ten feet long, about six feet high and hence held two cords of wood, usually tamarack from eastern Manitoba. Firewood could also be bought cut to length from the fuel dealers, but there was hardly a householder in Winnipeg who was not convinced the dealers short-shipped their customers on cut firewood. So it was mainly bought in four-foot lengths and sawed on the premises, usually by a man with a portable circular saw powered by a gas engine whose sleigh followed the wood racks around.

The cross brace at the rear of the rack was an ideal seat for ride-hitchers. So throughout the winter, wherever we were going we rode on the wood racks. Except, that is, if we were in a hurry. Then we caught rides on the back of light delivery rigs. Most of the teamsters who drove wood racks walked more than they rode. The horses could pull their loads only at a slow pace, and on cold days, which was most days, the drivers walked along beside their horses swinging their arms to keep warm.

Since snow removal, except by the spring thaw, was unknown in Winnipeg, there was plenty of snow for the sleighs all winter long, except on the bridges, on streetcar tracks, and at the main intersections. The Winnipeg Electric Company's revolving snow brushes kept the bridges clear of snow down to the pavement. When the wood sleighs got onto the bridges they would frequently get stuck halfway across. If the driver could not shovel enough snow under the runners from the sidewalk to get his team started, he would have to wait for a streetcar to nudge him along. There were times, on very cold days, when the streetcar itself would spin its wheels and only a second team hitched in front of the first would get the convoy of streetcars and sleighs started again. The teamsters were never intimidated by any stretch of snowless street or bridge, though.

The Winnipeg Electric Company also kept its surface lines around the city clear with the use of the huge revolving brushes mounted on work trolleys. These brushes when going full blast could create a cloud of flying snow and ice particles forty or fifty feet high and fifty or sixty feet across. The wood rack teamsters kept as much to the side streets as possible and away from the streets where the streetcars ran. However, they had to get across these streetcar routes and that presented a mounting hazard as winter dragged along. While the tracks themselves were kept free of snow, a mound gradually built up between the two sets of rails. Sometimes the sleighs high-centred on the centre ice mound. Sometimes the front runners got stuck on one set of rails and the back runners on the other. Sometimes an inexperienced teamster would try to angle across the mound, get into a skid, and spill the top half of his load into the street. A load of cord wood scattered across a busy intersection in the gathering winter dusk was the original traffic disaster area, even in the days when motor cars were scarce and trucks scarcer. There were enough of both on the streets even then to provide the ingredients for a traffic jam. And as sure as there was a traffic jam there would be boiling radiators and exploding tempers.

In all Winnipeg no temper exploded with the ferocity of that of Ginger Snooks; and only in an age of horses could any city have produced such a character. He was the original wild Irishman whose entire life was spent in a rage against the world. Ginger was a free-enterprising cartage man with a weakness for getting into deals with the city. His deals always went sour, however, so he was forever embroiled in threatened lawsuits, or in appeals to the city to change the provisions of the contracts. He had hauling contracts with the city that included carrying the manure from the city stables to the nuisance grounds, cleaning out privies located on city property, hauling wood and coal to soldiers' dependants, and hauling trash for the street-cleaning department. In between times he was engaged in a general hauling business and often combined city business with his own. Thus in the spring he would haul manure from the city fire halls to customers who required it for their gardens, collecting from both the city and the customer.

In addition to his notorious temper, Ginger Snooks had a vocabulary that consisted almost exclusively of the earthiest of Anglo-Saxon words. When Ginger Snooks invaded the City Hall it was a signal for all the female clerks to get out of earshot, and preferably out of the building, for Ginger had a voice that carried. Because of his many disagreements with civic officials he was in the City Hall so often that an alderman once suggested he should run for the City Council himself. The idea so appealed to him that he filed nomination papers at the next election. The local cut-ups who hung out at the Marriaggi Grotto thought it would be a wonderful joke on Winnipeg if Ginger were elected. So they set out to elect him and missed by only a hundred-odd votes.

Just about everybody who did not know Ginger Snooks at least knew of him and that included the kids in our neighbourhoods. The Harald Apartments at the corner of Westminster and Langside was on the route he took to his customers in Armstrong's Point and to the Sir James Aikins establishment. If Ginger crossed our paths at a safe distance from parental ears we would often run along beside his wagon and sing out an obscene limerick that neither scanned nor rhymed but, through the alchemy of youthful communication, seemed known to all the kids in Winnipeg. It has no printable translation, but it never seemed to bother the old man. He ignored it and us.

One day I was calling on my friend, Gus Badali, whose father was a wealthy Italian restaurateur who lived just north of the Aikins estate. As Mrs. Badali came out their front door with a couple of lady friends all dressed up for a shopping trip, Ginger Snooks passed on his wagon.

"Hey, Mrs. Badali," Ginger shouted at the top of his voice, "will anybody be home this afternoon because I'm plannin' on comin' round with your load of shit?"

Mrs. Badali and her friends were so embarrassed that they went back in the house to regain their composure. My friend Gus, not wishing to lose the opportunity of a lifetime to use some adult language in public, shouted back:

"I'll be here all day, Mr. Snooks, so you bring your load of shit around and I'll show you where to pile it." The Badali house had well-fitting windows so Gus escaped the whaling of his young life.

Whether it was for transportation, excitement, or only passing the time, horses were a basic part of our zest for life. And they were a factor, surely, in the aesthetic life of Winnipeg as well. What did Winnipeg ever need with a symphony when it had the sounds of winter all day long? It was true, as Irving Berlin wrote—although he had probably never heard of Winnipeg—that we used to listen for the sound of sleigh bells in the snow. And listening, we would try to identify the sound. The Eaton rigs were comparatively easy, for their sleigh bells were high-pitched and the fast pace of the horses gave them a six-eight time. The bells on the heavier horses that drew the dump wagons and coal sleighs were both deeper in tone and had a slower beat. Indeed, the only pleasant thing about the coal rigs was the sounds they made, both the bells on the horses and the tune the coal made as it rattled down the steel chutes into the basement. Most basement coal bins were afterthoughts put up with left-over lumber, packing cases, and pieces of cardboard. After every coal delivery the household had to be given an all-over dusting. And this had to be done again after the sons of the family had completed their weekly chore of taking out the ashes. This was one chore I never had to do. By the time I was big enough to do it, we were living in blocks. When we eventually moved back into houses I had younger brothers who were being taught the virtues of honest toil. Yet for all small boys, whether they had ashes to take out, wood to carry in, or kindling to split, there was comfortable reassurance in the sounds of winter, including even those of the coal wagons. The whine of the circular saw cutting through cord-wood and the clinking rattle of coal going down the chute added some reassuring warmth, and the omnipresent sounds of the bells told us that nobody was really alone, or had anything to fear from the darkness of an early winter night in Winnipeg.

CHAPTER SIX

On the Trail of Jack Krafchenko

For kids growing up in Winnipeg in the years around the First World War, the greatest desperado of all times was not Jesse James, Dick Turpin, or even Billy the Kid. His name was Jack Krafchenko and for several weeks in the winter of 1913-14 he brought all other matters of interest, all other conversation, to a standstill. By legend he was a gunman, confidence man, bank robber, murderer, and jail-breaker. He was also a certifiable lunatic but they hanged him anyway, on July 9, 1914. For the Strathcona and Machray school kids he was easily the most exciting thing that ever happened to our neighbourhood. Indeed, until Earl Nelson came along in 1927 and began strangling women, Krafchenko was the most exciting thing that ever happened to Winnipeg.

Jack Krafchenko was born in 1881 in Romania of Ukrainian parents, which by Winnipeg definition made him a Ruthenian, and he was brought to Canada with his parents at the age of seven. His family settled in Plum Coulee, southwest of Winnipeg near the American border, where for the next seventeen years the father was the village blacksmith. From his earliest youth Jack Krafchenko exhibited a violently aggressive streak. Ordinarily a placid, friendly boy, he flew into towering rages when crossed or disciplined. He was apparently a bright enough student but spent little time in school.

At the age of fifteen he was caught stealing a bicycle in Morden and appears to have been sent to jail, though the record is far from clear. In any event, he was launched on a career of crime that spanned two continents, according to the lurid accounts in the Winnipeg papers before his trial for murder.

Unhappily for any Krafchenko biographer, there are two or three versions for most of the stories that surround him. One story states that he left Plum Coulee and went to Australia where he became a professional wrestler, and that he wrestled extensively in the States under the name of Australian Tommy Ryan. Certainly, though he was only five feet six inches tall, he was extremely well muscled for his 160 pounds. His handsome face, however, was completely unmarked and his ears and straight nose belied the legend of his professional wrestling career. He came back to southern Manitoba around the turn of the century and posed as a temperance lecturer while writing a number of bad cheques. He was caught and sent to the penitentiary at Prince Albert for three years. En route he is alleged to have jumped through the window of a moving train while handcuffed. His guard jumped through the window after him and recaptured him. There were stories that he later broke out of Prince Albert penitentiary and that he had been convicted of armed robbery a couple of times.

The juiciest legend in the dossier was that he had gone to London from Canada and held up a bank there. He locked the manager in a cupboard and joined the crowd outside to watch the excitement when the police arrived. From England he went to Germany, robbed a bank there, and then went to Italy, still robbing banks. He wound up in Russia in 1905, where he married, and then returned to Canada in 1906. Between bouts with the law, he took up blacksmithing and worked at the trade steadily enough so that he became a foreman boiler-maker at the National Transcontinental Railway shops in Graham, Ontario.

Eventually he was done in by his temper. In the summer of 1913 he was demoted from his foreman's job for his violent outbursts. The demotion was such a humiliation that he quit. He came back to Winnipeg, hunted up his old criminal associates, and gambled and drank with them in the Moose

Club and the Pyramid Club, a couple of all-night boozeries. Then he went out and hung around Plum Coulee for some weeks visiting with his old Mennonite friends, of whom he seemed to have many. He travelled back and forth between Winnipeg and Plum Coulee several times in November and in the process joined with three of his Winnipeg cronies in a plan to rob the bank at Plum Coulee. They arranged for a car to take them out to Plum Coulee during the last week in November for the robbery. Unfortunately for them, the manager of the bank decided to take the day off and closed the bank early. Krafchenko stayed on at Plum Coulee; the others returned to Winnipeg. On the first of December he called on a local acquaintance named William Dyck and arranged to have Dyck drive him to Winnipeg after he robbed the bank the next day. According to Dyck, the arrangement was made by Krafchenko's holding a gun to his head and forcing him to agree to drive the get-away car. Why Dyck did not go to the police after Krafchenko threatened him was never explained, except that Krafchenko had such a terrible reputation that he terrorized everybody into silence.

The idea of Krafchenko robbing the bank in Plum Coulee was so transparently preposterous as to immediately indicate serious mental disorder. In that town of 150 people, just about everyone knew him. He had grown up there. His family had all lived there until a few years previously. To escape from the town after the robbery would be difficult, for little maintenance was done on Manitoba's mud roads after the first snow fell. Moreover, to try and get away in a car was even less sensible than using horses, since the cars of 1914 were kept running in cold weather only with great expenditure of time and energy on the part of the drivers. There was literally nothing about the Plum Coulee caper that made the slightest sense.

Yet rob the bank he did, all by himself the next day, of $4,700 in cash. After his departure from the bank with the money, the manager got out his gun and took after Krafchenko. He followed the robber and tried to force him to give up the loot. Krafchenko shot and killed him and was then driven part way into Winnipeg by Dyck. The only sensible act performed by Krafchenko during the entire episode was to provide himself with an oversized overcoat and keep his face hidden during the robbery in the hope that none of the local people who knew him could identify him. At least, he seems to have thought that was what he was doing. Those who saw the shooting identified him anyway.

The details of the robbery and murder were reported at length in all three Winnipeg papers the next day. The papers then proceeded to convict Krafchenko of the crimes and reported in detail his previous life of crime. For my father, the newspaper stories were full of fascination, for he claimed that he had once known Krafchenko. When my father came west in 1904, he had stayed temporarily with his brother James, who had homesteaded near Cartwright, forty or fifty miles west of Plum Coulee. He said Krafchenko had hung around Cartwright that summer and was forever getting into trouble with his gangster behaviour. This did not square with the newspaper stories that Krafchenko had been in Russia about that time but I, of course, was unaware of the fact then. As the manhunt went on, Father read every item aloud to my mother each evening, invariably punctuating his recital with the comment that he always knew Jack Krafchenko would come to a bad end.

On December 10, the police arrested Jack Krafchenko in a house at 439 College Avenue, which was tantamount to being next door to where we lived at 386 Salter Street. Our house was on the west side of Salter just north of Mountain, and College was the first street south of Mountain. The house where they got Krafchenko was on the north side of College west of Salter. So we could go out our back door, zip down the back alley, cross Mountain Avenue, and we were at the back door of the College Street house. We of course knew nothing of the arrest until the morning paper was delivered the next day. But for the next week the lane between College and Mountain was alive with boys of my age and one of them was usually me.

While Krafchenko was hiding out in Winnipeg his behaviour became even more psychopathic. He had three or four associates take part of the loot and hide it. He arranged to send $700 to his wife. He concocted wild plans to escape from the city dressed as a woman, and even had one of his pals buy him a complete woman's wardrobe. But he gave up the idea because he felt a woman would be too conspicuous riding on a freight train. When he rented the room on College Street he posed as a professor at St. John's College. In another house where he had a room, he posed as a doctor who had come to Winnipeg to assist in sewing an accident victim's leg back on. He even examined and treated an infected tooth of the landlady's son. The son immediately became suspicious of the doctor and notified the police. While the detective was interviewing the son in the kitchen, Krafchenko left through the front door. Nor did he take pains to remain hidden. He dropped in at the Moose Club and was frequently seen in his old haunts on Main Street.

One of Krafchenko's pals, predictably, turned him in. When he was arrested, the chief of police went out to the back fence and retrieved a bundle of the loot that Krafchenko's buddy had hidden in the snow at his direction. Neither the chief nor his detectives bothered to count the money. There was still at least a couple of thousand dollars missing and for the next week we combed and recombed that lane, and all the lanes around, in the hope of finding the money. We not only looked in the lanes. We were in and out of all the yards on the street. We searched back porches surreptitiously. We pawed around in the stables under the hay and into the oat barrels. We turned garbage cans inside out. Once the rumour spread through Machray school that one of the boys had found a dollar in the lane between Mountain and St. John's. Away we all went like a pack of hounds on a fox scent.

Eventually our zest for the cache cooled and we turned our attention elsewhere as Krafchenko disappeared from the front pages for a while. But not for long, or for good. Periodically he had to be taken before a magistrate for arraignment. The provincial magistrates did business in the law courts building on Broadway, and Krafchenko was kept in the near-by Vaughan Street detention jail. (It was in the yard of the Vaughan Street jail that executions were performed, and even in later years the clatter of hammers on scaffolding was a common sound for residents of the vicinity.) The Vaughan jail was a hundred-odd yards from the back entrance of the law courts and concern was expressed that Krafchenko, being such a desperado, would escape from custody on the way from jail to court. The authorities decided he should have a safer place of incarceration, and the city police station on Rupert Avenue was chosen. The cells at the Rupert Avenue building were on the fourth floor while the court rooms were on the second floor. So the risk of escape would be reduced because the journey from the cells to the court rooms and back was entirely indoors. The deep thinkers in the Attorney General's department did not, however, take into account the Keystone Cop qualities of the Winnipeg police force.

The city police decided not to keep Krafchenko in the regular jail cells. Instead they moved a cot into an old kitchen down the hall from the cells and locked him in there. On the night of January 10, he unlocked the door of his room with a dime-store skeleton key, stuck a gun in the ribs of his guards, locked them in a cupboard, and escaped through a hall window. While lowering himself to the ground on a clothes line, the rope broke and he fell heavily to the ground from a height of twenty-five feet. Though badly injured, Krafchenko disappeared into the Winnipeg underworld.

That winter, as always in those days, Winnipeg depended for its news exclusively on the newspapers and word-of-mouth rumours. So the first news of the escape came with the publication of the morning *Free Press* on Monday. The people who did not subscribe to newspapers got only garbled versions of what was happening from their neighbours. In our area of the North End, few of the immigrant families subscribed to the daily newspapers. They relied mainly on the foreign-language weekly papers to keep them informed. So in the Machray-Strathcona schools area, some of the wildest rumours flew back and forth, and we believed them all. The outraged indignation of the town was boundless. For some queer reason, my father took the escape of Krafchenko as a personal affront. He bought all the newspapers as they came out and read the Krafchenko stories over and over.

"Listen to this," he would say, "just listen to this." Then he would proceed to read long reports of the accusations that were flying back and forth between authorities. I listened avidly to every word Father read aloud. None of the kids I knew were yet able to read the papers, or inclined to even if they could. Many of their parents, moreover, were non-sub-scribers. So I could gain kudos by being able to dispense information about Krafchenko that was unknown to most of the schoolyard.

The provincial government did not even wait until Krafchenko was recaptured to launch a full-dress inquiry into the escape. Chief Justice Mather was named to head the inquiry and his commission got into operation in a matter of hours. Everybody who had any contact with Krafchenko was hauled before it and cross-examined mercilessly. Percy Hagel, Krafchenko's lawyer, was subjected to a verbal flaying and was even forced to explain why he had visited Krafchenko so often in the week before his escape. If Krafchenko had not been convicted by the newspapers before his original capture, he certainly was by their reports of the Royal Commission hearing. The newspaper reporters treated the affair as they would have treated a performance of *East Lynne*—as drama critics. They commented on the demeanour of each witness, and gave their assessment of the testimony as it affected Krafchenko, pro or con. The entire affair was handled, both by the newspapers and by the commissioner, as if Krafchenko was already a convicted murderer.

But if he was a murdering bank robber to our elders, to us he was a hero in the grand tradition of Jesse James, even Robin Hood. We were convinced beyond all doubt that he had to be hiding some place in our neighbourhood. It was this conviction that led us, over the next week, to tumble into our beds each night exhausted from our efforts to find him.

"Look," we told each other, "he's got to be around here some place. When he was hiding from the police last time, where did he go? He came right down to College Street. So why won't he come back right down here?"

The police came roughly to the same conclusion as the Machray school first-graders. To the authorities, Krafchenko was what was politely called a Ruthenian and impolitely called a Bohunk. He spoke both Ukrainian and German fluently and hence would be expected to seek shelter "among his own kind". He would have one very great advantage if he ducked deep into the North End. He would be among people who might not know that he was a fugitive with a price on his head. Like us, they saw deep significance in the fact that he had hidden out on College Avenue after the robbery, though strictly speaking the heart of the Ruthenian area was south and west of College and Powers.

During his flight from Plum Coulee he had used an artificial beard. Beards were not particularly common then, though they were by no means rare. Until Krafchenko was recaptured, men with black beards were trailed wherever they went by a bevy of small boys, but always at a safe distance. The kids of our neighbourhood confined their search mostly to the back lanes on the assumption that a wanted criminal on the run would want to sneak down lanes rather than walk down the front streets. In our searches we never went alone, and the kids my age always tried to tag along behind the older boys.

Every movement aroused our suspicions. If we heard a stable door slam, or a woodshed being opened, or even wood being chopped, we would "shush!" each other and creep up on the sound. Once half the Machray school pupils concentrated in the lane between Mountain and St. John's when a rumour spread that Krafchenko was hiding in a barn loft and that the police had been called. A lone constable eventually arrived and approached the barn with considerable caution. He went in, climbed the loft, and emerged with a couple of boys who had gone into the barn to smoke cigarettes.

In all our watching and besetting, none of us ever had any clear idea of what we would do if we ever blundered into the Krafchenko hiding place. Mostly we skulked around down the back lanes in groups of three or four listening for noises. And there always seemed to be noises.

"Hey, what's that?" someone would shout in a whisper and we'd all freeze in our tracks. We'd place our ears against the wall of the barn or woodshed and listen. If we heard anything we'd scatter back down the lane and then sneak back together on tip-toe. Only if there were some big boys along would we ever take steps to investigate. It was all a gigantic game of hide-and-seek and nobody was really "it". Looking for Krafchenko was a far cry from the times we had been looking for money before his escape. Then we seldom hesitated about going where our impulses moved us, even if it meant going where we had no business to be. But in the search for Krafchenko we mainly stood and shivered, partly from excitement and partly from the cold that was turning us from blue to white. And no matter where our search of the neighbourhood started, we usually wound up in the lane behind the College Street house where Krafchenko had lived while hiding out after the robbery. The landlady must have grown to abhor the sight of small boys and rubbernecking adults who always stopped to stare as they passed her house.

In our home, as in most homes in the neighbourhood with boys my age, Krafchenko put intolerable strains on the family ties. We were seldom on time for any meals except breakfast. We were warned and warned to come straight home after school; but we would turn up an hour late, usually breathless with wild tales of having seen Krafchenko on Boyd and Powers or running along Main Street. Yet if the schoolboys saw Krafchenko behind every open shed door and every set of whiskers, the adults of the town were no less gullible. The town's most prominent auctioneer spotted him one night walking down Higgins Avenue. He followed him over the Red River, spotted the house he entered, and then telephoned the police. A squad of cops turned up in the paddy wagon, which they parked a block away. Then they set up a portable wooden shield that they pushed before them as they approached the house. Eventually they got to the front steps, where one of them pounded on the door and shouted for Krafchenko to come out with his hands up. All that came out was a thoroughly frightened householder in his nightshirt.

My father's acquaintanceship with Krafchenko, whether real or imaginary, led to my getting a lot of attention from the kids at school. I had mentioned, boastfully no doubt, to the other kids that my father used to know Krafchenko when he lived at Cartwright. Whether they believed it or not, they repeated the story and soon it was all over the school and I was being pointed out as the kid whose old man knew Krafchenko. Naturally, there were doubters, particularly among the older boys, and I was accused several times of making up the story.

"Aw, gwan," they said, "your old man never knew Krafchenko. How could he know him when you didn't even live in Plum Coulee? If your old man's so smart why don't he tell the police where Krafchenko is hiding and get all that reward money? You're full of bull!"

"All right," I said, "I'll prove it to you. You come home with me and I'll ask my dad and he'll tell you. Come on, I'll show you who's full of bull."

The upshot was that by the time we got to our place I had about a dozen kids in tow, enough anyway to jam all the standing room in our kitchen where my dad was reading the paper.

"Daddy, these kids don't believe that you really knew Jack Krafchenko when you were out at Uncle Jim's farm. You tell them that you knew him, will you, Dad?"

My father marked his place in the paper and looked the kids over.

"Which one of you doesn't believe I know Krafchenko?"

he asked teasingly. The boys who had most seriously doubted my story remained silent for a while. Then one of them nudged and pointed to the boy next to him. The nudger said, "Orval here sure made a big thing about not believing Jimmie, but most of us just came along to see."

Orval half shrugged, glared, started to speak, and then stopped. My father took over and told them about Jack Krafchenko.

"He was a big blowhard," my dad said. "He used to hang around the blacksmith shop but he never worked. He just talked and bragged about where he had been." My father really didn't seem to know very much about Krafchenko except that he was really very strong for his size. He expounded on Krafchenko's feats of strength. The boys seemed satisfied and one of them asked if my father thought they would ever catch him. His father, he said, was sure that Krafchenko had made good his escape to Chicago. During that week the papers carried reports of Krafchenko being seen at several American points as well as across Canada. My father's faith in the Winnipeg police department was less than complete, stemming perhaps from their lack of interest in tracking down the culprits who had beaten and robbed him.

"They will catch him if he ever gets out of Winnipeg," he said. "And they'll hang him, too, you can count on that because anybody who would shoot down a fine man like Mr. Arnold in cold blood deserves to hang. If you ask me I'd say hanging is too good for him, particularly when you come to think that he's never done any good for anybody in his whole wasted life!"

The boys waited for more conversation, but my father quickly ran out of recollections of Krafchenko and the kids soon drifted out and away. I was disappointed in my father. He had told us a lot more about Krafchenko than he told the kids. And I could see that my friends were as taken aback by my father's anti-Krafchenko attitude as I was. While we followed every rumour of Krafchenko's appearance, none of us really wanted to see him captured. In the uneven contest between the hunters and the quarry, we were all on the side of the pursued. My father's expressed conviction that Krafchenko would hang hit us all where it hurt.

Days passed without our interest in the man-hunt abating very much, perhaps for the reason that there was not much else to be interested in at that time of year. Long before the end of the first week of his escape, the Royal Commission was filling columns of the newspapers every day. Eventually one of the guards broke down under a long cross-examination and incriminated himself and several others who had planned the escape during drinking bouts in the Clarendon Hotel bar opposite Eaton's. The guard and the others were arrested and the bag included Percy Hagel, Krafchenko's lawyer, and himself the son of one of the West's most famous criminal lawyers. It was not long before there was a stampede by everybody who knew anything about Krafchenko, his rob-bery, or his escape to confess to the police. Yet still Krafchenko remained at large and it was only after the police got onto the trail of a former clerk in Hagel's law office that the search heated up.

On the night of January 18, a dozen armed policemen led by Chief MacPherson surrounded the Burriss Block on To-ronto Street in the west end and took Krafchenko back into custody.

In the days after Krafchenko's escape, there was a general consensus that Krafchenko's jail break had been expertly planned, probably by a well-organized gang who had spirited him out of the country. The truth was that it was as badly bungled as everything else in Krafchenko's star-crossed life. The first mistake was in using a piece of old rope that broke under his weight. When he landed on the concrete pavement behind the jail, the fall tore his leg muscles and smashed some ribs. It was the middle of winter, but he had no coat or hat. No organized get-away had been arranged. Yet Krafchenko claimed he had managed to hobble down to Main Street, along Main Street for two blocks to William Avenue, and was struggling down William past the City Hall when a passing motorist stopped and offered him a lift. Krafchenko explained he had fallen on the sidewalk and dislocated his leg. The motorist drove him to the Burriss Block, where Hagel's former clerk lived, and helped him into the building. That was the last Krafchenko or anybody else ever saw of the passing Samaritan, who seemingly found nothing out of the ordinary in a sorely injured stranger wandering the street without an overcoat in the middle of a bitterly cold winter night. Had he become suspicious and notified the police he could have collected a $5,000 reward. If he had waited a couple of days the reward would have been worth $11,000. He was undoubtedly a non-reader of newspapers and so failed to discover that Jack Krafchenko had been his passenger. If Krafchenko's story of his escape was true, how did his benefactor manage to live in Winnipeg for the next week without becoming privy to that fact by the conversations about the escape that drove all other topics into limbo? That was and remains one of Winnipeg's most fascinating mysteries.

Krafchenko was taken in by Hagel's former clerk, and despite the price on his head he was sheltered and cared for until the police arrived. The clerk worked at the nearby Security Storage warehouse and Krafchenko asked him to fix up a piano box in which Krafchenko could be shipped out of the country. The police discovered evidence, in the form of food scraps, that Krafchenko had actually tried out the idea. But his injury was too painful to go ahead with the project, and although he was still armed with a loaded revolver he gave up without a struggle when the police arrived. He was rushed to trial at Morden the following April and was hanged in the Vaughan Street jail yard on July 9, 1914. Meanwhile, Percy Hagel was convicted of aiding in his escape and went to the penitentiary for three years. The guard who supplied the gun got five years and those who had participated in the planning of the escape got lesser terms. By then we had moved to Young Street and, having forgotten Krafchenko, were planning delinquencies of our own.

CHAPTER SEVEN

A Boy's-eye View of the Great War

The first money I ever earned was on August 4, 1914, and for a small boy it was a painful, even exhausting, introduction to the world of economics, labour, and human cupidity. I was awakened that morning by the shouts of newsboys running past the window of our suite in the basement of the Richmond Apartments.

"Hey, extra! Free Press extra! War declared! Germany invades Belgium! Extra! Extra!"

For the next half-hour the shouts came almost in waves as the boys rushed down Ellice Avenue and branched down the side streets. In those pre-radio and largely pre-telephone days, whenever anything exciting happened, like a disastrous fire, a shipwreck, or a big prize fight, the papers rushed out special editions. It was the circulation managers' responsibility to have key boys scattered all over the city whom they could telephone to round up extra-selling crews. In the downtown areas they would zero in on the newspaper offices. In the outlying districts the papers were delivered by truck to the regional depots where the boys would assemble. There was good money in selling extras, for we bought them for two cents each and sold them for five. Ordinary newspapers cost a cent and a half each and were sold on the streets for two for a nickel.

Most of the kids in the eight- to ten-years bracket who lived in our neighbourhood in 1914 sold extras. Several of them had regular corners on Portage Avenue at which they sold papers

101

after school. I had pestered my parents for permission to become a newsboy after we moved to the Richmond Apartments, but they always refused to allow it. My mother was afraid I'd get hurt and my father simply said I was too young. But they relented that August morning and my mother supplied the capital for the launching of my business career. She gave me a dime with which I could buy five papers. I rushed through breakfast and was off in a cloud of dust and small gravel for the *Free Press* building. I arrived at the back door out of breath and discovered a man sitting on a two-foot pile of papers.

"Where do you buy the extras?" I asked.

"Right here," he replied. "How many do you want?"

I handed him my dime and he slid five papers under my arm and I was on my way toward Portage Avenue. By this time Portage Avenue was crowded with men going to work, many of them reading the extra editions as they walked. I decided to cross Portage and head south toward the rooming houses around St. Mary's Church. I sold my first paper quickly, to a woman who ran out of a house in a kimono, bought a paper, and ran in again. At the next intersection I sold another. This time the customer only took a dozen steps and returned.

"Why you little crook!" he shouted, stuffing the paper at me. "Gimme back my nickel. That's the first extra they got out hours ago. Where's the second extra?"

That was the first I knew about a second extra. I had been swindled by a circulation manager who had simply been sitting on a pile of papers returned from the trucks that had taken out the first extra. There was already an army of kids on the streets with the later edition, so the only chance I would have to sell my papers was to find some late risers to unload them on. The prospect was hardly an attractive one. I gave the man back his nickel and started back to the *Free Press*, rehearsing all the while the speech I would make to the man so that I would either get my money back or be given a supply of new papers. On the way I decided not to overlook a chance of making a sale, so I went along shouting my extra to an unheeding world.

At the corner of Carlton and Portage I discovered a basic fact of newsboy life. I stopped on the corner to shout, "Extra! War's declared!"

I barely had the words out before I got a combination shove and kick from behind that sent me sprawling. I got up bawling from the sting of a scraped knee to encounter a tough-looking newsie a couple of years older than myself.

"What the hell are you doing on my corner?" he demanded. "Get the hell off this corner and make it snappy if you don't want to get beat up," he threatened, waving his fist.

I got lost quickly in the crowd that was eddying around us. By the time I got back to the *Free Press* the man who had sold me the papers was gone. So, choosing discretion over valour, I headed down the side streets and avoided the corners where other boys had established prior rights. I simply kept on walking and shouting and by mid-morning I sold two more papers to unwary housewives. Late in the afternoon I wound up near the new St. Boniface stockyards at the far end of Marion Street, a good three miles from home. I sold my last paper to a construction worker who had missed the first extra. He read the paper avidly as he walked along the sidewalk wheeling his bicycle beside him.

I asked him the way back to Young Street and he was so surprised to discover how far I had walked that he gave me a ride on the bar of his bicycle down Marion as far as the St. Boniface bridge. When I got back to the Richmond Apartments it was well after supper time and there was nobody home. My father and mother, it transpired, were out scouring the streets for me. I fell asleep on the steps of the block, where they found me when they came home. It was over a year later before they let me go extra-selling again but no small boy ever slipped a couple of coins into a dime bank with greater satisfaction than I did that night.

The war itself touched our family very lightly. The men of my father's family were all too old for service, while none of my cousins with whom I was acquainted was old enough. Two of my mother's brothers and one brother-in-law enlisted in

1915. My mother's sister had two small children when her husband went overseas and she had a very difficult time. There was no government assistance for the wives and children of soldiers. Their families were dependent on the largesse of the Patriotic Funds that sprang up all over after the outbreak of war. Millions were raised and distributed by the wartime charities, but when it was averaged out among all the recipients it was a very thin living indeed. Some idea of the scale of things may be gained from the fact that the first pension for widows was $249 a year, and the same amount was granted to soldiers who returned totally disabled from the war. Soldiers' wives had no alternative but to go out to work, in an age when there was little employment open to women except office cleaning and domestic service. My aunt, however, managed to get a job in a store and my mother looked after our cousins during the day while we lived on Young Street. But when we moved to the Harald Apartments on Westminster and Langside my aunt had to make other arrangements.

Like most of the other women of the times, my mother was always knitting; the Patriotic Fund provided khaki wool for volunteers to knit into socks and scarves for the soldiers. She kept her brothers in socks throughout the war, for she could turn them out at an unbelievable rate. We'd sit watching her knitting after supper and the steel needles would fly through the wool. The whole city, in the early war years, embarked on a frenzied knitting binge. Where all the wool came from we never knew. But great cartons of it would turn up at school and the boys were given the job of converting skeins into balls for the girls to knit with. The better girl knitters were allowed to knit socks and woollen mitts. The beginners were started on scarves and every now and then a little Grade Three girl would become so fouled up in her scarf-knitting that she would set everybody around to giggling. Then her work would all be unravelled and she'd start over again. Inexpert as the kids were in the beginning, they nevertheless turned out tons of hand, foot, and neck protectors during the war.

Second only to knitting was the Victory Garden crusade that swept the town about the middle of the war. With the shortage of farm labour and the demand for food for overseas, local food prices started to rise sharply. So it became the patriotic duty of everybody to plant Victory Gardens, and in Winnipeg there was plenty of room for them. The real estate developers had left the city pock-marked with vacant lots. These open spaces had provided us with do-it-yourself playgrounds very close to where we lived. We played baseball on the corner lots, and built bonfires on them in which we blackened potatoes, which we then ate raw under the illusion we had cooked them. We dug trenches in the lots and played soldiers, burrowed from them under the wooden sidewalks, and hollowed out secret forts all the kids knew about. Turning all these playgrounds into gardens we regarded as the ultimate in wartime outrages.

My mother and father seized with enthusiasm the opportunity to have a wartime garden. On the farms of Manitoba when my mother was growing up, the garden was the responsibility of the women of the household, along with the chicken-feeding and butter-making. My mother loved to garden and she put in a large one in the big Victory Garden layout on Young Street between Broadway and Westminster in 1916. There was no problem with planting the garden, it was the weeding that destroyed my interest. After every rain my mother would hand me the hoe and point me in the direction of Young Street. Very often she would go with me to see that the job was done properly. My father shared her enthusiasm but with only one arm he did an even poorer job of weeding and potato-hilling than I did. So mostly he built the smudges which helped to keep the mosquitoes away. No Winnipeg summer evening, in those pre-insecticide days, was ever tolerable outdoors without a smudge, and most householders saved their grass cuttings for smudge-making.

The fact that the gardens were operated under the imprimatur of patriotism never protected them from the marauding instincts of small boys. Garden-raiding was a favourite pastime and none of us ever went hungry when there were gardens around. We depended on them for our supplies of roasting potatoes and carrots. The rows of carrots, radishes, and onions all developed wide gaps that marked the passage of the boys of the neighbourhood. Such passage was not always peaceful. As our raids increased, the garden owners set up neighbourhood vigilante groups to police the fields. The fleetest of them were not above hiding behind fences and hedges and pouncing on us from behind. Some of them could even outrun us and when they did we were soundly spanked and painfully pummelled. Getting a whacking if we were caught was an accepted part of the game. But some of the sneakier gardeners developed a gambit which we regarded as the ultimate in dirty pool. Instead of chasing and trying to catch us, they would simply identify us. Then, when we were going about some other business, they would sneak up behind us as we passed their garden, or even passed their house, and apply heavy toes to the seats of our pants. But if we went home and complained we were usually in for a second punishment. My parents took the dimmest view of garden raiding, regardless of whose kids were doing the raiding.

The participation level of the public schools in the war effort seemed to depend a great deal on the principal. Some schools, particularly in the North End, went in for Victory Gardens on a grand scale. There was considerable vacant land west of Powers Street and Strathcona school put in a garden that took up most of a city block. Each room seemed to have had its own plot and there was a competition with prizes for the best efforts. How the project was managed in the summer when school was out I never knew.

I went from Grade One to Grade Three in Isbister school but the only patriotic exercise I can recall was knitting. Other schools had bugle corps organized and at Mulvey school, where I took Grade Four, we had an almost pacifist type of cadet corps that might very well have been the Loyal Temperance Legion. We were issued broomsticks to carry as rifles and were given red sashes to wear like Sam Browne belts. A rotund little man named Colonel Billman visited the school regularly and we were taught to march up and down the schoolyard and form fours. The Colonel doubled as a dancing master, and actually seemed to enjoy mincing around using his dancing steps more than doing the march routines. This was the closest to a physical education program that we ever had in public school, except of course for the public-school soccer leagues in which all the schools took part. The cadet corps by no means enjoyed the unanimous support of the community. The mothers in particular objected to their young sons being encouraged in martial pursuits by parading around with broomstick guns.

In our house it was my father who objected. A great deal of the propaganda pressure that was exerted on behalf of the war effort was produced by aging military types who were themselves well beyond the cannon fodder age. They were aided and abetted by lady patriots of the military auxiliaries. My father, with his missing arm, would probably have rated at the very bottom of the 4-D category. So it would have been perfectly safe for him to have played the role of the super-patriot. Instead he was utterly out of sympathy with the war, and I suspected at times that it would not have taken much to squeeze a mild expression of sympathy for the Germans out of him. Certainly there were bitter words when my uncles came in from Carman to enlist. Uncle Bill and Uncle Johnson were always very close and when one decided to enlist he made up the minds for both of them. They enlisted before coming to visit us and both were displaying the red, white, and blue ribbon on their lapels which the recruiting office provided pending their being sworn into the army. My father spotted the ribbons when they came in and launched into a bitter tirade. They shrugged off his criticism and ignored him for the rest of the evening. They were feeling very resentful toward my father but he never apologized.

Jobs were easy to get after the war was under way, and even though he drank heavily on paydays, my father managed to keep employed. But wages were low for the kind of work he could do and he seldom earned more than twenty dollars a week, on which he had to raise a family of three boys. What saved the family from utter disaster as prices rose during the war was his genius for talking people into things. Certainly it had to be a sales pitch of pure genius that enabled him to talk apartment block owners into hiring him as janitor. He was incapable of firing the furnace in the block, of hanging storm windows, or of shovelling snow. But one owner after another yielded to his blandishments and as a result we had free rent and a few dollars a month income from the janitor jobs. My mother, of course, did all the work, with the help of my brother and myself. And when my father was working, a man was hired to sleep in the furnace room and keep the boilers going in winter. In the main, my father kept his views about the war to himself and there was never any trouble with employers over them. But they erupted unexpectedly and disconcertingly around the house.

At Mulvey school our teacher was strong on patriotic songs. We began each day by singing all three verses of "The Maple Leaf Forever" followed by "Rule, Britannia!" and "God Save the King". For practice in memorizing the words and music, I frequently sang them around home. But when my father was home he would tend to explode in anger at "Rule, Britannia!"

The big thing in Winnipeg during the first year or two of the war was the parading by the bands through the streets playing martial music and luring the civilians to fall in to the parades. The parades were usually headed by a drum major in a black bearskin hat with a huge staff that he flung around in time with the music. Most of the musicians were in uniform. They were followed by a score or so of uniformed soldiers who marched ahead of the young fellows who had signed up during the past several days and were not yet in uniform. The vacant lots on Young Street where we played were close enough to Portage that we could hear the bands long before they arrived. We would tear off down the street and watch the parade going past and in particular watch the recruiting officers getting the people from the sidewalk to join in the parade, which of course meant that they were heading for the barracks to join the army. To get into the parade they had to shoulder aside a small army of kids who always brought up the rear. If the men sang as they marched we naturally joined in. Occasionally we would so out-number the volunteers that the officer in charge would sic a corporal on us and we'd break off and go home.

If our elders got half the thrill we did out of marching behind the band the wonder is that the parade did not denude the sidewalks of people when it passed. The main barracks was located on Osborne Street opposite Whitehall Avenue on the grounds of what is now the Manitoba Legislative Building. The parade followed several routes. Sometimes it would go north on Kennedy and turn east on Portage to Main, up Main to Broadway and back to the barracks. At other times it would cut across the old Hudson's Bay Reserve where the store now stands, turn west on Portage to Sherbrook Street, south to Broadway, and back to Fort Osborne. During the march the recruiters often got as many as a dozen or more men to join the parade and volunteer for service. I learned very early in the war that it was a mistake to say that I had been up on Portage watching the parade when questioned about my absence. Of all the wartime activities, my father disliked parades the most.

My mother never shared my father's antipathy toward the war. For her it was something very personal. Her brothers were fighting in France, and if truth, righteousness, and justice were not the monopoly of the Allies they would not have been there. She simply turned a deaf ear on my father's aberrant opinions. So did I after a while, for the counter pressure was tremendous. Even the elementary schools were hotbeds of patriotic fever. Occasionally we had returned soldiers turn up to tell us about their war experiences. On those days, most of us ten-year-olds went home wishing we were old enough to enlist and wondering how old you had to be to enlist as a mascot.

When the conscription crisis blew up in 1916, after the supply of reinforcements for the troops through voluntary enlistment began to lag, my father became quite outspoken on the subject. He was working for the city in 1917 when Fred Dixon and Dick Rigg in the legislature and George Armstrong and Bob Russell in the labour movement were manning the barricades against conscription. One of Rigg's legislative speeches against conscription was so stirring that A.V. Thomas, the *Winnipeg Tribune*'s legislative reporter, got completely carried away and stood up in the press gallery and cheered. He was fired, instantly.

As it turned out, City Hall seemed to be a fairly safe place for people with pacifist sentiments like my father. Several of the Labour members of city council were anti-war zealots and the labour movement itself, including the civic employees' union, was split over the issue. So when a monster anti-conscription rally was held in the Grand Theatre on North Main Street on the first Sunday in January 1917, my mother insisted that my father take me along for company. She was convinced that, with me along, he would stay out of trouble. There was the usual bevy of speakers, including Dixon, Rigg, and Armstrong, and the meeting was well under way in the packed hall when a group of soldiers stormed in from the back and headed for the stage with clubs and fists flailing.

I was naturally terrified at the shouting and the melee in the aisles. I grabbed my father by his good arm with both hands and pulled him with me in the stampede to the exits. When the assault on Dixon and Rigg took place we were out on the street and the police eventually arrived in sufficient numbers to restore order. But Dixon did emerge at length with a bloodstained handkerchief pressed to his head and there were many in the labour movement who were convinced that the cancer that carried him off ten years later was the result of the beating he took that day.

What impressed me most about the speeches was the way in which all the speakers peppered us with words I could not understand. I did discover one thing at the meeting that shook me a great deal. The United States was not in the war. I just naturally assumed that the whole world was united in a struggle to keep the Germans from slaughtering all the Belgians and French and conquering the rest of the world. As one of our teachers once explained, if the Germans won the war we would all have to speak German. The speakers at the Grand Theatre meeting kept asking, over and over, if this war was a crusade for justice, freedom, and national survival, why was not the United States in it? Why did we Canadians have to make such sacrifices while the United States maintained a hands-off attitude? But aside from this single point, the meeting was well over my head. I was similarly unimpressed a few years later by a boy evangelist who blew into town. He conducted revival meetings at one of the "Jesus Saves" churches and turned up one night on Market Square when it was Winnipeg's Hyde Park corner. He was a rosy-cheeked little fellow with a give-'em-hell brand of preaching and was supposed to be only twelve years old. He spoke with a high-pitched, squeaky voice but I was convinced that he was a midget in disguise. No kid that age could know all that this one seemed to know about the Bible! It was not long, however, before the Young Communist League was sending its twelve-year-old Young Pioneers out to disrupt Labour Party meetings by peppering the speakers with questions about dialectical materialism. Perhaps the next generation was just so much smarter than mine. Or perhaps they had better teachers. In any event none of the inspired oratory I heard during either the conscription controversy or the 1919 General Strike made any impression on me. It might as well have been in Swahili for all I ever understood of it.

Once conscription was adopted, the agitation against it seemed to peter out. Perhaps the entry of the United States into the war had something to do with it. I know my father tended to cool down a lot after that, but he was never really reconciled to conscription. He carried a downright distrust for soldiers with him as long as he lived. That I can understand, for I was with him when a recruiting sergeant gave him a right to the jaw that sent him to the sidewalk in front of the Post Office.

It happened in the late spring of 1917, when ladies from the battalion auxiliaries occasionally turned up on Portage Avenue to pin white chicken feathers on able-bodied civilians who were not in the army. The army had set up a recruiting stand in front of the Post Office and it was the job of the recruiting sergeant to accost civilians on the sidewalk and try to talk them into enlisting.

My father's job entailed taking the registered mail from City Hall to the Post Office each day and I had gone down to meet him after work and walk home with him on the day in question. He went into the Post Office and I stayed outside watching the recruiting sergeant being spurned by all his potential enrollees. Some of those he approached had probably been reacting with anger and the sergeant must have been having a very poor day. My father, who was scarcely five feet six inches tall, nevertheless walked with a square-shouldered stride that was almost a swagger. He turned to his left as he breezed out of the Post Office and almost collided with the sergeant.

"Well, now, you're a fine-looking specimen, my man, why aren't you in the army?" he said to my father. As he spoke he took hold of my father's left arm and half spun him around. My father always carried the armless right sleeve of his coat inserted in the right side pocket. As he was turned by the sergeant the sleeve fluttered out and upward in a movement that must have resembled a right fist coming up with a haymaker. The sergeant's reflexes took over and he responded instantly with a right fist that caught my father on the jaw with a smack and knocked him clear across the sidewalk where he tripped and fell.

"Daddy, Daddy!" I screamed and rushed to help him to his feet. He was shaking from head to foot as I helped him up, but from the way I was bawling the spectators must have assumed I was the one who was hurt. It was only after my father was back on his feet, and we were brushing the dirt from his clothes, that the sergeant saw the empty sleeve and realized what he had done. When I turned to scream something at him through my tears he was standing and staring in horror at my father's empty sleeve. Then he came over and tried to apologize and help clean off the dirt. The sergeant was quickly surrounded by angry pedestrians who had seen part of the action, or had been filled in by those who had. Soon he was being shouted at from several directions and a man came over to my father and said, "I saw it all and if there is any trouble I would be happy to be your witness."

My father had a small trickle of blood coming from his lower lip and he worked his tongue around in his mouth and spat a couple of times. He took the card the man handed him, thanked him, and we left. I turned around a couple of times and nothing seemed to be happening except that a policeman was walking toward the assembled group. I stopped crying and we headed homeward.

"When we get home, I don't want you to say a word about this to your mother," my father said. "She'll get all upset and start worrying because she'll think I may get in trouble."

"No she won't, Dad," I said. "No she won't, 'cause I'll tell her exactly what happened because I was there and I saw everything and it wasn't your fault."

"Never mind what you saw or didn't see. I just don't want your mother to be worried."

There was no way any eleven-year-old could have kept his mouth shut after such an adventure. We were barely through the door before I was blurting the whole story, and it took my father the rest of the night to explain to my mother that there would be no danger of the army doing anything silly like having him arrested.

The army closed its recruiting depot for the next week, and my father said that when it got back into business again a different sergeant was on the job.

CHAPTER EIGHT

Cynics Are Made by $50 Shinplasters

The jobs that were available in the child labour market during my boyhood were almost limitless in variety. Which was the most desirable depended more on the job seeker's view of his future than on the job itself. Some jobs provided both a good income and a foothold on an escalator that led to permanent employment. As a general rule, boys were still inclined to follow in their fathers' footsteps into trade and commerce. Thus carpenters' sons tended to become carpenters and doctors' sons to become doctors. Indeed, in later years it often seemed that entry into the medical profession was confined exclusively to doctors' sons, godsons, or near relatives. Throughout industry nepotism was just as much the name of the game as it was in the professions. The C.P.R., for example, prided itself on the number of father-and-son combinations on its payroll. When I was looking around for a career, my Uncle George suggested that I get started as a C.P.R. telegraph messenger so that I could learn telegraphy and get a permanent railway job. As a C.P.R. employee he volunteered to use his influence to get me in. For future employment in the railway-running trades a good first job was that of call boy for the engineers, firemen, and conductors. For the skilled shop trades the starting point was as a wiper, which led to apprenticeship. Grocers' sons got to be grocers by working in their fathers' stores. It was the same with the sons of druggists and of butchers. The chance to learn the trade was considered part of the inducement to take delivery jobs and running messages even for non-relatives. Many, if not most, of these jobs could be filled on an after-school basis, a fact that enabled employers of all types to get a lot of low-priced labour under the guise of "teaching the trade". The one after-school job that was a complete dead end as a springboard to a trade was delivering newspapers. But it always provided much better earnings than any other after-school delivery jobs, and for families where the need for immediate income outranked preparation for the future, it was the best job a boy could get.

Whether delivering groceries or delivering newspapers led to the earlier development of a bilious view of humanity could be argued either way. Having done both, I would cast my vote for newspaper-carrying. The grocer boys and butcher boys were mere go-betweens; carrier boys were risk-taking entrepreneurs. In the years before the development of chain stores, Winnipeg got most of its food from the friendly neighbourhood merchants and mostly it was bought on credit. A couple of Winnipeg merchants—Patterson and Black—launched an early cash-and-carry grocery chain. Yet even the "P and B Cash Stores" had to go back to both delivering groceries and charging them. The P and B store at Broadway and Balmoral, where I worked during one summer, tried to restrict its credit to the nearest payday. The manager of the store kept track of when all his credit customers got paid. Some were paid every two weeks and others only once a month. One of my jobs the day after every payday was to go around and collect bills.

"They'll pay all right," he said, "because they are honest enough people. It's just we have to keep after them because they are not too clever in money matters or else they would not be running up bills in the first place. If we don't keep after them somebody else will, and we will go short. If we go short we'll probably lose their business because they will go some place else because they won't want to face us when they owe us money."

All this was his preamble to acquainting me with the replies I was to make to counter any stalling on the part of the customers. On the day before my first bill-collecting excursion he gave me a short list of questions and answers to take home and memorize. The next day, before I set out with the bills, he combined catechism with order-filling.

"What do you say if a woman says her husband didn't get paid yesterday?"

"I say that is too bad and I will come back first thing in the morning."

"Suppose she says not to bother, that she will drop into the store and settle the account?"

"I tell her I have to collect the money for the groceries I have delivered so I will be around anyway."

"Suppose she wants to pay less than the full bill?"

"I say I can't take less and will have to ask you if she can pay less."

"Suppose you knock at the door and there is nobody home?"

"I come back ten minutes later and knock on the other door."

The important thing, he said, was to be firm. "Give them an inch and they'll take a mile" was a favourite phrase he used about his customers. So was "If they are hard up and can't pay all their bills, the first there gets his and the devil takes the hindmost."

It was surprising to me when I went out collecting how many of the excuses the grocer had anticipated popped up, and how familiar I was with them all from having heard my mother use them when she was short of money. It was no less surprising to discover how the customers came through with their payments when I used my employer's patented rejoinders. Yet whether they paid or not didn't really matter to me. I got paid, regardless. It was different for the newspaper carrier boys. When we failed to collect our bills we not only lost our profit on the papers we had delivered, we had to pay the newspaper for the paper as well.

Most of the dead-beats who skipped off without paying for their papers lived in apartment blocks. It was not that apartment dwellers were more dishonest than householders, they just seemed to move around a lot more, and could move out without being noticed. On the other hand, householders about to move away usually telegraphed their punches. Packing cases would be stacked on verandahs. Things would be piled outside. Any carrier with ordinary wariness would spot these signs and move quickly to collect his account. On the whole, not many subscribers set out deliberately to abscond without paying for their papers. Mostly they just took off without thinking about the twenty cents they owed. Regardless of motives, we still lost our money. Perhaps more curdling to our young spirits than defaulters were the housewives on our routes. Some of them could never be bothered to get out their purses and they had dozens of excuses for having us call back again and again. The worst were those who simply did not have the money and put us off with excuses. "Come back tomorrow." "I've only got a $10 bill." "You'll have to come back, I have company." "Oh, I'm just bathing the baby, come back tomorrow." Sometimes the excuses would string out until the subscribers were three or four weeks behind. Then, as boys in our early teens, we faced the dilemma that has confounded experienced merchants since debtors were invented: Did we cut our losses and give up hope of ever collecting the back account, or did we go along for another week in the hope of getting paid, and perhaps get in even deeper? Of this there can be not the slightest doubt, a newspaper route is the best short course ever invented to teach a boy how to survive in business with people as customers. It is no accident that so many successful businessmen owed their success to the tough hide and suspicious eye they first developed as newspaper carrier boys.

My first experiences as a carrier boy for the *Winnipeg Telegram* were so wild that I should have been scared off newspapers for life. Instead I went right back at the first opportunity and for two years delivered both morning and evening editions, but not for the *Telegram*. That paper was patently managed by feyish gremlins. If a paper route was supposed to teach financial responsibility and personal integrity, this one did its best to teach me all the wrong lessons. My only contact with the circulation manager who hired me was in the early summer of 1916. As a result of an arrangement my father had negotiated, he turned up at our suite in the Harald Apartments with a book of dated tickets, a list of the subscribers on my route which coincided with the names on the tickets, and a package of printed envelopes in which to enclose the money when making payments to the paper. The *Telegram* sold for ten cents a week. I was to visit each customer every two weeks, collect twenty cents, and remit twelve cents to the *Telegram*. There were about fifty customers on my route so that if I collected from all of them I would earn two dollars a week. With the formalities completed, the manager gave me a ride on the bar of his bike down to the corner of Cornish Avenue and Eastgate and showed me where my bundle of papers would be dropped off daily. Then he patted me on the back and rode away, into the sunset, as it were, for I never saw him again.

As the first boy on our corner with a paper route, I felt very grown up and superior as I went off to pick up my papers the first afternoon. During the next couple of weeks I became Winnipeg's only ten-year-old enrolled in a post-graduate course in basic economics, majoring in the impact on income of oversupply and ineffective demand. Once or twice during the week I was called back by subscribers after I had left the paper, to be told that they did not subscribe to the *Telegram*. Each time I consulted my list. The name was correct, the address was correct, but subscribers they were not and never had been. In the process of making my collections I encountered so many non-subscribers that my route shrank by almost a third.

Though the *Telegram* lagged far behind both the *Free Press* and *The Tribune* in circulation, what circulation the *Telegram* did claim was padded outrageously, if my route was any criterion. In house after house I was told that they did not subscribe to the paper, had told the paper and succeeding carrier boys they did not want it and would not pay for it, but still it was being delivered. Under normal circumstances I intimidated easily. My reception from my erstwhile customers drove me to tears. Not only did my potential income melt from $2 a week to $1, the *Telegram* was billing me for 50 papers a day and if I had to pay for the unsold surplus it would be touch and go to collect enough from the 30-odd actual subscribers to break even. My father's suggested solution was for me to take the money I had collected, the cards for the people who denied being subscribers, and my subscription list down to the *Telegram* and see the manager. Then they could cut down the number of papers I got, which meant reducing the work almost in half, and I would still be in business.

None of the Horatio Alger books I was then reading had any situation like this. But as a confused and hesitant ten-year-old I bundled up my money, collection book, and circulation list and headed for the *Telegram* office at Albert Street and McDermott Avenue. There was a sign on the door near the lane saying "Circulation Department". I knocked and when nobody answered I turned the knob and went in. It was empty. I wandered around, trying door handles that turned, and eventually I wandered into what must have been the business office. I picked out a young man who didn't seem busy and timidly explained my problem to him. Before I was halfway through he was nodding his head.

"The circulation manager isn't in today," he said, "but if he was I'm sure he'd say just what I'm going to tell you. This is a very common problem and I've heard him talk to other boys who have come in. Since the war started the *Telegram* hasn't been able to keep district managers. They leave almost as soon as we get them trained. They pad their subscriptions away up to win bonuses and then quit on us. So you must have a route where the district manager has quit. Well, I can only say that it will be very much worth while if you just carry on as you're doing for a week or two until we get a new man."

"But what about my lists and money and stuff?" I broke in. "Why should I pay for 50 papers a day when I only collect for 35?" I pulled out the *Telegram* invoice that had come with the bundle of papers the previous Friday. It was for 600 papers at $1 per hundred, or $6, and I had only collected $7 altogether. It was a problem. He went off to discuss it with a couple of other clerks. Nobody had any answers, and apparently little interest.

"Tell you what I'd do if it was me," he said when he came back. "Now if you actually had 50 customers on your route you'd make about $2 a week? Okay. Certainly it's worth $2 a week for you to deliver the *Telegram* six days a week for us. So why not do this: You collect from the subscribers you have and when you get to $4, for two weeks, that's all yours. Whatever extra you collect, that's the *Telegram*'s. You put that aside and when we get a circulation manager he'll want to square things up with you, so you give him what is left over after your $2 a week and that will settle everything."

But what about all the extra papers the people didn't want? He'd make a note for the delivery department and cut the bundle down to 35 papers. Meanwhile I was just to go along as I was. Nothing happened to the bundle. I still got 50 papers a day and delivered them to the original list, as the easiest way of getting rid of the surplus. One day while making my rounds I met a very angry non-subscriber at his door as I tossed a wrapper in his direction.

"Look, sonny," he said, reaching into his pocket and extracting a 50-cent piece which he held in his hand. "I've tried every way I know to persuade your newspaper to stop cluttering up my front step. I have even phoned Sanford Evans and threatened to punch him in the nose! I don't want the paper! I don't read it! I tell every delivery boy to stop leaving it! I refuse to pay for it! But still you persist in leaving it! All right. I want you to take this half-dollar. And every night when you come to my house instead of throwing the paper on my steps I want you to drop it down here."

He walked across the boulevard to the sewer inlet and

pointed it out to me. I went home that night the most bemused ten-year-old in the whole world, for I could understand nothing of a situation where I was told to give something away free and then was paid by the recipient not to give it to him. I never could puzzle it out but I did as he asked. After trying a couple of times to collect from the other non-subscribers, I gave them up as a bad job. Eventually, I located a butcher on Sherbrook Street who used newspapers as wrapping paper for his fish. He bought my surplus *Telegrams* for 15 cents a week. The bills for $6 for 600 papers came in every second week with the Friday bundle. I went on taking out my $4 from my fortnightly collections and putting what was left aside for the *Telegram*. Then one day as summer was ending, a knock came to the door from a man looking for an Albert Westly. My mother said he must have the wrong address because that was not our name. Then perhaps my mother knew the boy, he delivered the *Telegram*. My mother said that her son delivered the *Telegram* but his name was Jim Gray, not Albert Westly.

When things got sorted out it developed that the stranger was the new district agent for the *Telegram,* that Albert Westly was the name of the previous carrier for my route who had moved away. The previous manager had inserted our address on his records but had neglected to change Westly's name to mine. With that straightened out, he explained his immediate objective—to collect the $24 owed the *Telegram* for the papers I had been delivering for the last eight weeks. I went at once to my dresser drawer and retrieved all the envelopes I had been hoarding. When the *Telegram* agent did the arithmetic there was a deficit of about $16 between what his records showed was owing and the total contained in the envelopes. He listened to my explanation with mounting incredulity. My mother's strong point was never arithmetic. When she tried to assist in the explanation she made matters worse. It was not long before I was reduced to tears and my mother then sought to end the confrontation by gathering up the envelopes, pushing them on the *Telegram* man, and ordering him out of the house. He took not only the money but the collection book and circulation list as well. I was fired as a *Telegram* carrier and, he threatened, would likely be charged with theft when he came back with a policeman. We never heard of him again, though every knock that came to the door for the next couple of days made me shake with apprehension. By then the new district man had undoubtedly been embroiled in even zanier adventures in the tangled affairs of the *Telegram*'s circulation department. Incredibly, the paper was able to survive well into the 1920s.

Being fired from my first real job, and being threatened with the police, left me so emotionally drained that I just moped around home for several days. As a ten-year-old with a paper route I was a personage of stature among the kids of the neighbourhood. Merely having a *Telegram* paper bag on my shoulder impressed the other kids, or so I believed, for I had successfully crashed the preserves of twelve- and thirteen-year-olds. Now what would I tell the kids? Certainly not that I had been fired from my paper route. The whole truth was too complicated, so I told the half-truth—that I gave up the paper route because school was beginning the next week.

I collected two invaluable dividends from my short experience as a carrier boy for the *Winnipeg Telegram*—an absolute mastery of public school mathematics and an insatiable appetite for the printed word. The simple business of collecting dimes and nickels, of making change and counting money, did more for my understanding of arithmetic than hours of drill in school. My paper route forced me to solve more problems in arithmetic in the course of making a few collections than the average boy did in a year. In any event, arithmetic was one subject on which I had to spend very little time from then on.

Learning to read at four or five when we lived on Rennie had given me a head start over the other boys and girls of my age. And because I was good at it, I naturally read more in school than the others. When I became a carrier boy I discovered newspapers for the first time, and with them the great world beyond our neighbourhood. The front pages were filled with stories of the war, the daily crises in Ottawa, and the home front scandal centring on the new Legislature Building in Winnipeg. I understood almost nothing of the main stories in the *Telegram*. At first I pestered my father to explain them to me but he gradually developed such impatience that I gave up and went looking for things I could work out for myself. Out of this developed a curiously oblique interest in the war that had nothing to do with the battles being fought. The *Telegram*, like all the Winnipeg papers, carried detailed biographical sketches of the local men who were killed, wounded, decorated, or invalided home. I turned to these stories as other kids turned to "The Katzenjammer Kids", "Mutt and Jeff", and "Buster Brown".

My interest in reading was carried even further forward by a fringe benefit accruing as the son of apartment house janitors. Apartment house dwellers, I have said, moved around a lot. It was the duty of the janitors to clean up the suites after departing tenants, many of whom simply moved away leaving things they no longer needed. So we regularly fell heir to great piles of magazines, and occasional stacks of novels or collections of books. The Great War came toward the end of the "collected works" era of book publishing. Book salesmen roved the country with sample cases full of the book spines put together like accordions to demonstrate how "The Collected Works of Lever" would look on a bookshelf. People, seemingly, bought book collections by colour scheme rather than for content. In any event, we fell heir to the various sets of collected works abandoned in vacated suites. Some, such as those by Scott, Dickens, and Mark Twain, we kept and read. Others we sold to a second-hand bookstore on Portage Avenue near the Wesley College. During the year we lived in the Harald Apartments I must have hauled a half-dozen coaster-wagons-full of books to the second-hand store.

We also occasionally salvaged copies of the Henty and the Alger books and, best of all, copies of the English boys' books such as *The Boy's Own Annual* and the American periodical

"The Youth's Companion". The Winnipeg winters kept most of us housebound after dark until we were into our teens. I was three years older than Walter and six older than my brother Bob so there were few games we could play together. We were reduced to reading by force of circumstance, and as members of the janitor's family we happily fell heir to more than enough material to keep us reading all winter.

My infatuation with the printed word got me into no end of trouble on my next paper routes. When we moved to the Rozell Apartments on Clark Street in 1917 I managed to get a *Free Press* route, although I was still a year short of the minimum age that the paper had set for its carriers. My route covered Wardlaw, Stradbrook, and Bell avenues and contained almost a hundred subscribers, from whom I regularly netted between $3 and $4 a week. The *Free Press* was everything the *Telegram* was not. It had a regular depot in a store front on Osborne Street where all the carriers in the area got their papers. In order to carry this route, my father bought me a bicycle behind which I could tow our coaster wagon on Saturdays when the papers were too heavy to be carried in two bags. On other days we folded the papers into what we called "wrappers" and fired them at front steps as we rode past. But when there was something exciting happening in the world, I'd stop a safe distance from the depot and read the paper. My mother used to say she could always tell when something big had happened because I was late for supper. Many of the subscribers on my route seemed to have a fixation about getting their paper promptly. If I was a few minutes later than usual those with a phone would telephone the paper to complain. We were fined a nickel for late complaints and a dime for missing deliveries. A collection period seldom passed without my having several fines added to my paper bill.

In 1919 I branched out into morning delivery as well and then I acquired the habit of curling up in the hall of a nice warm block halfway through the route to catch up on the news. It was this practice that eventually got me fired from my morning route for ignoring a persistently complaining subscriber on Roslyn Road. He always complained if his paper was late. His worst complaint, however, was my neglect to place his paper inside the storm door so he did not have to retrieve it from the verandah in his nightshirt on a 40-below morning. On such mornings I did my route on the dead run to keep from freezing and so threw his paper in the general direction of the front door. I ignored the warnings of the district manager until one morning he greeted me at the door of the depot with the word that I was fired. Not at the end of the collection period, not the end of the week. He meant that very morning because he was going to do the deliveries himself until he got a boy to replace me. I was to accompany him that morning and bring my list of subscribers in that afternoon. It was twenty years later before I understood his mad rush to take over my route. The subscriber I had treated so cavalierly was E.H. Macklin, the publisher of the *Free Press!* However, in having me fired, he had issued no ukase against my being rehired for a different route, and in a matter of weeks I was back on the *Free Press* morning circulation department staff.

It was the Roslyn Road route that landed us with a great moral crisis that shattered the family aplomb for weeks. It developed during the week before Christmas and, despite the season of the year, gave us a jaundiced view of mankind that survived well into the New Year. Christmas is as close to heaven as things ever get for newsboys. When collections are made during Christmas week the tips fall like snow into waiting hands. We normally picked up more in Christmas tips than we would make in a month of normal deliveries.

The moral crisis developed the year I was fourteen. My brother Walter, who was eleven, used to help me with the morning route and had a route of his own after school.

The luxurious Roslyn Apartments were on his part of the route. While he was making collections during the week before Christmas, he interrupted a Christmas party in the suite of one of the sons of Winnipeg's biggest packing-house family. When the door opened to Walter's ring the noise from inside, he reported later, made it difficult to make himself heard. But he shouted and the man with the paper hat leaned against the door jamb, reached into his pocket, withdrew a fistful of bills, and, peeling one off, said:

"Here y'are son. Merry Christmas! Keep the change, boy, Merry Christmas!"

A woman came to the door, linked her arm through the man's, reached down and kissed Walter on the cheek, and wished him a Merry Christmas too. He pocketed the bill and went on with his collections. We reached home about the same time that night, emptied our pockets on the dining room table, and began to count our loot.

"Hey, Jim, look what I got," Walter said, "a 50-cent shin-plaster!"

I had never heard of a 50-cent shinplaster. We got lots of the little 25-cent paper notes but a 50-center was something new. Walter held it up for my father to see.

"Somebody has been fooling you," my father said, "there's no such thing as a 50-cent shinplaster. Let me see it."

He merely glanced at it before letting out a yelp.

"My God, boy, this is no shinplaster, this is a $50 bill! Where did you ever get such a present?"

The money-counting stopped while Walter provided all the details, though he sputtered a lot at the discovery that he was the owner of a $50 bill.

My mother came in from the kitchen and we passed the bill back and forth. For such a big bill it wasn't all that impressive. Numeral 50's were in the top corners with capital L's on the bottom. There were a couple of stern-looking bank officials portrayed on the front and a picture of a bank on the back. It was the ordinary green colour of most other bank notes.

Walter had already begun cataloguing the things he wanted to buy with his windfall when my mother interrupted.

"First thing I want," he squealed, "is a pair of real shinpads, and then I'm gonna get—"

"You'll do nothing of the kind, of course," my mother interjected. "You'll put on your things and take that money right back to the man."

Walter and I were so shocked by this order that it seemed ages before we could recover our breath. My father still held his City Hall job, though his grip on it was beginning to slip. Most of our earnings from papers went to buy our clothes and what was left after a small allowance helped with the cost of living. But such windfalls were different and we had been counting on doing our Christmas shopping with some of our Christmas tip money. We both exploded at once at my mother's decision.

"But Mom," I pleaded, "the man is a rich millionaire! You

should see his big suite in the Roslyn. He owns a big packing plant. He'll never miss the money!"

"But Mom," Walter broke in, "he had a whole fistful of money. He had thousands of bills I bet and more in his pockets. Maybe he even had his other pocket full. Mom, in all your life you never saw so much money, not even in Eaton's cash registers."

It was no use. My mother was adamant. "The man made a mistake. That's all there is to it. If you kept that money knowing he had made a mistake it would be the same thing as stealing. No one in his right mind would ever give a paper boy a $50 Christmas tip. He made a mistake and you must take the money back."

"But Mom, we can't do that," Walter argued. "There is this big party on with a bunch of men playing music and dancing and singing. They don't want us botherin' them. Let's wait till tomorrow."

My mother recognized a trick when she saw it and became more determined. We appealed to my father, who had taken no part in the argument.

"All right," he said. "That is enough. I want both of you to put on your coats and take the money back and give it to the man. Tell him you did not realize he had made a mistake. Then if he gives it back to you as a tip you can keep it. But until he does, you cannot keep the money. And that is all there is to it!"

We took the $50 bill back with heavy hearts and dragging feet. It was not so much giving the money back that made us miserable, for neither of us would have had more than a small part of it to spend. But this tip should have set off the kind of family celebration that previous windfalls had caused, and generated a euphoria that would last for several days. In poor families where money counts for so much, unexpected riches do something to lift everybody's spirits in a way that better-off families can never experience. When my father had said that our 50-cent shinplaster was a $50 bill we simply could not hold still with the excitement his announcement set off. Then it was over and we felt worse than if Walter had never been given the money in the first place. But try as we might, we could not recapture the mood as, on our journey to return the money, we took turns suggesting devious ways of getting the subscriber to reconfirm his gift. None of the ideas was any good and we were left with the hope that the party was over and the people had gone some place else. The party was still going with such gusto that we had to ring the bell a couple of times before anybody answered the door. Then a stranger came and went off to get our subscriber. He was not quite as happily drunk, apparently, as he had been. He had some difficulty understanding the nature of our mission until a couple of his guests became volunteer interpreters. In the end, he took the money, mumbling it was the smallest he had and said he'd pay us next week. Then he shook hands, wished us both a Merry Christmas, and stumbled back into the party. Somebody shut the door.

At home that night my mother delivered her favourite homily on honesty. Nobody, she said, ever lost by doing the honest thing. Despite what it might seem like at the time, bread cast upon the waters always returned a thousandfold. That man would always remember us as honest boys and there was no telling what favours he might do. At the very least he would have a handsome tip for Walter when he went back on his next collection and there would be more satisfaction in having honest money honestly come by than riches we were not entitled to. The way my mother went on, it almost seemed she was getting more satisfaction out of sending back that money than she could have got from keeping it. If we had kept money given us by mistake, she kept repeating, it would never have done us any real good and we'd always have had it on our conscience. All Walter and I had on our conscience as weeks passed was a corroding resentment of the fate which prevented our meat packer from establishing an all-time record for Christmas tips. When Walter made his next collection, the subscriber paid his account without any reference to the $50 mistake.

"Did you have a nice Christmas?" the subscriber asked, by way of making small conversation. Walter allowed that he did and reported his receipt of a pair of shinguards and hockey stockings. The man thought that was nice, as he shut the door on Walter and the subject of Christmas and all that it entailed that year. Obviously the giving and the return of the $50 bill had made no lasting impression on his mind. We kept hoping, for some weeks, that he would be reminded of it somehow, but he never was.

CHAPTER NINE

Poor Boys and Rich Millionaires

*T*here was one advantage in growing up in poverty as we did—we never had to learn how to be poor. We were, therefore, exempt from the trauma experienced by people who, having once known affluence, were reduced to poverty. The Honourable Stuart Garson once recalled, when he was Premier of Manitoba, his vivid memory of being ordered to take the groceries he was delivering around to the back door by the maid of a family whose home he had frequented as a guest before his father went broke in the crash of 1913. The elder Garson had developed the Manitoba limestone quarries at the town that still bears his name. He was a successful contractor who had several large buildings under construction when the crash came. He lost everything and died soon after. His son got a job delivering groceries and worked his way through school and college. He never forgot the humiliation he felt carrying his grocery bag to the back door. Yet when, at the age of ten, I was ordered around to the back door by a uniformed maid I thought nothing of it. It was at that moment that I first discovered that there was a "filthy rich" segment of our society, as well as the segment to which we belonged and to which I had previously assumed that everybody else belonged as well.

Wherever we had lived the kids always used the back doors, both at home and when calling on our friends. While we waited, we sat on the back steps or hung over the back fence. With the exception of Eaton's drivers, all deliveries were made to the back doors because that was where the kitchen was. Indeed, it was only on the rarest of occasions, in fact a real *occasion,* when anyone ever came to the front door. On the day I discovered the upper class I would probably have gone to the back door anyway except that the people kept an angry-looking dog chained up in the garage. Being afraid of the dog, I had simply walked up to the front door and rung the bell.

Poverty undoubtedly put strains on marital ties, for I can remember my mother complaining that she got so tired "living from hand to mouth all the time". As a girl growing up on her father's farm, she probably had fewer comforts of life than she enjoyed in the city. But on the farm there was always an abundance of food in the pantry, most of it homegrown. So it was a simple matter, when the spirit moved, to cook a roast, roast a turkey, make half a dozen pies, or whip up a layer cake. In Winnipeg "living from hand to mouth" meant doing everything on mini-scale. My mother made bread in smaller batches. We never tasted steak until we had grown out of our teens. Only rarely were there roasts, and turkey was served only at Christmas, if somebody gave us one, and they usually did. Ours, I suspect, was far from a healthy balanced diet. Perhaps during the late summer and fall we stored up enough vegetable vitamins to last us through the winter. We had to because there were no imported vegetables on sale during the winter, certainly never at prices we could afford, and we had ripe tomatoes only as long as ripening could be retarded by picking them half-ripe and wrapping them in paper. Oranges were something we got only in our stockings on Christmas morning.

Wherever we lived my mother managed to scout around and find some vacant land to plant a vegetable garden. What we couldn't eat fresh from the garden she preserved for the winter. Thus we had fresh butter beans one night, beans and peas the next, carrots and peas the next, sometimes with cauliflower and peas in cream sauce, or mashed turnips and buttered carrots, sliced ripe tomatoes with vinegar and sugar, and lettuce with vinegar and sugar for as long as it could be grown without going to seed. In the winter there were ripe cucumber pickles and green cucumber pickles, green tomato pickles, mustard bean pickles, carrot marmalade, and preserved citron which was the favourite dessert in our family. Sometimes we had homemade soup twice a day and homemade pork and beans substituted for meat twice a week. We ate a standard breakfast of rolled oats porridge or Cream of Wheat, and as much homemade bread as we could hold, covered with molasses or Rogers' Golden Corn Syrup, both of which we bought by the gallon.

My mother also leaned heavily on eggs and poultry. She bought the eggs in thirty-dozen crates from old friends on the farm. The eggs cost as little as ten cents a dozen, delivered in Winnipeg, and she preserved them in water-glass so that a crate of eggs lasted several months. She also bought farm-killed chickens a dozen at a time, and froze them outside to keep for the winter.

When we lived in the North End we ate pretty much the way our Jewish, Ukrainian, and Polish neighbours ate. We went light on meat and heavy on bread, vegetables, and dairy products. Our meals, however, lacked the variety that the immigrants achieved through their reliance on European menus. The Jews could do a dozen things with chicken or beef brisket that my mother never heard of. And of course the Slavs all relied heavily on garlic to flavour everything they cooked. My mother had a prejudice against garlic more pungent than the garlic itself. And she strongly disapproved of our eating raw vegetables, except lettuce, tomatoes, and cucumbers, because she believed that they would give us worms. Finally, she distrusted spices for a reason I never knew. My brothers and I naturally accumulated a number of irrational food prejudices under her tutelage that took us years to outgrow. But I never outgrew a taste for homemade bread and molasses, or hot fresh bread and brown sugar, or lettuce or tomatoes sprinkled with vinegar and well sugared and salted, or fresh-picked butter beans, peas, and carrots.

What tastes the boys of the wealthy homes were developing at this time I never learned. We sometimes went to the same schools. When we did, we played in the same schoolyards at the same games and were often the best of friends. But we never visited each other's homes. And that was true wherever we lived and regardless of economic status. When we called on our friends, we whistled, shouted, or pounded on the back door. If they failed to come out, we assumed they were not home, or were being kept in. So we went on with what we were up to without them. A result of this environment was that we on the wrong side of the tracks grew up in complete unawareness of how the other half lived. There was no newspaper advertising, magazine advertising, radio advertising, or television advertising to create in us a thirst for the finer things of life, or even for the bogus things of life. On our safaris through Jerry Robinson's, Eaton's, or the Hudson's Bay, we undoubtedly got peripheral glimpses of expensive furniture and clothing. If so, it made no impression, for what sub-teen has the slightest interest in such things?

If any of the kids I chummed with in my younger years noticed that my knickers were homemade from the salvagable parts of one of my father's worn-out suits, nothing was ever said. Probably, for all I knew or cared, because everybody else wore made-overs and hand-me-downs. If we had ever known there were rich classes and poor classes, and had been concerned about it, we would not have defined a poor boy as one who wore hand-me-down clothes. To us, a really poor boy would have been one who had to wear girls' buttoned shoes to school. On the other hand, we would never have considered a girl who wore boys' shoes as being poor *per se*. Except that girls' boots were buttoned and boys' were laced, there was little difference in the sex of boots for children. Families with both girls and boys to keep shod could not afford to pay too much attention to the difference. When the handing-down process was operating, foot size and not design was the determining factor. Except that, while it was common to see little girls in boys' boots, boys seldom seemed to wear girls' footwear. If we had to define a rich kid, it would have been one who always wore "store boughten" clothes and got his hair cut in barber shops. Home barbering was the universal rule in all my growing-up neighbourhoods. There was one other factor that separated us from the better-off kids. That was the care we were taught, even compelled, to take of our clothes. Once, for example, we were playing an important baseball game and we had a man on second who tried to reach home on a single to right field. As he turned the corner at third base we could see it was likely to be a very close play.

"Slide, Artie, slide!" we screamed. But Artie failed to slide and was tagged out as he tried to dodge around the catcher. He was immediately accosted by the rest of us who shouted criticism at him for not sliding. He silenced us all with the simplicity of his explanation.

"I couldn't slide," he said, "'cause my mom told me I couldn't play ball unless I promised not to get my pants dirty on account of I gotta wear them to school all next month."

On another occasion one of the boys in our class at Kelvin school got his sweater tangled in the revolving spindle of a metal working lathe and it was pulling his arm steadily closer to the lathe while acting as a tourniquet on his upper biceps. When Alfie discovered he could not shut off the machine he screamed in panic and a near-by boy tripped the switch. By the time the lathe stopped, the sweater sleeve was wound into the lathe clear up to Alfie's armpit. One of the boys tried to turn the lathe backwards by hand to release him but the sweater was so tangled up that it could not be moved. At last the teacher produced a knife and cut away the shoulder of the sweater while Alfie, who was at least fifteen, cried unashamedly.

The teacher, meanwhile, accompanied his knife-using with a steady stream of invective. "There," he said, "let that be a lesson to you all! This boy might well have lost his arm if he had been wearing tougher material! And I have told you all that the most dangerous thing you can do is approach a lathe with shirt sleeves dangling! And look at you! I can see half a dozen who have paid no more attention than Alf, here! Look at those sleeves! Look at them!" He pointed to the careless boys and turned angrily to Alfie.

"Oh stop your damn blubberin', boy! You're not hurt all that much to be making such a fuss! It could've been a lot worse, I can tell you!"

"It ain't my arm, it's my sweater," Alfie said when he got control of his feelings. "It's my new sweater and my father said if I so much as tore it he'd whale the devil outta me. And now look at my sweater. It's ruined! What am I gonna do now?" he asked.

We all went back to our machines, checking our sleeves as we went.

"You can tell him you might have lost the use of your arm for life," the teacher grunted as he left. Alfie went back to his lathe with a look that indicated he knew he was in for a whaling no matter how good his excuse.

The reason so many of us were very careful about our clothes may very well have been that we had to buy them ourselves. I can never remember having to go hungry when our family fortunes hit bottom before prohibition came in. It was in the non-food costs that the economic crunch was most painful, and it was this pressure that nudged most of the boys of my generation onto the labour market. I doubt if my father ever earned more than $20 a week in his life. Certainly he earned less than that in the jobs he held in Winnipeg in the early years of the war. Henry Ford, it is fitting to recall, scandalized the manufacturing industry of the United States in 1914 when he announced that he was setting a basic minimum wage of $5 for a nine-hour day in his plants. At this time the average wage in industry was $11 a week.

The regular workday in pre-war Winnipeg was from 8 A.M. to 6 P.M., six days a week, though some of the government and commercial offices quit at 5 P.M. or 5.30, and some closed on Saturday at 1 P.M. The standard work week was at least forty-eight hours and in the summer the building trades often worked up to sixty hours, to make up for the twelve to fifteen

weeks they were idle each winter. The labour aristocracy was
the men of the railway running-trades, who on the average
made about $1,400 a year. At the other end of the scale were
the common labourers, who earned less than $600 a year and
worked an average of only forty-two weeks a year. Even with
their long hours, none of the building trades managed over
$900 a year. Certainly Winnipeggers who earned more than
$20 a week were in the great minority, and over a year's span
the weekly average was probably less than $15, even with the
skilled trades included.

If wages were low, however, everything else was in propor-
tion. The cottage we lived in on Salter Street rented for $12 a
month and that was about par for the smaller modern accommodation. On the outskirts of the city, beyond the sewer and
water mains, in Brooklands and in parts of St. Boniface and
St. Vital, a five-room house could be rented for less than $10 a
month. Many of the older houses had toilets but no bathroom, so urban bathing was done as it was on the farms, in
tubs in the kitchen on Saturday night. Water was heated in a
tank that attached to the kitchen stove. In the summer we
always had to choose between cleanliness and an overheated
house. In most houses there was no way of heating enough
water to bath in without turning the inside of the house into
a sauna bath. The exception was those cases where the
cookstove was moved into the back shed for the summer. So
mostly we took sponge baths by standing in the tub and using
as little water as possible. A house with a complete bathroom
and perhaps a jacket heater in the basement to heat the water
would have rented for $15 to $18 a month. At the outbreak of
the war men's suits were selling for as low as $10. Nobody
except ladies with expensive feet wore *shoes* in those days. Men
and women both wore boots and in 1915 a good-quality pair
of boys' boots sold for $1.25, girls' boots for $1.50, because they
had buttons instead of laces, and men's and women's boots
for $3. A good-quality woman's winter coat could be bought
for $12 and ordinary women's dresses began at $2.50 and went
as high as $5. Occasionally there were clothing sales at which

boys' knickers could be bought for as little as a quarter and when we were in the market for clothes my mother always watched for the sales and put great faith in Eaton's Thursday Bargain Day. It was, therefore, financially possible at the outbreak of the war for a man earning $15 a week to raise a small family in comparative comfort, provided he worked steadily and lived frugally.

In the days before supermarket pre-packaging, everything was bought in the large economy size. Thus my mother always bought lard in the 3-pound pails that ranged in price from 40 to 45 cents a pail. Jam in 4-pound tins retailed for 65 to 70 cents. Tea sold for 3 pounds for $1, potatoes were 100 pounds for 75 cents, rice was 50 pounds for $2.50, a 98-pound sack of flour sold for $2.75, a 25-pound bag of white beans was 60 cents, butter was always quite expensive at 3 pounds for 75 cents, rolled oats in cartons sold for 5 pounds for 20 cents and 10 pounds for 20 cents in bulk. With the cartons the customer got a dinner dish. It was literally true that a boy could take a dollar to the store and come home with his coaster wagon full of groceries.

Nevertheless, despite the low price structure, life was very hard for our immigrant neighbours with large families. And it was soon to get very much worse. Not long after the Great War started the "enemy aliens" began to get the critical attention of the home front. Before the war immigrant families managed to make some degree of economic progress when husband, wife, and children worked. The men got all the dirty jobs—street cleaners, construction labourers, railway car sweepers, and shop wipers. The women cleaned offices at night, worked as chambermaids in hotels and hospitals, went out house-cleaning by the day. But soon the agitation started to have all "enemy aliens" fired and their cleaning jobs turned over to the wives of overseas soldiers. As I have mentioned, there was no separation allowance for wives and children in the First World War, and war-widow pensions were pittances on which no one could subsist unassisted. The immigrant women saw their jobs slip away while the agitation spread to reserve other jobs for loyal and patriotic Canadians. Almost from their arrival there was great economic pressure on the immigrant families to put their sons and daughters to work, as there was as yet no compulsory school attendance act in Manitoba. It was, therefore, possible for children to leave school after Grade Three or Four and go to work if they were big enough and strong enough. As the war progressed, employment expanded and so did the use of child labour. However, the School Attendance Act of 1916 made attendance at school compulsory until age fourteen, so that while the immigrant children gained educationally, the family suffered financially. Then everybody, WASPS as well as "enemy aliens", was caught in the economic squeeze when the price spiral developed in 1916. Not only did food and clothing prices rise sharply, but the quality declined in just about everything. Blue serge suits began to turn a purplish red after a week of exposure to the sun. Compressed paper replaced leather in the soles of shoes. Not only did the price of clothing double, the shoddy material made it necessary to replace items twice as often. Thus the real cost of living rose much faster than bald comparisons of prices would indicate.

Food prices kept pace with the rise of other commodities. The price of flour went to $4, to $5, and then to $7 a sack. Potatoes, beans, rolled oats, syrup, and meat almost doubled in price. Wages advanced slowly if at all, so that by 1916 incomes that had been barely adequate, in frugal and sober households, were now wholly unable to sustain family life.

The School Attendance Act of 1916 drove all the under-14-year-olds who had quit school back into the educational system. But the economic pressure of rising prices drove them out again into part-time employment. Before the development of the supermarket, small merchants did most of the food business in Winnipeg. There were hundreds of jobs in the retail trade filled by schoolboys after school, at nights, and on Saturdays. The girls, too, nibbled at the labour market. While it was against the law for them to work during school hours, no law prevented them from working with their mothers as charwomen at night. The telegraph companies provided part-time work for boys as messengers, and the railways used others as "call-boys" to travel the city arousing train crews at nights. The drug stores had messenger boys and the junk yards employed boys on Saturday, sorting scrap.

The point I am emphasizing is that child labour was a fact of life in Winnipeg and it was the normal thing for boys when they reached ten years of age to be on the look-out for odd jobs, not to earn spending money but to supplement the family income. Statistics for the period are fragmentary where they exist at all. But the contribution of child labour to family income was of sufficient importance by 1921 for the Census to take cognizance of it. In that year it reported that there were 26,498 families in Winnipeg with earnings of $42,000,000. Working children, 7,800 of them, contributed $6,243,000 to those earnings. There is no record of what the facts were in 1916, when the great inflation began, but wherever we lived there was a frantic scramble among all the kids for the part-time jobs that were available. The greatest favour any boy could do for another was to turn his part-time job over to him if he got a better one, or just had to give it up.

When my parents got the janitor's job at the Richmond Apartments in 1914 it was an economic lifesaver. It was a small block and no pay was attached to the job, just the provision of a free suite in return for the janitor services. With heat and shelter provided, we managed to survive on what my mother could earn and on my father's income between his bouts with the bars. But as prices took off they could no longer make it. Then they got the job looking after the Harald Apartments on Westminster Avenue and Langside Street. It was a much larger block and while there was more work there was also fifteen dollars a month in cash in addition to the free suite. A year later we moved to the Rozell Apartments on Clark Street where the pay was twenty dollars a month and a free suite. I had got my first job at age nine delivering fish and chips for the Bristol Old English Fish and Chips store on Ellice near Langside. It entailed a lot more sitting and waiting than anything else, but it paid fifty cents a week. When we moved to Westminster I had to give up the job. There were no grocery stores in the neighbourhood and I wound up with the paper route for the *Winnipeg Telegram* that I described in the previous chapter. The *Telegram* was the poorest of the Winnipeg newspapers, but it was stridently Tory and my route must have been the most Tory in Canada. It took in the whole of Armstrong's Point—Eastgate, Middlegate, and Westgate—with a few subscribers on the bottom ends of Langside and Furby. In Armstrong's Point I first discovered that there was another side to our society, that this was it, and that this was how it lived.

I picked up my bundle of papers in the vestibule of an apartment block at the foot of Langside Street. The *Telegram* scarcely ever exceeded a dozen pages, so carrying the papers was no great burden. When I began my deliveries at the first house on Eastgate, I entered into a world as new and as magnificent as any in the Arabian Nights. Indeed, there were no houses in Eastgate or Westgate or Middlegate. There were only castles, huge castles three full storeys in height, some with leaded glass windows, and all, certainly, with dozens of rooms. They were built in an assortment of architectural styles and peopled by names from Winnipeg's commercial and industrial Who's Who. I was so awe-stricken by the sheer size of the houses that I almost tiptoed up the walks with the papers. When I finished my deliveries I rushed home to break the news of my discovery of this fabulous new world to my mother and father. That night the whole family walked down to Armstrong's Point, down Eastgate into Westgate and then up and down Middlegate. I acted as guide as we went along, pointing out the houses where I delivered my papers. My father and mother were obviously as impressed with the magnificence of the homes as I had hoped they would be. We were seeing a world we never knew existed, though it was only a long block away from the Harald Apartments into which we had recently moved.

How could this be? How could anybody live in a small city

like Winnipeg for four or five years and not become inti-
mately acquainted with its parts? It was easy to do for the
simple reason that there was no public transportation into
Armstrong's Point or into the area immediately across the
Assiniboine River in what was called Crescentwood. There
was nothing to take outside families into these areas, and
there was no way of getting in except on foot. "Taking a walk"
was a universal summer pastime in Winnipeg and whole
families took nightly strolls together. But most of this walking
was done close to home. The early Winnipeg planners, taking
cognizance of the way people tended to live within their
neighbourhoods, saw to it that the city had plenty of
neighbourhood parks for sitting in and strolling about.

Small boys occasionally went exploring abroad by hitching rides on delivery rigs, but these were aimless excursions
consisting simply of riding as far as the rig went and hitching
another ride back home. Younger adults took longer walks.
North-enders promenaded down Main Street to Portage
Avenue and west-enders along Portage Avenue to Main
Street. "Going for a walk" merely took the walkers around a
neighbourhood; "going for a walk up town" had an objective,
like window shopping or going to a movie. To have walked
from the North End to the West End would have been
pointless, for there was nothing in any one residential district
to attract walkers from any other residential district. It added
up to this: Just about everybody living in any of the areas we
had lived in would have been as surprised as we were to
discover the existence of the palatial houses in Armstrong's
Point.

Small boys, however, never stayed awed for long and
within a few days I was throwing the wrappers on the front
steps in Armstrong's Point as casually as I did on the steps of
the plebeian houses on Langside and Furby streets which
were also on my route. I got over the magnificence of the
houses, but I doubt if I ever really got over the rich environment. At the end of the second week, I had to make the
rounds collecting for the paper, so with my collection book in

hand I started out on Saturday morning to ring doorbells and get my money. Everything went off without incident until about the fifth house on Eastgate. The inside door was ajar and after I rang the bell I heard a rustling noise in the hall followed by the click of heels on the hardwood floor. The door was opened by the most beautiful girl I had ever seen. She was dressed entirely in black, with a neat white miniature apron and a sort of nurse's cap on her black curls. I had trouble saying anything, but in the end I blurted:

"*Telegram* collection, twenty cents please for the past two weeks."

The most beautiful girl in the world froze me in my tracks.

"Go to the back door," she said as she turned on her heel and shut the door with a mini-slam. That was all. No explanation. No rebuke. No please. Just "Go to the back door."

I was so taken aback that I had walked clear out to the street before I noticed a path around to the back of the house. I hesitated to take it even then, however, because of the fierce-looking dog in the huge garage at the rear. However, I convinced myself that the dog's chain would not reach to the back door and besides it probably didn't bite anyway. I was prepared for a similar unfriendly reception when I rang the back door bell. This time the surprise was friendly. The woman who answered was dressed all in white. She even had white stockings on and I could not then recall ever having seen a woman in white stockings before.

"Well now," she said in a deep brogue of some kind, "what are we havin' here now?"

"I'm collecting for the *Telegram,*" I said, "twenty cents please."

"Well come on in and I'll just see if we can find twenty cents for you."

I went into the biggest kitchen in Winnipeg. There was a great stove that took up most of one side. On the adjacent wall was a butcher-shop-type door. In the centre was a butcher's block and a long table and above the table was a rack for pots and pans. There were a couple of other tables, at one of which

another white-garbed woman sat kneading butter between two round, flat bats. She had cut a whole pound of butter into small cubes and was leisurely rounding them into balls. The woman who had opened the door was so friendly that I could not resist asking her what the other woman was doing.

"Have ye never seen butter balls before, boy? We're makin' butter balls, that's all."

But why? I wondered. What could you do with butter balls after you'd gone to the trouble of making them? My face must have mirrored my bafflement so plainly that the woman volunteered the explanation. Butter balls were served on the bread-and-butter plates at dinner. But I still didn't really understand as I pocketed my twenty cents and headed for the door.

"Here, my boy, hold yer horses a minute. How'd ye like a fresh-baked cinnamon roll with one of those butter balls spread all over it?"

She didn't wait for an answer but went over to a table that was draped with cheesecloth and extracted a bun from under the cloth. Then she sliced it neatly on the butcher's block and, taking a knife from a drawer and jabbing it into a butter ball, quickly spread the butter on the bun.

"There now," she said, handing me the bun segments, "that's all they is to it, only mind you don't jab it like that when ye come to dinner!"

She liked that little joke and was still laughing as I made my way down the walk to the street. It was a joke she never forgot. For as long as I delivered papers there she reminded me about the butter balls whenever she handed me my Saturday morning treat. The day brought other women in white as well as women in black to the doors, but nothing further happened. That was butter-ball Saturday and I could hardly wait to report to my mother on the size and magnificence of all the kitchens I had been in. Most of all I had to describe the butter balls. It was a disappointment to discover she knew about butter balls, that they had often made them on the farm when company came for Sunday dinner. But they were a surprise to my father so I felt better on that account.

My exposure to Armstrong's Point gave rise to one area of bafflement for which little enlightenment was obtained. How did anybody get so rich that they could build such houses and employ so many servants? Some of the houses seemed to have five or six people just working in them. I pestered my father but he had few answers. I got out my collection book and we went over the names of my subscribers. My father recognized name after name.

"There's Thomas Ryan, the big shoe merchant who owns that big building behind the fire hall. You've heard of Stovel's printing, well there is Mrs. Stovel . . . Mr. Bain has that big wholesale company . . . and Lady Schultz. Her husband was a wealthy doctor. And look, here is Mr. Speirs of Speirs-Parnell the bakers . . . and Mr. Chevrier who owns the Blue Store on Main Street . . . and Sir Charles Tupper the famous lawyer . . . and Mr. Jackson the contractor . . . and the Reverend C. W. Gordon the famous author and Senator McMeans who is a rich politician . . . " My father had heard of practically everybody on my route. But merely identifying the subscribers begged my question: How did people get rich enough to live in such houses? It seemed as my father went over them that you could get rich doing just about anything. But how? I fell asleep night after night searching for the answer to that question. It never came.

My Armstrong's Point paper route did not last long, as I have explained. Indeed, I had barely got the front-door–back-door business straightened out when the *Telegram* circulation manager took back the route. Many of the houses were quite content to have me call at the front door for my money. Sometimes I was even asked in to wait and from the glimpses I got from the front hallways the insides of the houses were fully as impressive as the outsides. There were richly carpeted staircases, living rooms full of upholstered chairs the like of which I had never seen before, walls hung with tapestries and family portraits in oils, stuffed deer heads, and one house even had a stuffed bear standing erect in a corner by the hat rack. Standing in the hall of such a house naturally triggered my imagination and I wondered what it would be like to live in such luxury and slide down such shiny banisters.

Even more impressive than the insides of the houses were the insides of the garages. In an era when the motor car was still far from common, and there were fewer than ten thousand in all Manitoba, most of these houses had two cars in each garage. Why any family needed two cars I never did figure out except, perhaps, to have a spare on hand in case the other broke down. Once, when a huge Packard was sitting in the Ryan driveway unattended, I climbed into it and sat at the driver's seat. Mr. Ryan came out and saw me and, instead of running me off, came over and explained to me how all the levers worked. I said it was a wonderful car and I sure wished we had one like it. "I've never had a ride in a car," I said. The man was astounded.

"What?" he said. "You haven't? Well you just move over and we'll fix all that." I moved over, and he adjusted the switches and levers, put on a pair of gloves, and cranked the car into life. I held tightly to the side as we wheeled out of his driveway, then out across Cornish Avenue and down Sherbrook Street to Portage Avenue.

"Gee," I said, when he slowed down to turn onto Portage, "this is better than an open streetcar!"

Mr. Ryan thought that a huge joke and repeated my compliment several times on the way home. He asked me my name when I thanked him.

"Say, that is a nice name, isn't it. Jimmie Gray, eh? Well, Jimmie Gray, you've had a ride in a Packard Twin Six and now nobody can ever say again that you've never had a car ride."

He reached out and shook hands with me. That was a double first, for I could not recall any other adult ever having asked my name or shaken my hand. Mr. Ryan went into the house chuckling to himself.

"Better than an open streetcar," I heard him say for the fourth or fifth time. I couldn't figure out what was so funny. It really *was* more exciting than riding on an open streetcar.

CHAPTER TEN

Scabbing Was a
Faceful of Dish Water

The Winnipeg General Strike of 1919 was the climacteric from which the city never fully recovered. It lasted for thirty-seven days during which upwards of twenty-five thousand strikers brought the economy of the city to a halt. Nothing like it had ever happened in Canada before and nothing approaching it has happened since. Involved in the strike were bitter struggles between ideologies, between craft and industrial unionism, between national and international trade unionism, between entrenched capitalism and militant, near-revolutionary labour leadership, between Anglo-Saxon racism and common decency. When the strike was lost, hundreds of families saw their livelihoods destroyed. In the histories of the event, most of the emphasis has been on the major issues, on the unleashed forces that had such a devastating effect on the economy and political life of the region. But there was another side where all the strains were picayune and personal, where nothing much was involved except the impairment of human relationships at the family level. This damage was naturally greatest in the families where the father lost his job as a result of the strike and was forced to try to remake his life in an impossible environment. Yet even in those families which escaped serious damage from the strike, the wounds that time had seemed to heal kept breaking out and suppurating for years afterward.

Our family survived the strike without too great an economic loss. Compared to many others, we came out relatively
undamaged. In fact, the 1919 affair was less disruptive to our
family life than the 1918 strike of the civic employees. The
advent of prohibition in 1917 and the ending of the open bars
helped my father solve his liquor problem for the next three
years. It was only when bootleg beer became openly available
in the downtown hotels after 1920 that he gradually slipped
from the pledge. Toward the end of 1917 he got a minor
clerical job in the City Hall handling the mail and the statio-
nery supplies. The job in all likelihood paid less than twenty
dollars a week and probably closer to fifteen. But with the
janitor's suite in the Rozell Apartments, plus the small stipend
that went with the suite, and my paper route money, our
family achieved a level of unaccustomed affluence. Certainly,
our 1917 Christmas was the best I could remember. Unhappily
it was a short-lived period of prosperity. The owner of the
Rozell Apartments came back from the war after Christmas
and decided he needed a full-time, able-bodied janitor. We
moved to the only housing we could find at a rent we could
pay, a semi-modern cottage at 126 Bryce Street. The move
precipitated a financial crisis that became permanently endemic to the family. In 1918 there was no way in which our
family could survive on my father's wage. Yet as a man
approaching fifty and handicapped, he had little chance of
bettering himself by changing jobs. His only hope for the
remote future was somehow to wangle an increase in pay and
then work himself into a better job in the civic service if one
developed. That was an uncertain prospect at best, for the
wounded already were coming home from the war and
returned soldiers were being given job preference over civilians. But, forlorn or not, it was about the only hope he had.
In the meantime, the present became a period of economic
torment.

While my parents were trying to adjust to the shattering
blow to their standard of living, the 1918 strike threat loomed
over City Hall. My parents were confronted not only with a

complete loss of income if the strike did develop, but with the prospect of the permanent loss of my father's job as well, if he went on strike and the strike was lost. The mere mention of the word "strike" soon became enough to bring on my mother's migraine. Until I was almost twelve I never heard a cross word pass between my mother and father except when alcohol was involved. It was almost as if my father, unlike most alcoholics, realized when sober that he had built up an imposing burden of demerits when drunk, and was trying to balance the books. If it had been within his power, my mother would have been as badly spoiled as a Jewish mother. He turned over his pay to her and would buy clothes for himself only after her urging became irresistible. He walked to work and back to save carfare. He even encouraged my mother to cut his hair when she was cutting ours. His greatest pleasure was in sitting by the table after supper reading aloud to my mother while she sat darning or sewing.

Except for reading, however, our family would have qualified as a laboratory specimen of what latter-day social jargon labels the "culturally deprived". C.P. Walker had provided Winnipeg with one of the finest theatres in the country and it was ablaze all winter with road companies from New York, light opera from Ireland, and operatic stars from the continent; the Pantages and Orpheum vaudeville theatres were uninterrupted by the war; the movies were beginning to attract large crowds; there was a music teacher in every block in the North End to give the Jewish, Ukrainian, and Polish kids massive doses of musical instruction weekly. There was a good deal of music in my father's family. One of my cousins had studied in Germany and had had a short fling as a concert pianist before retiring to the management of a piano store in Toronto. Nobody in our family, however, could carry a tune, though I once developed a mild urge to take piano lessons. The closest my brothers and I ever came to exposure to culture was occasional attendance at Saturday matinees at the Mac's Theatre on Ellice Avenue or the Starland on Main Street to see a Charlie Chaplin two-reeler and Pearl White in a "Perils of Pauline" serial. I doubt if my mother or father ever attended a theatre, legitimate or vaudeville, or went to a concert or even to the movies. Neither danced, played games of any kind, or in fact took very much interest in the world at large, except vicariously from books and the newspapers. In plain truth, for them the whole world seemed to revolve around each other and their family.

Then, out of the blue, came the 1918 strike and something went out of our family life, something that never wholly came back again. If my mother could ever have understood what the word "strike" meant in its industrial context she might not have been as vehement in her opposition to it. For her the word had only one meaning—hitting something. For her "going on strike" conjured up visions of workers ganging together to beat up an employer until he capitulated to their demands for higher wages. Nobody understood the need for higher wages better than she did, and she conceded that the only way to get more money was to ask for it. But to couple the request for a raise with a threat to strike somebody caused a mental block in my mother's mind that my father was never able to overcome. As the negotiations between the City and its employees began to come unravelled, she listened to my father's attempted explanations with mounting impatience.

Her fear that my father would lose his job perhaps prevented her from even trying to understand the complicated issues that were arising at the City Hall. For many months the Civic Employees Federation had been working on a plan to reclassify the salaries of the entire service on the basis of the work performed. The pay rates for people doing identical work varied widely from one department to another. The effect of the reclassification would have been to raise wages substantially for just about everybody, and this the City Council resisted mightily. On the other hand, the Council recognized that the cost of living was getting out of hand. This led the City to offer a "war bonus" of two dollars a week for single men and three dollars a week for married employees. A three-dollar-a-week raise would have lifted our family finances much nearer the point of solvency. But the Federation rejected the "war bonus" and stood by its demand for reclassification.

"Men make me sick!" my mother would explode in the middle of my father's explanations. "*We* need more pay and the City employees say *they* want more pay. The City Council wants to pay you three dollars a week more than you are getting but you say you won't take it because it isn't reclassification. What difference does it make what you call it as long as you get your raise of three dollars a week?"

"Don't keep saying 'you, you, you'," my father protested. "It ain't me. I got nothing to do with it. It's the union and it's run by men who have worked for the City for years so they must know what they are doing."

"But, how can they?" my mother came back. "It don't seem reasonable. Here the City wants to give you three dollars a week more on account of the cost of living but you don't even get a chance to say you'll take it. Some other fellow steps forward and says you can't take it. What right does he have to take food out of your children's mouths, Harry Gray, you just tell me that!"

The arguments replaced after-supper reading and sometimes went on far into the night. My brothers and I slept three in a bed in the bedroom behind my parents' room. My brother Walter was a very light sleeper and slept next to the wall. The arguments in the next room frequently awakened him and since he could not abide being awake alone, he would nudge my brother Bob awake. Then one of them would wake me. Our under-cover pushing, tickling, and pinching continued until somebody cried out and this brought my father in with his razor strap. He would peel back the covers, hit us a couple of stinging swats with the strap, and go back to bed. We got strapped more in the months before and during the 1918 strike than we had during all the previous years of our lives.

Relations between my mother and father were badly strained before the strike, and they got steadily worse after it started. The argument over reclassification got lost in the shuffle after the City Hydro and the waterworks' employees struck for more money on May 2 and 3. Then the teamsters struck on May 7, and the firemen went out on the 14th. By that time half the unions in the city were out on strike, either for higher wages on their own account or in sympathy with the civic employees.

How long my father was actually on strike I cannot remember, for my recollections of the 1918 walkout are hopelessly tangled with those of the 1919 strike. I do recall, however, his coming home one afternoon, either from work or from a mass meeting in Victoria Park, with word that the strike was about to be settled by the government appointing a board. The men had agreed to that and it was now up to the City Council. That night the City Council ruined everything. When the settlement proposal went before it an amendment was added that civic employees would individually have to sign affidavits that under no circumstance would they ever go on strike again. After signing, they could all go back to work while the issues were arbitrated. Mention of the "Fowler Amendment" was sure to start an argument in our house for the next couple of weeks. Up to that point my father had been comparatively passive in his support of the strike. I suspect that my mother's blind opposition to the idea of a strike had forced him steadily into a stronger position than he might otherwise have taken. Along came the Fowler Amendment and he became a ranting militant.

He came home from a meeting with a new phrase—"yellow dog contract"—and announced that he would rather starve than put his name to such a shameful piece of paper. My mother's reply set them at each other with my mother crying and my father shouting and neither hearing the other.

"Well, you'll get your chance to starve, yellow dog or no yellow dog," she screamed at him. "We are out of food and out of money and out of credit and the rent is due. From now on you just try doing the cooking for this family and see how you like it trying to stretch things the way I have to stretch them." She tore off her apron, flung it on a chair, and retreated behind her bedroom door.

The 1918 strike gave birth to the polarization of Winnipeg society between labour and capital. When the firemen went on strike, the businessmen organized the "Committee of One Hundred" dedicated to maintaining law, order, and the public services. Volunteers manned the firehalls and were kept busy answering false alarms. When grass fires or bonfires got out of control, the strikers were blamed for starting them. When at last the street railway employees joined what had become a general strike, the federal Minister of Labour, the Honourable Gideon Robertson, took a hand. He talked the City Council into abandoning the Fowler Amendment and arranged for a local citizens' group to function as a conciliation board. They brought in reclassification, my father got a small raise in pay plus the "war bonus", I got a morning paper route as well as an evening route, and we survived after a fashion until the 1919 general strike.

This time all the civic employees went out and were out for almost two weeks until the City Council declared their sympathetic strike illegal. My father then went back to work along with the others, although the strike itself went on for at least three more weeks. While he was on strike he spent a great deal of time at the Labour Temple and Victoria Park, like most strikers who had nothing to do. The clear victory that the strikers had scored in 1918 unquestionably made people like my father overly confident that once the 1919 strike became general it too would succeed quickly. It was a tragic miscalculation. Though my father went back to work when ordered to by the City Council, he still spent the weekends at Victoria Park, and my mother insisted that I go along to try to keep him out of any trouble that might blow up.

The route from our home on Bryce Street to the Labour Temple on James Street took my father past the Industrial Bureau on Main Street, the headquarters of the "Committee of 1,000" which was organized by the business community to beat the 1919 strike. Once, after the regular police force had

been fired and the vigilantes sworn in, my father got into an altercation with one of the vigilantes while passing the building. He was so severely jabbed in the ribs with the butt end of an axe handle that for days he carried a gruesome-looking bruise that covered some painfully cracked ribs. I don't think my mother ever precisely sorted out in her mind what she expected from my going along with my father. Certainly a skinny little thirteen-year-old was unlikely to provide much assistance in a brawl. But as had happened in the Grand Theatre riot, at least I frightened easily enough to run at the first sign of danger and tried to take my father with me. The fact that nothing much ever happened when I was along reinforced my mother's conviction that I should go with my father.

The pitched battles that took place on Main Street and Portage Avenue during the 1919 strike never happened when my father and I were around. The closest we ever came to a riot was the day when the strikers burned the streetcar in front of the City Hall and clashes between the special police and the strikers killed one man and sent thirty to the hospital, while scores were placed under arrest. Our journey to Victoria Park was delayed that day by a long argument between my mother and father whether he should go at all. He had developed a shorter and shorter fuse about the strike and had had flare-ups with several people in our neighbourhood over it. My mother feared that his tongue would provoke some of the special police into giving him another clubbing. As the bitterness of the community heightened, my mother's anxieties increased. Unhappily, whenever she tried to talk my father into staying home her arguments always strayed over into the area of the strike itself. The 1918 strike for higher wages and job classification had been hard enough for her to fathom, but the 1919 "sympathetic strike for collective bargaining" was utterly beyond her comprehension. The idea of my father being involved in a "sympathetic strike" on behalf of bricklayers, carpenters, and sheet metal workers who, she believed, made twice as much money as he did was so preposterous that she closed her ears and mind to my father's arguments. I suspect that my father agreed with her on that point but he was driven increasingly by circumstance to support of the strike. A paramount reason was his inability to earn enough money to support his family as the cost of living got completely out of hand. The exposure of outrageous profiteering in the war industries had a profound effect upon him, as did the shoddiness of wartime clothing and shoes. Finally, he could not forget that the aldermen who had fought every step of the way against the efforts of the civic employees to improve their standard of living in 1918 were deeply involved in the efforts of the "Committee of 1,000" to break the strike.

So it was that while my father himself did not stay on strike for its duration, he became ever more bitter toward the strike-breaking "Committee of 1,000". My mother not only feared that he would get hurt again, and more seriously, but that he might also do something that could cost him his job. Whenever he announced his intention of going to Victoria Park, she objected with rising anger. Sometimes she succeeded in talking him into staying home. But on this particular Saturday he was determined to go. When at last he put on his hat to signal the end of the argument, she called me in to go with him. I objected. I had my papers to deliver that afternoon and would surely be late if I went with my father.

"Then take your paper bag and bicycle with you and when the meeting's over you can go for your papers," my mother said. My father vetoed that idea. He said any boy who showed up at the Victoria Park with a newspaper bag emblazoned with "Free Press" would be mobbed. Then I should take my bicycle but leave my bag at home and stop by for it en route to the *Free Press* depot, my mother countered. I'd still be late, I insisted.

"Oh, for heaven's sake, stop being so difficult," my mother said. "Let Walter pick up both your papers and you can get yours from him whenever you get home." Walter helped me deliver half my route. With the postal workers and telephone operators both on strike, there was no way for subscribers to complain if the papers were late. Indeed, it was probably a surprise to most readers to get a paper at all since the supplies of just about everything else were drying up. Many of the wholesalers were closed, and the retail stores that stayed open ran with depleted stocks.

Because it was late when all the arguments were settled, we cut around behind the Industrial Bureau on Main Street and took a short cut to Victoria Park along the C.P.R. transfer tracks that paralleled the river. Taking the short cut caused us to miss all the action, which we would have seen if we had gone to City Hall the usual way.

When we arrived at Victoria Park it was empty, for the strikers had already broken up and moved to the City Hall. By the time we walked that far the riot was over, the crowd had been dispersed, and the street was being patrolled by dozens of armed special police with white arm bands. They allowed us to turn into Main Street but when we stopped to talk to passing strangers about the overturned streetcar, a special policeman rushed up and ordered us on our way. Yet everyone who knew anything about the riot seemed eager to share his news with everyone else. It was as if all the men walking south stopped to talk with all those walking north, if only for a minute. Despite the special police, knots of spectators gathered, and were broken up only to regather with different components a few yards away. As we got farther away from the City Hall the ad hoc news exchanges lasted longer, so we reached Portage Avenue with a pretty complete strikers' version of how the riot had started. The mounted special police had charged into the crowd, had been driven back, and then had charged again with guns blazing. At Portage and Main we encountered remnants of the mounted patrol still on duty, riding up and down ordering people to keep moving and not to congregate. When I reached home at supper time to deliver my papers I found the *Free Press* had replated its Saturday edition as an extra paper. From it I discovered that there were almost as many versions of the riot as there were eyewitnesses. The people we talked to had blamed the special police for starting the riot. The *Free Press* blamed the "alien Reds" for firing on the police and war veterans and causing the bloodshed. In any event, the riot ended the strike and left behind enough bitterness to outlast several generations. It was a long, long time before the relationship that existed between my father and mother before the two strikes was even partly restored.

Aside from the internal family turmoil, the worst thing that happened to us in the 1919 General Strike was the totally unexpected walkout of the newspaper pressmen, which put all the Winnipeg dailies out of business. When it became clear that there would be a strike in 1919 and that my father would be involved, my mother began hoarding her food supplies against the emergency she was sure would develop. The loss of even a few days' pay would put an impossible strain on our family budget. As it was, for the last several days before each payday our meals were noticeably skimpy. When the newspapers stopped publishing for a week the six or seven dollars she could count on from my paper routes disappeared. While the *Free Press* got back into business within a week, there was no way for us to recover the lost revenue. When the paper did start publishing, my father developed a curious ambivalence toward my resuming deliveries; although he was on strike himself at that time he did not object to my going back to my paper routes to deliver the newspaper that was most extreme in its opposition to the strike. I suspected that some sort of secret treaty had been negotiated between my mother and father in connection with the paper routes. The income was so vital that we would have gone hungry without it. My father probably gave in to my mother in face of that alternative, but he never had to like what I was doing. Nor could he stomach what appeared in the *Free Press*. Soon after he began to read the paper he would angrily rumple it and fling it from him with a string of curses.

Living as we did on Bryce Street, and delivering my evening route along Stradbrook and Wardlaw avenues and my morning route along Roslyn Road and the streets off River Avenue, I moved in an atmosphere that was overwhelmingly hostile to the strikers. Except for an area adjacent to the C.N.R. shops, south Winnipeg was populated largely by supporters of the "Committee of 1,000" and generally subscribed to the extreme position taken by the *Free Press* that the strike had been fomented by "alien Reds" aiming at establishing a Bolshevik dictatorship in Canada. But here and there within this area there were bound to be small pockets of strike sympathizers like my father and one or two of our neighbours. I encountered two such sympathizers on the first day that the *Free Press* resumed publication. Instead of firing the papers at the front door as I rode my bicycle along the sidewalk, the usual practice, I called at each house to tell the people that the *Free Press* was back in business and would remain so for the duration of the strike. This procedure was ordered by our district manager when we got our papers. The first twenty-five or thirty calls I made evoked favourable and sometimes enthusiastic responses. Then I encountered one subscriber who single-handedly brought the reaction into balance.

"Hello, Mrs. Logan," I called, as I caught sight of one of my customers through the screen on the front door. My shout caught her attention and I could see her halt whatever she was doing in the kitchen, which was down a short hall from the front door. "It's the *Free Press* paper boy," I said, "back in business again and here's your paper." Receiving no response, I judged she had not heard me. So I repeated my call and was in the process of opening the screen door to hand her the paper when I got her reply—full in the face.

I had triggered such an outraged reaction that she grabbed up a pan full of dirty dishes that had been sitting on the back of the stove since lunch, rushed to the front door with it, and flung it at me as I opened the door—dishes, dishwater, and all. Her aim was perfect. I got it all from head to toe, including a mouthful and a messy dish that plopped against my shirt front. With the slop-bath came a torrent of vituperation that would have done a truck driver proud.

"Take your filthy rag and get off my steps and don't you ever come back again or I'll set the dog on you, you filthy little Judas scab!"

Her abuse poured out as she exploded through the door and shoved me slithering backwards down the steps and out to the sidewalk. I grabbed my bike and papers and pushed off down the street with her strident voice following till I was out of earshot. The episode happened within a block of home, so I went to change my clothes and wash the dishwater out of my hair. My mother's reaction was predictably indignant and for a while she was all for calling the police and having the woman arrested, except that with the strike on there was no way of calling the police. I changed my clothes and went back to delivering my papers.

The second episode that day, near the end of the route on Bell Avenue, also caught me by surprise. A couple of young men reached out and grabbed me as I passed them on the sidewalk. While one of them held me, the other seized my *Free Press* bag and jerked out the dozen papers I still had to deliver. While I screamed at him to leave my papers alone, and tried to get loose, he tore them up one after the other.

"There, you stinkin' little scab, that's what decent people

think of your —— yellow sheet that ain't fit to use for ass-paper. You oughtta be ashamed to bring that rag into a decent neighbourhood to poison the minds of decent people. Let this be a warning to you! Next time you show your face with this —— rag it will be you that gets torn apart as well as the papers!"

"And let this be a lesson to you!" the man who had been holding me said as he released me with a push and then gave me a kick in the pants that hurt so much I was sick to my stomach all over my clean shirt. They had disappeared up the street long before I regained enough composure to take off tearfully for home. Who the men were I never discovered, but I approached that end of my route fearfully for the duration of the strike.

It was in the same area, however, that I started on an adventure that gave my memories of the 1919 General Strike a happy ending. So complete was the shut-down of Winnipeg that even the bread and milk drivers had stopped work until they were ordered back on the streets by the General Strike Committee so that the basic needs of the women and children could be met. To protect the drivers from attack by angry strikers, their rigs were posted with signs that said the deliveries were being made with permission of the General Strike Committee. It was the wording of those signs that ultimately played an important part in sending the strike leaders to jail for seditious conspiracy after the strike was broken. The ice wagons on which the householders depended to keep their milk and butter fresh were, however, off the streets for much longer. The ice companies opened their storage places for the people who could get to them to pick up their own ice. We had no icebox and my mother kept her milk and butter in a small dug-out that was reached through a trap door in the kitchen floor. On very hot days she put a block of ice in a large pan on the floor of the dug-out. One hot Saturday midway through the strike she sent me with my wagon to the Arctic Ice warehouse on Harkness Street at the foot of Bell Avenue. An employee lazing in the sun waved his arm in the general direction of the interior of the building when I asked if I could have some ice.

"Take what you want," he said. "You'll find an axe in there to chop off what you can carry." I backed my wagon up to a block of ice and chopped into it the way I had seen the iceman do, and a large chunk broke off and slid onto my wagon. I covered it with a sack and started home along Bell Avenue, which was tree-lined and cooler than River Avenue. I was barely past the old Children's Home before a man sitting on the steps of one of the bigger houses spotted me.

"Hey, boy," he called, "what you got in that wagon? Ice?"

I hesitated before answering, recalling my recently painful experience in the neighbourhood. But he seemed friendly and I nodded.

"Hey, don't run off, wait just a minute and let's me and you make a deal. How about selling me half that block of ice. You don't need all that much."

"No," I said. "I'm not selling ice. I'm just taking this home for our milk."

"Well, there isn't an icebox in Winnipeg that'll hold a piece that big. Come on, I'll give you a nickel for half of it." I hesitated. He went on. "Tell you what I'll do, I'll give you a dime for half of that ice." Without waiting for me to accept, he went into the house and came back with a large dishpan and an ice pick. He handed me the money and then went to work on the block of ice. While he was chipping the woman next door came out and spotted what was going on. Without asking she rushed back indoors and returned with her dishpan. I tried to tell her that I was taking the ice home but she would not listen. Instead she ignored me, and asked the man what he had paid me. She reached into an apron pocket and took out a dime and handed it to me. I was twenty cents richer but fresh out of ice.

The custodian of the ice house was still in the same spot when I got back and he waved me in to the ice as casually as he had done the first time. I cut off another chunk and this time headed down River Avenue to avoid being waylaid on

Bell Avenue. It was no use. A woman spotted me from the second floor of the Moxam Court, shouted out the window for me to wait, and came running with a pan for some ice. As I became completely surrounded by women with pans for ice it dawned on me that I was giving too much ice for too little money so I started charging fifteen cents for the larger pieces and a dime for the smaller ones. Within a couple of hours I sold better than two dollars' worth and there was no end in sight. I was still a couple of blocks from home on my fifth or sixth trip and my wagon was empty again. Soon I stopped trying to avoid customers and went looking for them. There were a number of apartment blocks in the neighbourhood and I needed only to attract the attention of one woman tenant and she would rouse all her neighbours to the presence of the iceman. Soon the silver in my pocket was converted into a small wad of folding money. By early afternoon, my take approached five dollars and I contemplated an afternoon of even more profitable business. Alas, the boom collapsed as suddenly as it had arisen. The custodian locked up the ice house and went home.

I never did get any ice for my mother that day, but the profit took the edge off her disappointment. With it we went down to Hardy and Buchanan's on Osborne Street and laid in a wagonful of groceries. When my father discovered what I had been up to while we were having supper I thought he would choke with anger, or at the very least fling his plate at me.

"To think that a son of mine would turn into a scab for the Arctic Ice Company . . . ", his voice trailed off into sputtering silence.

"He wasn't a scab for any ice company," my mother said, rushing to my defence. "He was hauling ice for women with babies who needed ice to keep their babies' milk. And the food you're eating, mister, came from that ice, and so did the shoes I got back from the shoemaker for you, and so will the food we'll eat next week." Her voice, like my father's, trailed off into nothing and we finished eating our supper. By the time the next Saturday rolled around ice was again being delivered by the regular icemen and I was out of the ice business by whatever definition—either as a scab for the Arctic Ice Company or as a succourer of babies in hunger and distress.

CHAPTER ELEVEN

The Delinquent
Who Never Was Caught

I did a short stint as a police reporter for the *Winnipeg Free Press* in 1937, and I was lolling at the reporters' table in police court one morning while the crown prosecutor and the police magistrate processed a normal weekend run of malefactors with their usual efficiency. It was the practice, in those days, for the crown prosecutor to discuss his docket with the magistrate before court opened. Quite often, after a guilty plea had been entered, the prosecutor would say, "This is the case I mentioned to you, your worship."

The magistrate, an old crown prosecutor himself, would glance at the prisoner in the dock, nod his head and mumble almost inaudibly, "H-m-m-m. Six months in jail."

This practice had been going on for so long that both the prosecutor and the magistrate were astounded when I stirred up a public outcry by writing a news story that described the chummy liaison between the prosecution and the bench. Thereafter, when the prosecutor went to visit the magistrate before court opened, he left his docket behind and abandoned the phrase "This is the case I spoke to you about", except when memory lapsed.

But on the morning in question the old practice prevailed and jail sentences were being handed out at a goodly rate. Then proceedings came to a short halt while the magistrate found his place on the docket and finished looking up the notes he had made before court opened. The charge was breaking and entering. The accused, a tall, gauntish fellow of my own age, fiddled with his sleeve while waiting to hear his fate. I glanced up and saw that he was looking at me rather intently with a sort of half smile of half recognition. His lips moved, ever so slightly, as if he were saying "hello".

I returned his half smile, but for the life of me I could not place him. The prosecutor droned over his long record of arrests and convictions for minor offences, mainly petty theft. The magistrate glanced at him and gave him another two-year jail term. I ran my finger down the docket on the table, came to his name, and stopped. I recognized it instantly and was transported back to the Isbister schoolyard more than twenty years before. The recollection ruined that day for me—and the next and several days after that. Whenever I recalled the episode, a paraphrase of Bradford's quotation ran through my mind: "But for the grace of God, there goes Jimmie Gray."

The name of the man in the dock was Philip Newfeld, and I was along the night he got caught stealing a bunch of bananas and made his entry into a life of crime. I was along because he was my hero. He had saved me from a beating one day in the Isbister schoolyard and he was my friend for life, or so I had believed at the time.

Like my other schools in Winnipeg, Isbister housed a mixed bag of pupils. It was surrounded by what we called terraces—row houses attached to each other in blocks of ten or twelve units. The units contained three, four, and five bedrooms and often held three or four families. However, on Balmoral and Spence streets, north of Ellice, there were a number of large single-family houses on thirty- and forty-foot lots. J. W. Dafoe, the editor of the *Free Press*, lived on Balmoral Street and flooded his back yard in the winter to turn it into a skating rink for kids from blocks around. There were Italian immigrant colonies on Young Street nearer Portage and on Young and on Langside streets near Sargent. We lived in the Richmond Apartments on the corner of Ellice Avenue and Young Street.

Life in the Machray schoolyard had been tough enough. I was a year older than anyone else in my Grade One class and tall for my age to boot. It seemed that no game we played was ever completed at recess or before school without a couple of fist fights and wrestling matches. I seldom managed even a draw, but the process of losing taught me who to stay away from, and by the following spring when we moved I had found my place in the pecking order and managed a tolerably peaceful existence. But at Isbister school the whole process had to be gone through again, with a succession of tough young Italian kids substituted for tough young Ukrainian and Jewish kids. On balance, Isbister seemed worse than Machray, mainly because of a short, bow-legged Italian kid named Johnny Orestes, who took a dislike to me when he first laid eyes on me. I was barely into the yard on my first day at school when he came over, sized me up carefully, gave me a push, and said, "Hey, kid, you wanna fight?"

I didn't and said so. That was a mistake. Soon we were rolling around on the ground with him punching and me trying to hold on to his arms. I must have caused some kind of allergic reaction in Johnny Orestes. Whenever we came within yards of each other he wanted to practise his punching technique on me. Then one day Phil Newfeld interceded. For no reason I could understand, he stepped in and grabbed my nemesis by the back of the sweater, jerked him around, and gave him an open-handed slap to the jaw that could be heard at least across the street. Johnny let out a howl, tried to wiggle free, and got another slap. Phil was in Grade Three and was a good two or three years stronger and taller than Johnny.

Phil gave Johnny a push that landed him on his seat and stood over him. "From now on you leave the kid alone," Phil said. "He ain't done nothin' to you, you stinkin' little wop. Go pick on somebody else for a change or next time I'll knock your teeth in!"

On the ground, Johnny was still defiant. "You just wait," he sobbed. "You just wait till I tell my brother on you."

Phil Newfeld lived on Langside Street, half a block down

the lane from our block. Until I got well settled into Isbister school I waited to walk home from school with him. Eventually Johnny Orestes lost interest in beating me up, but my attitude toward Phil Newfeld was that of a willing servitor. Yet except for the peace-making episode he mainly ignored me. Although I was almost as tall as he was, I was two years younger. He ran with kids of his own age or older, and I belonged with the little kids, the second-graders. Whenever his group played vacant-lot baseball or any of the hide-and-seek games they usually chased us away.

Winnipeg, in those days, was overrun with peddlers of every conceivable variety. Mostly they drove one-horse rigs filled with fruit, vegetables, ice cream, popcorn, and sometimes even furniture and hardware, with pots and pans hanging from hooks attached to the roof. Every peddler looked with a bilious eye on the young boys of the city. For our part, we regarded all peddlers' rigs as natural targets for smash-and-grab thievery. We might spurn carrots, beets, or turnips when served on our plates, but if we could grab a bunch from a peddler's rig we'd devour them with relish. For their part the peddlers seldom left their rigs unguarded. Often they carried their own younger children along and we learned early in life to take no liberties with them. They were usually armed with broom handles and knew how to use them. Other peddlers carried barking terrier dogs to protect their goods. It was a snarling terrier dog that led to Phil Newfeld's downfall.

A fruit peddler who lived on Young Street near Sargent used to go down our back lane on his way home at night. Phil once tried to snatch a basket of fruit and was grabbed and painfully bitten by the peddler's little white dog. He had a bandage on his arm for several days and discussed, in sidewalk strategy meetings, how he and his gang could get back at the peddler by stealing a whole stalk of bananas. Eventually they came up with an elaborate scheme. The peddler always unloaded his rig, except for the banana stalk, when he came home, and took his fruit into a back shed. In his back yard he had a small barn for the horse and a space for his rig surrounded by a high fence with a gate that was always kept locked. After supper he would take his ease in a rocking chair on the front verandah of his house. Phil's problem was how to keep him on the verandah while he broke into the yard and grabbed a big stalk of bananas. The big kids worked out something, but when we tried to tag along they ran us off. We went along anyway, at a discreet distance. We hid behind garbage cans and watched as Phil and another boy went over the fence. They were back in a minute with the banana stalk, complete with the slats and sacking shipping cover. They had failed, however, to take the acute ears of the little terrier into account. It began to bark as they pushed the crate over the fence. We ran for home when we heard the dog bark. We were well down the lane before we turned to look back. Phil and another boy were surrounded by a dozen angry Italians who were shouting and calling for the police. Eventually a patrolman turned up and a while later, at home in bed, I thought I caught the sound of the paddy wagon's bell as it headed for Sargent and Langside.

That was the last we saw of Phil until he returned to school in the fall. He had been taken in hand by the juvenile court, was paddled severely, and spent the summer holidays in detention. I skipped a grade at Isbister and went into Grade Three that fall. This brought me a grade closer to him. But we seemed farther apart than ever. For one thing, he had become something of a loner. For another, my mother and father were always warning me against being seen with him. He was a bad boy who had been arrested by the police. He was bad company and I should avoid him. However, the fact that he had been arrested by the police and had been in jail, as we called it, made him a neighbourhood celebrity for the boys in our group. So I would have been friendly with him, even though I no longer needed his protection. But he drifted out of our orbit and I never saw him again until that fleeting minute in police court.

For a moment after he left the court I thought of going up

to the jail to see him. But what, after all, did we have in common? I thought better of it and settled for sending him up a package of cigarettes.

"There," I kept telling myself, "but for the grace of God went Jimmie Gray." The only difference between Phil and me was that he got caught stealing and I never did.

Respect for private property is by no means an easily acquired characteristic. There is nothing much sacred about private property for people who do not have any, which took in most of the families of the kids I ran around with in early childhood. We all learned early there was little point in asking our parents to buy us something we yearned for, whether it was a bag of marbles or a coaster sleigh. Mostly the yearning only led to thoughts of where and how the desired objective could be pinched. The word "stealing" was never used by the boys of my age—perhaps because the act always sounded a lot worse when our parents warned us against stealing than when we went out to pinch something. Thus we scoured the back alleys for anything we thought might be salable to the Jewish junkmen who travelled the same alleys. If we found something, we'd sell it for a penny or two and then watch for the chance to pinch it back from the rig and resell it to the next junkman who came along.

Occasionally scrounging the back lanes yielded rich and unexpected dividends. We started out one morning with sacks in which to gather bottles. If we could collect a number of the same kind of whisky bottles the junkman would give us a dime a dozen for them. In this safari we came upon an apartment block where there had been a small fire and which was being remodelled. There was a lot of lead pipe lying around outside, so we filled our bags with all we could carry and hurried home. The junkmen were always asking, "You got lead? You got maybe some brass?"

The first junkman who came along refused to buy our lead. "That's new," he said. "That's new and you steal. No buy stolen stuff. You boys take back where you stole."

We protested that we found it in the lane and told him

where. It was no use. It looked new to him and he refused to buy. When we examined it more closely we could see that it was rather new looking, not that any of us could tell new lead from old lead. There was no thought of returning it, however. We brought out hammers and axes and battered the lead pipe until there was no longer any question of it being new. The next junk dealer along paid us fifty cents apiece for our stock, which was more than we ever made in several Saturdays of bottle collecting. We rushed back to the apartment building for more but were halted short of the site by a shouting match going on between the workmen and the foremen, over who was responsible for leaving the lead pipe lying around where somebody could steal it. We quietly returned to bottle collecting and said nothing to anybody.

In the spring of the year, the fifteen-cent store at Donald and Portage was overrun by small boys bent on pinching a bag of marbles when the clerks turned their backs. Curiously enough, we never seemed to pinch anything of much intrinsic value. But we gave storekeepers fits. Whenever they saw two small boys come in they kept a wary eye on both, with special scrutiny of the non-buyer, for he represented the potential loss. In the North End, most of the stores were run by Jews and this created a special problem for junior-grade shoplifters. Most Jews had large families and usually they lived behind the store with the living quarters separated from the store only by a curtain hung across an open doorway. There was always an elaborate hook-up of bells into the living quarters to warn the proprietor when someone entered the store while it was unattended. If there were more than two or three customers in the store at once, one of the proprietor's family would probably be watching from behind the curtain. I know of nothing as chilling as the sudden scream from a head poked through the slit in the curtain: "Papa, Papa, look quick. That skinny boy just stole a piece of halvah!"

We dropped the halvah and ran for our lives, often pursued by half the storekeeper's family! If a storekeeper's son ever caught us in a schoolyard fight over something else, we got some special whomps just in case we had sneaked anything into our pockets from the store.

I was never caught. Except once. That episode should demonstrate that larceny was no respecter of environment, that given an opportunity country boys can hold their own with city boys in the liberation of other people's property.

I was visiting my cousin Harvey in Kenton one summer when disaster struck the summer fair at Harding, the next town down the C.P.R. line. A big hailstorm had turned a blistering day into a chilly evening and the Kenton baker, who had set up an ice cream concession at the fair, was left with two large churns full of ice cream. By the time he got the stuff back to Kenton it had melted. In addition to running his bakery and confectionery he also owned the town ice house, which was located behind his store. He buried the ice cream in the ice, refroze it, and announced that he was going to have a clearance sale of his left-over supply. The only trouble was that the refrozen stuff was excessively flaky and was not amenable to being scooped into a cone. So he sold it by the cup or by the soup plate, with everybody bringing their own containers.

His sales pitch fell flat with everyone in town except Harvey and me. We tried the ice cream and it was not only tasty but we got a lot for a nickel. We ran out of nickels before we slaked our appetites. Then Harvey devised an ingenious scheme for raiding the old baker's treasure trove and eating our fill for free. The baker was a garrulous old guy and liked to jaw with customers, even with kids. The plan was for one of us to go into the front of the store and engage him in conversation while the other sneaked into the ice house and loaded up a couple of platefuls of ice cream. After a couple of days the old baker began to get suspicious at all the attention we were paying him, a suspicion that heightened when he discovered that one of his tins of ice cream had been emptied. It was my bad luck to be doing the raiding when he acted. He listened for the opening and closing of the ice house door, stopped Harvey in the middle of a sentence, and rushed out the back door. He slammed the lock on the ice house and I was caught. Clad only in short pants and a light shirt, and bare-footed, it was not long before I began to worry about the cold. At first I thought Harvey had locked me in as a joke. But I was afraid to holler for fear of attracting the attention of the baker. I compromised by shouting in a whisper to Harvey to let me out. But as time passed and nothing happened it began to seem a lot colder than it actually was. The ice house itself was a converted barn in which the ice harvested in the winter from a near-by lake was stored under a thick blanket of sawdust. About all the sawdust really did was slow down the melting, for the rickety building barely protected the contents from the sun. There were cracks between the boards through which I could see part of the baker's yard and the lumber yard next door. After a while I stopped worrying about getting out and wondered what would happen when I did. My Aunt Millie could blow up a storm over what seemed like nothing. What would she do if she discovered we had been burgling the ice cream? And suppose the baker had gone for the town constable? I still had a couple of dishes full of ice cream and as soon as I thought of the policeman I dumped the incriminating evidence back into the freezer and buried the dishes under the sawdust. At last I started a frantic search for a pry of some kind to break the door open. There was nothing. I tried to find a loose board I could push off the wall. Again nothing. I was on the point of convincing myself I was freezing to death when Harvey came back with my Uncle George, who ransomed me by paying the baker for the ice cream we had stolen. For the next couple of days Harvey and I weeded the garden and manhandled the operating lever on Aunt Millie's muscle-powered washing machine.

The most elaborate caper I was ever involved in took place while I was going to Fort Rouge school at about the age of eleven. On the east side of Main Street where the Federal Building now stands was the old Industrial Bureau, which took up most of the block. It was a kind of convention centre and a place in which goods manufactured in Winnipeg were displayed in glass showcases in the corridor that ran the length of the long building. We used this corridor as a halfway warming station in winter when we were on our way downtown from our homes. The display around which we always stopped and drooled was the one in which boxes of chocolates and candy bars were displayed. We always tried the door on the showcase on the chance that somebody had accidentally left it unlocked. They never had. Eventually somebody thought of breaking into the case and pinching a box of chocolates. The thought became an obsession. For weeks we tried to think up a workable plan.

One boy suggested we arm ourselves with a screwdriver and go down and pry the door open. The first time we tried that, the screwdriver was too large to be inserted. The next time, with a smaller one, we exerted so much pressure that it cracked the glass and we fled in fear lest someone had heard the crack. After that we stayed out of the Industrial Bureau for a few weeks just in case we had been seen and somebody might be waiting to collar us if we returned. It turned out to be my idea that proved successful.

"Hey," I said. (All conversations in my boyhood started with "Hey".) "Why don't we find a key that will open the lock? We got lots of old keys around our place. You know, like keys to sewing machines and bureaus and cabinets and stuff."

The gang liked the idea, so before we tried again we collected a bagful of keys and prepared to try them out. Nine-tenths of them were the wrong shape or size but we ended up with half a dozen that would at least fit into the hole in the lock. We discarded all the unusable keys and redoubled our search for keys shaped to fit. The lock resisted all our efforts until one day we inserted a key and it worked. It was a shattering surprise and we quickly relocked the door and left the building to discuss when and how we would carry out our raid.

Great train robberies have been staged with less preparation than we gave our candy bar heist. When did we think the hallway would be the emptiest? What should we do with the loot? What should we wear? How many lookouts should we post? How many kids would we bring into the caper? Who would unlock the door? How would we signal danger? Should somebody be leader to decide what to do in case of an emergency? What would we say if we were caught in the act?

For the next couple of weeks we cased the joint as few joints have been cased before. We discovered there were some offices off the main corridor but the people working in them seldom came into the front of the building. The only person we had to worry about was the janitor. The raid had to be carried out on Saturday, we decided, because a couple of us had paper routes and could not get away after school. There was, however, more traffic through the place on Saturday, particularly early in the day. We settled on a time late in the afternoon, after we had delivered our papers.

Everything went off perfectly. The lookouts signalled "all clear". The key worked in the lock. Three of us filled our paper bags quickly with boxes of chocolates, and our pockets and the insides of our shirts with candy bars. Then we bolted for the doors and were off down the street toward our rendezvous under the Main Street Bridge over the Assiniboine River.

We had agreed that we should all walk naturally down Main Street after the heist so as not to attract attention. Race horses would have had difficulty keeping up with the highly unnatural pace we set. We got to the bridge and ducked down the path under it gasping for breath. Then we unloaded our bags, spread out our loot, and started to divide it. But first we tore the wrappers from some candy bars and took great anticipatory bites into them. But not quite. Instead of the luscious chocolate bars we had expected, the wrappers encased only blocks of wood.

We stared at each other in horrified surprise. Then we tore open the boxes of chocolates that had looked so attractive on the stands. Those which had been opened for display, and which we had covered as we took them out, contained only compressed cotton batting painted to resemble chocolates.

The unopened boxes contained only sawdust. One of the boys shied a chocolate box into the river. We were as dejected a bevy of thieves as ever assembled. But there was still a little larceny left in our souls. How about taking the chocolate bars into Joe's confectionary opposite the school and exchanging them for real bars when he wasn't looking? Or how about taking them to school and selling them to the girls at two for a nickel?

Nothing came of these ideas. We had drained ourselves of both energy and initiative in planning and carrying out our raid on the candy case. The total failure of something on which we had counted for so long with so much hope all but destroyed our taste for candy, if not for thievery. Perhaps it was the scope of this ghastly failure that kept another project from ever getting off the ground.

A new boy named Ross Marr moved into a big old house down near the Wardlaw end of Clark Street on which we were living. We rode back and forth to school together and one day he invited me to inspect something he had discovered in the half-finished attic of his house. Someone had built an elaborate small hiding place between the ceiling joists of the second floor. From above it looked like ordinary flooring. But if you stepped on it in a certain way a floor board sprang up to reveal a compartment about two feet square and six inches deep, lined with tin.

Wow!

He had told no one of his find, not even his parents or sisters. But no boy can keep a secret from everybody, so he told me. At first our speculation centred on who had installed this secret compartment. The war was on and it was easy to conjure up visions of the house having concealed a nest of German spies with all the secret incriminating documents hidden away in the attic until they could be smuggled to Germany. These speculations ran dry fairly rapidly. We could think of nothing important going on in Winnipeg that the Kaiser would be interested in. Anyway, if there was, it would be in North Winnipeg among the pro-Germans and not in good old patriotic Fort Rouge where the best people lived.

Our alternative explanation was robbery. Perhaps a gang of jewel thieves had lived in the house and had hidden their loot in the compartment until the police search cooled off. We made judicious inquiries at home to see if our parents recalled any big jewel robberies in Winnipeg in previous years. We both drew blanks. My friend discovered from a sister who was a stenographer that he could find out who had lived in the house in previous tenancies by checking in the city directory. None of the names he turned up sounded like spies, bank robbers, or jewel thieves.

If we had no answers, we still had the secret hiding place. And what was the good of a secret hiding place if you had nothing to put in it. Obviously, it would only fulfil its function if it contained contraband of some kind. There was no sense having a hiding place if you used it to store old shoes. We had a place to store some stolen goods. What we needed were some stolen goods. We discussed what we could steal and where we could steal it in order to fill our cache. We considered breaking into the school and stealing something. But what?

"How about a box of pencils and a box of chalk," Ross suggested.

That failed to excite me but I couldn't think of anything else in school worth taking. Besides what could we do with a box of chalk except store it away? We never did figure out what to do with Ross's secret hideaway. Eventually we forgot about it, not through a rush of honesty to the head, but simply because we could think of nothing worth stealing that could be stolen.

Surely a very thin line divided the Phil Newfelds from the Jimmie Grays of Winnipeg. We simply couldn't figure out how to launch ourselves on a career of crime, and probably lacked the basic courage it took to get the other boys started. In the raids we staged on the fruit wagons and junkmen's carts, and in the Industrial Bureau caper, we were just plain lucky not to be caught. That enabled time to help us to outgrow our criminal tendencies by diverting our attention in another direction.

My interest was permanently diverted from thievery by the finding of a first baseman's mitt. I was riding down River Avenue one day on my bicycle and there, lying well out from the curb, was a baseball mitt. There wasn't a soul on the street as I picked up the mitt, hung it over the handle of my bike, and rode home to examine it. It was a well-worn but still highly serviceable mitt. My mother insisted I take it back to where I found it and inquire around for its owner. Whoever lost it, she said, would be looking for it. I made a few inquiries, of elderly ladies with shopping bags and elderly gentlemen cutting grass, and was happy that none of them had lost it. It was a better mitt than I had ever hoped to own. I took it to school and showed off my prize to the other kids. But when the word spread I had found the mitt two boys immediately rushed to the principal to report that I had found a mitt their brother had lost. Their efforts to prove ownership failed; I kept the mitt and spent the next years looking for ball games to get into rather than for display cases to break into. From then on the only things I was really interested in stealing were baseballs; and it was not really stealing by our definition. I simply stationed myself on Balmoral Street whenever there was a baseball game and waited for foul balls to come over the fence. Other kids grabbed the balls and returned them to gain entrance to the games. I snagged and kept enough balls to keep the Fort Rouge school in baseballs all summer.

CHAPTER TWELVE

Sex Is Not for Jockeys

My career as a jockey was the shortest on record. In fact I never did get to ride in a race. Like so much else that happened to me, it was something I blundered into accidentally while looking for something else. Finding a first baseman's mitt had turned me into a baseball nut of the first order. I carried it with me wherever I went that summer. I rode by the Fort Rouge schoolyard half a dozen times a day on the odd chance the kids would be playing ball. If they were not, I would spend the time bouncing a baseball off the school wall. I never missed going to Wesley Park at Ellice and Balmoral when the Arenas or Dominion Express were playing. In the spring of 1920 the Western Canada Professional League was organized with teams in Winnipeg, Regina, Saskatoon, Edmonton, and Calgary. The Winnipeg team, the Maroons, played on a diamond in the infield of the race track at River Park, where the Winnipeg Electric Company operated an amusement centre at the foot of Osborne Street.

When the league opened I was there with my mitt, dreaming of the day when I would be a professional baseball star. But mainly I was watching for a chance to snag a foul fly that might come my way. We were always losing our baseballs, or knocking the covers off them. For replenishment of our supplies we depended on foul balls that we snagged when they were hit out of the parks. At Wesley Park the league kept a couple of ballplayers outside the fence on Balmoral Street. They were supposed to chase the foul balls or the kids who caught them. This cut the odds way down, but if we were caught with the ball we turned it over quickly. That got us seats behind home plate where we could watch the stuff, mainly curves, the pitchers were putting on the ball.

At River Park, the only fences were those enclosing the race track and there was a wide expanse of grass on both sides of the foul lines. The Winnipeg Maroons had a very tough mascot named Izzy Klein who, when he caught us, would take the balls away and whack us a couple of stiff ones in the process. After he caught me a couple of times and forced me to disgorge, I decided to put more distance between us. I gave up the hole I had under the fence near the right field foul line and found a loose board away over near the southwest corner of the fence. I figured that if I could grab a long foul fly down the third base line I could be outside the fence before Izzy could get there from his position along the first base line. On the other side of the board I had loosened to get into the park were the race-track horse barns, the discovery of which both surprised and thrilled me as I squeezed through the fence for the first time. It was not only the stable area, it was the stable area full of horses, all getting ready for the race meet that would open in a few days. My passion for horses antedated my love affair with baseball. I had become horse-crazy during our North End period, probably when I was getting over St. Vitus's dance, because I seemed to be alone on the street a lot and delivery men and peddlers often let me ride on their wagons. Whenever I saw a horse stopped on our street I'd rush around and pull grass for it to eat. There was usually a stable or two in every city block where small boys could gather and watch horses being shod, or combed, or just being horses.

A summer or so before I discovered the race track, I spent a month on Simpsons' farm at Roland. The Simpsons had raised my mother when she was orphaned in early childhood, so they were sort of *ex officio* grandparents to us. On the farm that year the pasture was scarce and I used to herd the cattle up and down the road allowance on horseback. My mount was an old mare named Jude and at first I rode her in a beaten-up stock saddle, but later I rode her bareback. No one ever gave me any riding instruction. One of the Simpson boys simply saddled up the mare, jumped on, and showed me how to herd the cattle by getting behind them.

"Just give old Jude her head," he said, as he boosted me into the saddle, "and she'll do the job. But watch when you head in this direction or she'll take off at a gallop for home."

My job was to graze the cattle slowly up one side of the road allowance for a couple of miles and down the other, keeping them out of the stinkweed which, I was warned, spoiled the butter. Nobody warned me about sow thistle, however, and when they came to a big patch I let them polish it off. That ruined the milk for the next couple of days. Cow herding was and is the dullest farm job ever invented, but I played at being a cowboy, made smoke smudges to ward off mosquitoes, and left the cattle to graze unattended while I picked saskatoons and chokecherries. By the time the summer was over I could leap onto the barebacked mare without help and if anybody had asked I would have said that I could ride a horse very well. And of course I regarded Jude as my own and wondered and wondered how I could get to keep a horse in our back yard on Bryce Street.

My ardour for baseball cooled the day I discovered the horses. There were horses everywhere—running horses, trotting horses, and pacing horses. Like all farmers, Mr. Simpson was a trotting-horse man. He drove a pair of matched sorrels in a buggy and on the kitchen wall he had a picture of Dan Patch from a Minneapolis Stock Food calendar. But Jude was a saddle pony and I quickly opted for the running-horse barns. I spent the rest of the morning just wandering around and looking. I watched a driver adjust the dreadfully complicated pacing-horse hobbles and ogled stablemen rolling cotton batting bandages on horses' ankles. The odours of Absorbine, arnica, and Save-the-Horse mingled deliciously with that of the ammonia from the fresh manure being cleaned from the stalls. Saddles, bridles, and harness were soaped and hung up. Then, as if on signal, all activity ceased for the late morning siesta. The race track inhabitants, man and beast, retired for a nap. I watched some jockeys and stableboys playing dice on a blanket spread on the floor of an empty stall and then went home.

I could hardly wait until the next morning to get back to the track to be on hand when things were happening, like the harness horses racing the running horses around the track. I hurried off after breakfast before my mother could think of chores for me to do, or reasons why I shouldn't go back at all. But while it was well before nine when I arrived, the work was half over. The running-horse people were almost through

exercising their horses and the harness men were taking over the track. I was surprised to discover they did not race against each other. Other equally surprising discoveries came during the next couple of days.

For example, I discovered almost at once that a small boy standing around on a race track will inevitably have somebody shove a halter shank into his hands. I was watching a horseman taking a blanket off a horse he had been walking in circles in a ring between the barns.

"Here, kid," he said, "you want to cool him off?"

I waited for a translation and it came quickly.

"Come on, if you want to walk the horse till he cools out, and I'll give you a dime."

I thereupon entered upon my new career as a "hot walker". When a horse has been exercised or raced he works up a sweat that quickly reaches a foamy lather. Before he can be returned to his stall he has to be walked as slowly as possible and permitted to sip water occasionally until he has completely cooled off and dried out. Walking hots is the worst job on a race track. The horses can be held to a walk only by lacing the chain end of the halter shank through the halter and under the jaw. For the first few minutes it is a brute-strength struggle between walker and horse. Then, as the walker's arm is about to part with the shoulder, the struggle eases. By then his shoes are full of pebbles from the walking ring, his throat is parched, and he is lathered in the sweat that once covered the horse.

That was the year that running races were introduced to Winnipeg for the first time as a result of challenges which developed between the livestock commission agents at the Winnipeg and St. Paul stockyards. The commission men in both cities used horses to work the cattle from pen to pen in the stockyards and occasionally they would race each other over the neighbouring fields. A number of wagers were arranged to be settled by the running of the Stockyards Derby at the Winnipeg track. Other races of a quarter to a half mile were also arranged. Several local livery men had horses they thought could run, so in all there were forty or fifty runners on the grounds that summer. I latched onto a steady job as a hot walker and for the next several days never earned less than a dollar for my work.

Neither my mother nor father knew anything favourable about race tracks. My mother got race-horse trainers confused with horse traders, whose reputation for nefarious dealing was as wide as the prairies. She was all for forbidding me to go back when I came home with my first race-track dollar. If she had even suspected the open-air drinking, carousing, and gambling that went on, she would, to use her own expression, have "skinned me alive" for going within a mile of the place. But she didn't know and such was the burden of inflation that every penny my brother and I could earn helped put food on the table. So, reluctantly and with misgivings repeatedly expressed, they let me go back. Unfortunately my new windfall stopped when the racing season ended a few days later.

When I went back out to Simpsons' that summer I naturally tried riding the way I had seen the jockeys riding the running horses. I shortened the stirrups on the stock saddle and kicked old Jude into a canter while trying to stay in a jockey crouch. I came down on the saddle horn with such force that I abandoned that idea instantly. Then I tried riding her bareback with my knees gripping as tightly as possible high up on her withers. But my knee muscles were so hopelessly inadequate and my balance so unstable that I was clutching her mane for dear life most of the time. When I lost my hold I fell off on the road. Then I found an old back-and-belly band and rigged up a set of stirrups on it, but that didn't work very well either.

When I had a brush with serious injury the Simpsons put an end to my experiments. Their gate was located halfway down a one-mile stretch of dirt road. I decided one day that I would see how fast Jude could run the half-mile between the corner and the gate. Using my bellyband saddle I got her into a canter, and soon she was galloping full tilt down the road with me gripping my watch in one hand under the reins. I foolishly expected the mare to continue her gallop down the road because I assumed she was going too fast to make the turn at the gate. She made it anyway and I went off over her head, narrowly missing Mrs. Simpson, who was emerging from the gate. The chewing-out hurt more than the bruised nose and knees, and the next day I was sent off to help with the stooking.

The following year I began to itch for the return of the race horses as soon as the baseball season re-opened. Pari-mutuel betting was introduced to Winnipeg that year and this brought several carloads of race horses up from Minnesota early in June to await the opening of racing. The Winnipeg livery stable owners moved their runners out to River Park along with several new horses which the stockyard owners had acquired after their experience the previous year. The barns quickly took on a more colourful look. The American owners had their medicine chests, pails, and feed buckets all painted to match their racing colours. The colours also made it possible for each to identify his property instantly; getting other people's property mixed up with their own has always been a characteristic of gypsy horsemen. I fell in with the Americans and quickly got steady jobs walking horses for them and helping around the barns on Saturdays and Sundays. I had a morning paper route that year and it gave me both a chance to visit the tracks in the morning and an alibi for being late for school. I'd get up an hour earlier and complete my route by 6.30. I could bicycle out to the race track, work for a couple of hours, and be at school by 9 or 9.30. The explanation that "my papers were late" was an acceptable excuse if it didn't happen too often. In any event the end of the school year was at hand and the teachers were as tired of school as we were. Discipline relaxed noticeably after the first of June.

In addition to walking horses, I was also taught to muck out stalls, bed down horses, soap saddles and bridles, and fill the rope hayracks, all with a maximum of horseplay and practical jokes. I ran all the fool's errands any stableboy runs.

I made the rounds asking horsemen for the loan of a left-handed halter shank, being sent from one trainer to another all over the track. Then it was a three-pronged foot pick and a front leg run-down bandage. Very quickly I developed my own defences. When I was asked to fetch something I pretended not to hear until the request was repeated and I could listen for the sound of somebody snickering. But even when I caught on, I was caught out. One day one of the owners was bridling a horse for a workout when he shouted to me to get a tongue tie from the medicine chest.

"The joke is on you this time," I laughed. "You don't catch me on that one. Boy, I'd be a tongue-tied dumb-bell myself if I ever got caught on that one."

I was really delighted with myself until he walked over to the medicine chest and extracted a foot-long, inch-wide piece of cotton cloth. He proceeded to tie it around the horse's tongue and knot it under the jaw to keep the horse from getting the tongue over the bit when it was running.

I lived and learned and mostly I was obsessed with the idea of riding the horses. So I pestered the Americans at every chance to let me ride their horses for them. None of them believed I could ride until one day Ross Willmert let me take his stable pony and canter a couple of his horses around the track on the halter, with the shank reefed around the horn of the pony's saddle. Then he put a flat saddle on the pony and walked onto the track with me. He shortened the stirrups until my knees almost touched above the pommel. Then he lengthened them about halfway between jockey length and regular length.

"Now let's see you take him once around the track at a trot and then a slow canter but don't let your seat touch the saddle."

It was an ordeal. I discovered, however, that by gripping hard with my calves and pushing hard on the stirrups and using the knotted reins on the pony's neck I could keep my balance quite well. By the time I got back to where the owner was standing my legs were almost numb and I could hardly stay on. He put me on a walk-a-quarter-canter-a-quarter routine for the next hour, watching my performance casually from the rail. Next day when the work was done he asked me if I wanted to go for another ride and I jumped at the chance and of course I did much better. Mr. Willmert had a couple of horses which had gone lame racing in Minnesota and he was getting them ready to race later on in Brandon or Regina. He was a man of about forty and he asked me one day if I'd like to go around the circuit with him and learn to ride by exercising horses.

The idea of becoming a jockey had never really interested me. For one thing, I had assumed I was too tall, even though at five feet I weighed only ninety pounds. The jockeys and exercise boys on the track were a head shorter than I and resembled tall midgets more than anything else. Nor was I particularly attracted to the idea of sleeping in tack rooms or feed rooms. I was, in fact, far more taken with the horses than with the people, whose language and habits were far rougher than any I had ever encountered. I worked up what enthusiasm I could, however, and said I would try to talk my mother into letting me go.

The immediate upshot of the exercise was that the horsemen stopped calling me "skinny" and started calling me "jockey" as a joke. It was a curious fact that race-track people didn't seem to be concerned about names of anything but horses. They pencilled the names of their horses on their stalls. Some, like the owners of Phil Patch, the locally famous trotter, had printed nameplates for all their horses screwed to the doors. So names like Spizzareene, Echo, Sunny Day, Prairie, Little Miss, Jingo, Yorkroad, Olds Eight, and Stradbrooke Boy stuck in my memory from my first exposure to the race tracks. But the names of their owners disappeared quickly if I ever knew them. Mostly the grooms were known by the names of the horses they rubbed, so the horse's name became the person's name and all exercise boys and riders were called "jockey" or just plain "jock". Exercise boys were the butts of most of the jokes because physical reprisal from them was unlikely except perhaps from the drug addicts, or hopheads as they were called. And a completely green embryo apprentice like me was everybody's target.

The first day of the races I rushed out to the park after school because there would be hot horses to walk. The races were half over when I got there and after finishing with the horses I was sitting on a bale of hay resting when Willmert and a jockey named Bobby Small called me over. They had been sitting with their heads together in an animated conversation for quite a while.

"Hey, Jockey, you know where Argle Street is?"

I couldn't recall ever having heard of it. Willmert had a piece of paper on which was written: Annie's 38 Argyle Street.

"Oh," I said, "that's Argyle Street. Sure I know where it is. It's down near the C.P.R. station."

"Swell," said Willmert. "Bobby and I want to go down to this place and see a guy who wants to make some bets on our horses. Highpockets has got Dohan's car to take back but he don't know where Argle Street is. So why don't you come with us and you can go home from there?"

During the days immediately before the races the stable area was overrun with bettors in search of trainers with tips to give on possible winners. The traffic increased noticeably on the first day of the races as the owners and trainers exchanged inside information in return for $2 tickets on their choices. They were as eager to provide the tips as the gamblers were to get them. So I accepted Willmert's reason for going downtown without question, but I had a good reason for not wanting to go. My bike was in Gyp Emmertt's tack room and I would have to come all the way back out to River Park for it and I would be very late getting home.

"That's all right," Willmert said. "Here's car fare and here's a dime for a soda." He handed me a couple of dimes. It wasn't the money that convinced me; it was the automobile ride. Getting a chance to ride in a car was so rare that all the kids I knew jumped at every opportunity. We rode off in style in Dohan's Buick and I found the place for them without

difficulty. But Willmert refused to concede Argyle was pro-
nounced my way. He kept repeating aloud, "Argyle, Argle,
Argle, Argyle. Man these Canadians sure have a funny way of
saying things, huh Bobby?"

When we got there they refused to let me go just yet.

"Come on with us and you can have a bottle of pop with
us and sit for a while and then you can take off." I went.

It was a big old house on a corner lot with a verandah that
went down the front and around the side. It had obviously
been built well for an early Winnipeg first family but it had
fallen on evil days. The yard was covered with weeds, the
verandah was falling apart, and the windows downstairs were
all covered with heavy wire screens behind which the blinds
were drawn. We mounted the steps and Willmert gave the bell
a couple of twists. A small hole no bigger than a quarter was
bored in the door. The inside cover slid back and an eye
appeared.

"Yeh, who there?"

Willmert said, "Bill Calhoun sent us."

The door opened and we stepped into a huge hallway with
a wide set of stairs that rose in a half circle to the second floor.
Under the landing a door led through to what was probably a
butler's pantry or kitchen. The hall was finished in dark wood
panelling and dark burlap, like a set in a horror movie. A
single electric bulb swung from a cord that had once been
part of a chandelier. While I was inspecting the premises
introductions were being made. The woman who opened the
door spotted me.

"Oh oh," she said, "who's the kid? Whuffo yo' bringin' a
kid in heah fo'? Yo' know Ah cain't take no chances on havin'
no kid in heah, man! Ah cain't let no kid come in heah fo' god
sake . . . Go on sonny, scat, on yo' way, home to momma!"

The door-opener turned out to be a buxom Negro
woman. She was not only the first Negro I had ever seen; hers
was the first deep-southern accent I had ever heard. I stood
entranced at her voice as she stepped around to try and push
me out the door.

"Whoa, Annie, whoa," said Bobby Small. "This ain't no kid. This is Ross's new apprentice. He's going to take him around the circuit and make a jockey out of him same as me. Next year he's goin' to ride here and win you lots of money when you bet on him. He ain't no kid, Annie. He's a jockey same as me."

Annie was far from convinced, but as she looked me up and down she stopped trying to nudge me to the door and turned to lead the way down the hall.

"If he ain't a kid, wha's he doin' in short pants? If he's a jockey, why ain't he dressed like one? Tell me that. Just you tell me that."

"Because he's just beginning, that's why," Willmert replied. "Okay, so he's just a kid yet. But he ain't really just a kid either."

I was embarrassed to the soles of my feet by the argument. I wanted to run out the door and shut out the voices. But Ross Willmert was a new friend. He liked me and I liked him. He treated me like an adult and the one thing in life I wanted then was to be grown up. I had a feeling, too, that if I ran off I'd be letting him down by allowing the Negro woman to best him in the argument. Besides, it was easier to go along as a sort of passenger rather than make a decision.

The bottom floor of the old house had obviously undergone some major modifications at the hand of a very rough carpenter. A large archway that had once opened into what was probably a very large living room had been closed up and two doors now provided access, presumably to two rooms. A smaller archway on the other side was also closed in and a single door insured privacy. We went down the hall to another room that may originally have been a library, den, or sewing room. It was furnished with a round dining-room table and several nondescript hard chairs. There was one half-empty and several empty glasses on the table. Annie sat down at the glass that contained the colourless liquid. At last she seemed reconciled to my staying.

"If yo' boys is lookin' fo' some good Scotch, yo' picked a

bad day," she said. "A couple of moralities was jus' here and cleaned me outta m' Black Label. Ah'm due fo' a raid 'bout now so Ah let mah stock get down. No use loadin' up on good booze fo' them to confiscate. 'Sides, if Ah got mo' 'n a few bottles on hand they think Ah mus' be gettin' rich an' they staht gettin' greedy, iffen yo' know what Ah means. But Ah got some local gin what ain't bad, since y' see Ah'm drinkin' it mahself. But Ah got lottsa beer, iffen tha's what you'd like."

While she was talking I realized where I was for the first time. I was in a bootleg joint, a "blind pig" my mother called them, and I had to fold my arms to keep from shivering from shock. My mind reeled with premonitions of disaster. What if the police came in and found me here? Would I have to go to jail? And what kind of a fit would my mother throw if she discovered that her son had gone into a "blind pig" with a couple of race-track characters, after all I had seen of the evils of alcohol? I was torn by an almost uncontrollable impulse to flee, and by an overwhelming curiosity to see the adventure through to the end. I stayed. My companions ordered a couple of beers for themselves and a bottle of pop for me.

Annie came back with her glass recharged when she brought the beer. She drew a drape halfway across the door and visited with her customers. Every now and then she glanced at me and muttered, "Man, Ah sure hope the moralities don't come back and fin' this kid in here." After a while she stopped worrying and ignored me. I was sitting far enough away that I heard only snatches of the conversation between Willmert, Small, and the woman. When Small got up and went out through the draped door I became conscious that there was a lot of traffic in the house. Annie answered the door several times, ushered people into the other rooms, and several times there was the sound of steps going up and down stairs. The floors were devoid of carpeting so sound carried.

When Small came back Annie brought some more beer and said to Willmert, "Well, honey, you goin' upstairs or not?"

"No, I guess not tonight, Annie, but I tell you honest now

why we really came here tonight. What we really come here for tonight was to get our new jock laid."

Suddenly my mind was a mass of flashing lights. I was not only in a "blind pig", I was sitting in a brothel on the edge of Winnipeg's red-light district. A boy growing up in Winnipeg would have to be deaf, dumb, and blind not to know about what went on in its red-light district. Our sex education was well taken care of by the time we were twelve by the kids a year older. And I had been at Simpsons' when the stallion man arrived so I knew how the animal kingdom procreated. And by this time the terms "blind pig", "bootleg joint", "gin mill", and "booze joint" had become current. There was plenty of crime news in the newspapers in which both places were identified. But until that moment I had never even suspected that a whore house and a bootleg joint could be one and the same.

I began to sweat to the point that I felt faint. My face burned. I ducked my head and kept my eyes on the floor as Willmert went on. "We sure didn't fool you much, Annie," he laughed. "Sure he's a kid, but we told the truth too. If I'm going to take him around the circuit with me I want to get him started right. I don't want him to get messin' around with these tack-room floozies that come around the race track or kids running away from home. So I said to Bobby one day, what I'd give if somebody had taken me in hand when I was his age and taught me a few things it took years to find out. And Bobby says, let's get the jock started right by taking him to a real pro for starters. Then he won't spend years making a fool of himself till he learns what it's all about."

I felt betrayed. Fool's errands were one thing. But this! And still for some reason I have never been able to understand, I made no effort to flee. I stole a glance at Annie expecting her to explode with anger. Her face was wreathed in smiles.

"Oh you right! Oh my you know you right! You know lots of grown men come in here, lots of grown old men come in here an' they don't know from nothing. No suh. From nothin'. An' you know why? Because nobody never taught them nothin'. 'Cause they started out messin' round with some lil ol' school kid. An' —— is the mos' impo'tant thing in life because if it ain't none of us ain't goin' be heah."

The next few minutes of conversation were anatomically clinical. Hearing Annie use in casual conversation all the four-letter words we had learned at play, or had seen chalked on fences, shocked me beyond belief. Like most boys I had used them all, yet it had never occurred to me that the words were ever actually spoken in conversations between the sexes about sex.

Willmert, or the gin, had triggered Annie into a torrent of opinions on the subject of sex education. "It is the most impo'tant thing what is. Everybody's got to know about it; but where you go to learn to —— ?" she demanded. "It's mo' impo'tant than 'rithmetic, or spelling and such. But they got whole big schools teach you read and write. But fo' the mos' impo'tant thing in life they got nothing. Look at this po' little jockey here. How he gonna find out about life? He goin' start messin' round with some l'il girl who don't know as much as he do. And he don' know nothin'. And by the time he learns somethin' he'll have wasted half his life and spoiled it for the girls as well.

"So yo' right. This is the way it should oughtta be done. You start out with a good teacher. You learn you lesson real good and then you can pass on what you learned to the girls and you don't spoil everything fo' them either."

She went on and on and the men chipped in with recollections of their own fouled-up love-making and it was all punctuated by uproarious laughter—at my expense. I became more and more embarrassed and wished only that I had never let them talk me into coming. At last one of the men said, "Well, come on Annie, let's get on with the job we came for."

The room rocked with laughter and Annie got to her feet.

"Time fo' yo' first lesson, jockey," she said, putting her hand down the front of my shirt.

I exploded out of the chair, tore open the door, and was off down the street before even I knew what I was doing. I took the streetcar out to River Park, got my bicycle, and rode home. I never went back to the barns that summer, not even to see the horses. Once, on the last day of the races, my resolve weakened. But when I got to River Park I was waylaid at the grandstand by the sight of thousands of Winnipeggers pouring their money into the newly installed pari-mutuel wickets. Behind each wicket was a metal contraption for recording the bets and as the wagers were made the machine operations would sing out, "Five dollars to win on Little Miss," and snap a handle that registered the bet.

It became apparent to me very soon that the bettors were slow learners when it came to understanding the difference between straight, place, and show. Many who bet on horses to place or show—to finish second or third—threw away their tickets when their horse finished first, or straight. I found this out after I had idly scavenged a handful of tickets from the ground and compared them with the numbers posted on the results board. My abiding interest veered sharply from horses to money. On that historic afternoon I found and cashed more than fifty dollars' worth of winning tickets that the bettors had thrown away in their ignorance. I went home with money in every pocket and I emptied them one after the other in front of my mother's bulging eyes. I doubt if she could have been more ecstatic if I had come home with $50,000, for we were in a desperate economic downspin at the time, and the money saved our family from imminent disaster. If Willmert and Small had not tried to teach me the facts of life in a Winnipeg brothel, who knows what might have happened to us? In any event, it made it easier for me to get over my angry embarrassment, my humiliation even. The next year when the horses came back I went out to the barns to renew acquaintance with Willmert, who never mentioned the episode, though our paths crossed regularly for the next decade. By that summer my long bones had started on a rampaging growth and I edged toward six feet in height. My stillborn career as a jockey was filed and forgotten.

CHAPTER THIRTEEN

The Great Ticket Capers–
Pari-mutuel and Ice Cream

*A*lexander Pope once said that he had been betrayed into common sense when some intruder stole his pen. I have often wondered how many enterprises have been betrayed into success because some innocent asked a stupid question that none of the knowledgeable would have thought or dared to ask. A child's mind that is uncluttered by stored-away facts often goes to the heart of a situation in a way that a knowledge-mired mind can never do. Children are direct actionists, and a child's mind in action can effect the most profound changes in adult procedures. After my fifty-dollar windfall at the River Park Race Track, my brother Walter and I gave the management such fits that they were forced to bring in new regulations almost daily to circumvent us.

It took the excitement engendered by my finding and cashing the fifty dollars' worth of pari-mutuel tickets a long time to die down in our house. Never before had there been such a windfall in our family. And at the height of the inflation in 1921 there were a hundred places for the money to go. My mother decided that it would be spent mainly for winter clothes for us kids, but only after she put aside enough to buy me a new set of Automobile D hockey skates, as a special reward. When we came back to earth the next step was obviously to discover when there would be some more horse races and some more lost tickets to recover. My father made inquiries of the newspapers and found that there would be no more races until the following spring. We dropped the subject until the middle of March. From there on we watched the papers avidly for news of the opening of the races. When it was announced that there would be a race meet late in June we began making plans.

My father decided that our chances would be improved if I took my brother Walter along to help in the scavenging. The race meet, however, opened on a Thursday, a school day, and if we stayed in school all day we would miss half the races. So my father wrote notes that got us released at recess and we hopped on our bikes and pedalled like mad for River Park. My brother still went to Fort Rouge school while I was in my first and only year in high school at Kelvin. I got to the track before him and had already found and cashed two small tickets by the time he arrived. Like the bettors Walter had trouble, at twelve, understanding the difference between straight, place, and show. So he was continually running up to me waving tickets which he thought were good but which were losers. As a long-time expert I got so out of patience with him that he stopped asking me. When in doubt, he would take his tickets to the pay-off wickets and ask the cashiers if they were good or not. Late in the afternoon to his immense delight he discovered a $5 ticket that was worth $16, which was more money than I had collected for my several $2 tickets. Mostly the tickets we salvaged were $2 show ducats, worth perhaps $3 or $3.50 at the most. The bettors knew if they placed a $2 straight bet and the horse won that they won. But some thought show meant finishing second and that place meant finishing third. When they tried to cash a $2 place ticket on a horse that came in third there was an argument at the cashier's wicket. And there were arguments at some wicket after every race.

On the second day I seemed to detect a change in bettor behaviour. They began to take out their anger at losing by ripping up their tickets. There were more torn tickets than whole ones lying around. Thus we had to focus our attention on the torn ticket numbers. If we located a winning ticket we would have to paw around on the ground and find all the pieces, some of which had blown away and some of which had become mixed in with other pieces of torn-up paper. By the time I collected all the pieces and fitted them together, several other races would have been run. When I appeared at a cashier's window with a torn ticket for the second race while he was cashing tickets for the fourth, I created a lot of confusion. He didn't know whether to cash my ticket or not. There was a long conference between the cashier and the man in charge and in the end they gave me the money. An hour or so later I turned up with another torn ticket and the whole process was repeated. It was not that there was any problem from the fact that I was just a kid. The horsemen commonly sent exercise boys down to cash tickets for them. And people who came with their children often sent them to buy their tickets while they stood in line to get their money for their winning bets. But the pari-mutuel clerks were already being driven round the bend trying to explain the system to the Winnipeg populace, and Walter and I were problems they could just as well have done without. Turning up with torn tickets two or three races late not only messed up their paying-out routine, it forced them to change all the neatly balanced figures they had compiled for the early races. That night they went off and dreamed up a regulation which was codified the next day in a newly painted sign on the pari-mutuel shed. It read:

ALL TORN OR MUTILATED
TICKETS MUST BE CASHED
WITHIN 30 MINUTES AFTER
RACE IS RUN.
The Management

It was an almost fatal blow to our enterprise, for it was seldom possible to locate all the pieces of a torn-up ticket within that time limit. Only a bettor who tore his ticket by mistake, or who quickly recovered the ticket he had first thought to be worthless but which was in fact a winner, could retrieve the pieces and beat the deadline.

So we concentrated on whole tickets and precipitated another crisis that led to another change in the regulations. My brother discovered a $2 straight ticket on a long shot that had won and paid $30. He rushed up to the wicket to cash it. But instead of giving Walter the money the cashier shouted out to the supervisor, "Hey, Mr. King, this is probably the ticket you were asking about." He held the ticket aloft while Walter and I held our breath wondering what was going on. Both of us were shaking with excitement at the size of his bonanza but I became somewhat alarmed when the cashier held up the ticket.

Walter and I were alone at the wicket since the next race was about to be run. Mr. King came down the passage behind the wicket and a man who had been standing at the central information counter came into the wicket area behind us. He and Mr. King started bombarding us with questions from both sides. Where did we get the ticket? What wicket did we buy it at? We *could* have bought the ticket, but Mr. King knew where we got it—on the ground in the betting ring. After all, we had been around with enough torn-up tickets for our faces to be familiar to him. There was no point in trying to convince him we had bought the ticket. There was, moreover, no way in which we could prove that the ticket was ours. But neither could the irate bettor, who claimed he had thrown away a winning ticket, prove ownership. And how could Mr. King know for sure that this particular ticket was the one the man had lost, if he had lost one? It could have been lost by another bettor.

Whether Mr. King was more out of sorts with the bettor or with us was difficult to determine. "If you damn kids don't quit making a nuisance of yourselves, I'm going to call the cops and run you in," he threatened. "You've got no right on this race track anyway when you should be in school!" Then he turned to the bettor.

"And if you haven't got sense enough to look after a ticket on a $30 long shot you deserve to lose it. If you want my opinion, I don't think you lost it. I think you threw it away."

Walter and I just stood there and said nothing while the bettor and the supervisor argued. In the end, the supervisor said, "All right, I'm going to decide this once and for all. I'll give you each half of what the ticket is worth."

That seemed about as good a deal as we were likely to get and I was quite prepared to settle for the $15. But not Walter, who was a lot tougher than me.

"Oh no you don't," he said. "Just because this man comes up and says he has lost his ticket you are not going to give him half my ticket. That is my ticket," he said jumping up and down and pointing to the ticket in Mr. King's hand. My brother had a wild temper as a boy and sometimes it got out of control. I had a feeling that would happen soon and I put my arm around his shoulder and suggested that we should take the half that Mr. King offered.

"You keep out of this," he yelled at me. "It ain't your ticket! It's my ticket! I found it and that board up there says it is worth $30 and I want my money!"

This outburst from a half-pint twelve-year-old so took Mr. King by surprise that he just stood there looking at Walter. Here was this creepy little kid challenging him and his whole system. And my brother was right. He *had* brought the ticket to the wicket and would automatically have been paid for it if the bettor had not previously been around complaining about losing his ticket. My brother shouted, half crying, "Finders keepers, losers weepers! And how do you know this man didn't see me pick up this ticket and then rush over to you and say he lost his ticket so he could claim mine? How do you know?"

This question so outraged the disconsolate bettor that he took a slap at Walter and knocked us both into the side of the wicket. I lashed back with my elbow and from his grunt I guessed that the exchange was about even. Mr. King thought for a minute and then told the man to come down to the door into his office. He handed the ticket to the cashier and said, "Give the kid the money." What happened between Mr. King and the bettor I never discovered. But the next day there was a new sign over both the sellers' and cashiers' wickets.

POSITIVELY NO TICKETS
SOLD TO OR CASHED FOR
ANYONE UNDER 18 YEARS
OF AGE.

Our get-rich scheme was being strangled by regulations. But the races for the spring were over anyway. When the horses came back late that summer we were both back at the track scavenging tickets. The pickings thinned out considerably. We were joined in our searching by a dozen other kids and a sprinkling of adults, for the word about lost tickets had got around. By this time I had restored my relations with Ross Willmert and the people around the barns. I found several tickets which I got them to cash for me.

Again it was brother Walter who became involved in a development that added to our knowledge of the underside of human nature. He had located a torn-in-half ticket while I was back at the barns and decided to ask an adult bettor to cash it for him. Again it was for one of those lucky long shots and was worth twenty-odd dollars. He explained to the stranger that he had found the ticket, and that it could still be cashed if the stranger would take it to the information booth where they handled torn tickets. The stranger took Walter's ticket, cashed it without difficulty, pocketed the money, and refused even to listen to Walter's demand for it. I came upon the scene a few minutes later when Walter was trying to get a riot started. All I could hear was his tearful shouts, "Give me my money! You give me my money! I want my money!" All the while he was pulling at the stranger's sleeve and coat and once even made a grab for the man's pocket. The latter was trying to ignore Walter and getting nowhere, so he simply kept him at arm's length. Several other men became interested in the disturbance and my brother gasped out his story to them.

"The kid's lying," the man said. "It was my own ticket and I tore it up by mistake. He's a little thief, that's all. He is trying to steal *my* money."

The bystanders began to take sides and I saw that mostly they were siding with my brother. Eventually the man broke free of the group and headed for the exit at a running walk, with my brother following along with tears falling and his temper rising. He followed the man all the way to the streetcar, grabbing at him and trying to snatch the money out of his pocket.

When we reported the incident that night my mother was shocked almost speechless. "Well, I never!" she said. "Well, I never! If that's the kind of men you boys are with at the race track, that is the end of that! From now, no more race-tracking! No more, you hear! I'm not going to have boys of mine associating with riffraff that would steal money from a child."

My mother needed every cent we could bring home, but she didn't need it badly enough to expose her boys to "that kind of man who'd steal from a child". Neither my mother nor my father, however, ever raised any moral doubts about our scavenging operations, which at its lowest common denominator was profiting from the misfortune or stupidity of our fellow men. The fact that thrown-away tickets were involved probably clouded moral judgments all around. If I had found a watch or purse or some other tangible valuable on the race track, my parents would have insisted that an effort be made to locate the owner, that we could only keep what we found if the owner could not be found. Lost pari-mutuel tickets were somehow different.

I didn't bother trying to talk my mother out of her ban on further scavenging. The races were about over for the year anyway and what with all the new regulations the ticket-retrieving business was hardly worth the effort anymore. Anyway, it seemed that whenever we discovered an easy way of making money some kind of disaster always overtook us. That had happened in my collision with the Public Parks Board two years before, when my cousin Harvey and I cut such a swath through the cost-accounting procedures of the Winnipeg Public Parks Board that the Board was compelled to recast its method of dispensing ice cream and other toothsome goodies from its refreshment booths. No adult had spotted the flaws in the Parks Board system until a couple of twelve-year-olds came along, and it was a system that had worked to perfection for years. If we had not gone swimming at the Cornish Baths, the system might have rolled along until the Baths were eventually torn down and no one would ever have discovered its fatal flaw.

My mother never knew about that one, but if she had she would have had no problem with moral judgments. She would have regarded our activities as sneak-thievery and have been outraged by them. Yet not until it was all over did I ever regard our caper as a subject for moral judgment. We were only playing a game of wits, with money, ice cream, and candy as the prizes.

I doubt if any other Winnipeg family made more use of its parks than we did in summer. My mother loved picnics and every Sunday when the weather was fine she would pack a lunch and we would take the streetcar to Assiniboine, Kildonan, or River Park. The Winnipeg Electric Company operated open streetcars in summer that were the delight of our lives. The passengers were protected on one side by a wire mesh that ran the length of the car. The car was completely open on the other side with steps that ran its entire length. Passengers could get on and off simply by grasping a hand hold on the seats and stepping aboard. By the time that cars reached the parks there were as many passengers standing on the footboards and clinging for dear life to the sides as there were inside. The cars rocketed along at thirty miles an hour, generating a breeze that blew hats off and women's hair around. Two things always happened on these Sunday trips. Somebody would start to sing "Tipperary" and everybody would join in, with one song leading to another. And some child, sitting next to a woman in a new dress, would become

suddenly carsick and throw up in all directions, but mainly on the dress.

There was room enough in Winnipeg's huge parks to accommodate thousands. There were large playground areas equipped with sand boxes, swings, teeter-totters, and merry-go-rounds. The playgrounds were bedlam all day long as new groups arrived continually to replace those who had become exhausted or bored. There was unceasing competition—between swing riders to see who could pump their swings the highest, and between merry-go-rounders to see how fast and how long they could go before dizziness took over completely. Kids got conked and bowled over by the swings, they got flung off the merry-go-rounds and had sand thrown in their eyes. There was lots of squealing and screaming and crying, but parents never seemed overly concerned and supervision of the playgrounds was satisfactorily casual. There were also vast open areas where off-spring could be turned loose for baseball or cricket. There were not only family picnics but company picnics, church picnics, and neighbourhood picnics. To service the appetites of the civilian armies that descended on Kildonan and Assiniboine parks the Parks Board had large refreshment pavilions. To be served it was necessary for the customers first to buy tickets from a cashier's booth which were then exchanged for ice cream, soft drinks, sandwiches, etc., at the counters.

In addition to its parks, the Board also operated a number of indoor swimming pools throughout the city. We discovered the Cornish Baths on Cornish Avenue near the Maryland Bridge when we lived in the Harald Apartments, and we continued to patronize them on Saturday mornings after we moved to Fort Rouge. When my cousin Harvey came to visit us with his family his first interest was always in going to the pool. One day as I was getting out my nickel for admission to the Cornish pool my fingers picked up a ticket I had been saving from the previous Sunday when the Assiniboine Park pavilion had run out of ice cream before I could exchange a ticket I had bought for a cone. When I had gone to get my money back the cashier had been absent so I simply put the ticket away until our next visit. And this was how I discovered that the tickets used at the refreshment counters in the parks were identical with those which the woman in charge of the Cornish Baths tore off a roll and handed to us when we plunked down our nickels for admission.

That discovery would not have rocked our world except for this fact: Nobody collected the tickets at the baths. There was merely a square cardboard box into which the tickets could be dropped if the impulse moved anyone to do so. Otherwise the tickets were dropped onto the floor of the corridor or locker rooms. There were tickets everywhere, and why they bothered issuing them I never did figure out. But there they were, red and yellow tickets with Public Parks Board on the face, and a large figure 5 on the back of the red children's tickets and a 10 on the back of the yellow adult tickets.

As we undressed Harvey and I talked about our discovery.

"I wonder what would happen," I said, "if we picked up some of these old tickets that are lying around on the floor and tried to buy some ice cream with them when we go to the park tomorrow."

Instead of answering, Harvey picked up a dozen tickets and then said, "Let's try when we go on the picnic."

As we left the baths, we stopped at the cardboard ticket receptacle and picked up a couple of handfuls of tickets each from the floor. I saw the woman behind the counter watching, so I asked, "Can we have some of these old tickets to play with?"

"Take the whole boxful if you like," she replied, "it'll save me carting them down to the furnace." The carton was over half full of tickets that likely had been deposited over the past week, probably forty or fifty dollars' worth.

Boys' shirts in those days were equipped with elastic threaded around the bottoms and they ballooned somewhat over the tops of our pants. We stuffed handful after handful into our shirts until the box was half empty. At home Harvey and I sorted out our ticket collection into neat little packages of five-centers and ten-centers and ran off our brothers who wanted to play with them. Normally when we went to the parks we held off getting refreshments until very late in the day. Then if my mother could afford it, we could each have an ice cream cone. If not, there was always lots of cold lemonade which she brought with her. On our next visit Harvey and I could hardly wait for the refreshment stand to open. With a lot of inward shivering and shaking we each handed an attendant a Cornish Baths ticket and asked for an ice cream cone. They were promptly forthcoming without a second glance at the pasteboards. We polished off the cones in short order and decided to press our luck. We went back and ordered cones for our whole party, ten of them in all, and ran back to the picnic area where our parents and brothers and Harvey's sister Mabel were assembled. My mother and Harvey's mother spoke the same question at once: "Where on earth," they asked, "did you boys get the money for all that ice cream?"

Harvey thought faster than I did. "It's my treat, folks," Harvey said. "I've been saving up for my holidays and this is my treat."

Only my cousin Mabel, who was a year older than Harvey, boggled at her brother's explanation. Disbelief was written all over her face.

"There's something fishy going on, Mom," she said. "That little sneak never bought a treat for anybody in his whole life. Boy, what a tightwad!" She kept looking first at Harvey and then at me as she ate her cone and then went on, "There's got to be something fishy going on, Mom! Just you look at that Jimmie's face. Did you ever see a guiltier-looking kid than that in all your born days?"

My mother chipped in to say nobody could go by that. "That boy always looks guilty, even when he hasn't done anything," she said. "I don't understand it. Walter can do something that I know he has done. And I'll ask the boys who did it and Jimmie will look as guilty as sin and Walter will look as innocent as a lamb." It was not an explanation that I liked particularly but it got the subject away from the ice cream and Harvey's generous gesture.

Harvey and I snuck off from the other kids to discuss our treasure trove and how best we should proceed from there. We had enough tickets hidden away at home to keep us in ice cream for the rest of the summer. But affluence brought problems and we began to consider ours. To convert our tickets into ice cream we had to go either to Kildonan or Assiniboine Park. One was five miles west of where we lived and the other five miles north. As my family only went to the parks on Sundays we would be ticket rich and ice cream poor during the week. How could we get to the parks during the week? Or how could we convert our tickets into cash with which we could keep the ice cream and candy moving during the week? We went back to the pavilion and ordered ice cream sodas while we pondered the problem.

I noticed that the traffic tended to get congested around the ticket seller's cage when the people from any large outing all came in at once for refreshments.

"Hey," I said. "I know what. See all those guys and kids standing in line. Suppose I go and buy a cone and walk over to the people in the end of the line and say, 'I've got a couple of tickets left if you want them.' Then they'll buy them and not have to stand in line."

"That's a swell idea," Harvey said. "But let's both do it."

We each extracted twenty cents' worth of tickets from our pockets and sidled up to some people at the end of the line. They gladly took them at face value and we pocketed the money and left.

Our world got brighter and brighter to a point where we feared it would burst. That night we went home sated with ice cream and candy and began to concentrate our attention on how to get to the other park the following week. Harvey's family was going home to Kenton the next day but arrangements had already been made for him to stay on with us for a couple of weeks. A day or so later we discovered that several of the other kids on the street were going to a Sunday school picnic at Kildonan Park. Harvey wanted to know whether we could go along. The kids were noncommittal but Harvey rushed in anyway to tell my mother we had been invited to a Sunday school picnic and pleaded for permission to go. What mother would deny a visiting nephew permission to go to a Sunday school picnic and take her son along? Not my mother. But first we went back to the Cornish Baths and got permission from the attendant to clean out the cardboard receptacle. We did not want to run short of tickets at a Sunday school picnic.

During the balance of his visit, Harvey discovered more Sunday school picnics than there were Sunday schools. Mainly we just hopped on the streetcars and took a chance there would be big picnics of some kind in progress when we got there. Because Kildonan Park was easiest to get to, we went there most often. Most days we returned with our stomachs stuffed with ice cream and candy and our pockets full of money. Then Harvey went home and I was by myself. By that time we must have consumed ten dollars' worth of ice cream and candy apiece and I had almost fifteen dollars in cash hidden away at home.

My uncle was the C.P.R. station agent at Kenton and his

family was ever so much better off than ours. Harvey was allowed to keep any money he earned running errands. So it was second nature for him to keep the money he collected from converting the tickets into cash. But the first thought I always had about money was to take it home to my mother to help with the household expenses. From my first paper route I had earned almost two dollars a week when I was just ten. I would keep only a dime to spend and turn the rest over to my mother. Harvey and I used to take our loot out and count it now and then when nobody else was around. Harvey got a great kick out of his. But having all that money gave me such a deep feeling of guilt for holding out on my mother. One day to salve my conscience I took out my five-dollar bill, went outside for a few minutes, and then rushed in and gave it to my mother with the explanation that I had found it on the street. She gave me a hug and a kiss and I felt worse than ever because I still had more than ten dollars hidden away. But I did not feel badly enough to find it in the street too and donate it as well. Curiously enough, it was another altruistic gesture I made on the spur of the moment that brought my whole financial world crashing down around my ears.

It was a long walk from the streetcar to the refreshment booth in Kildonan Park and I stopped to watch a group of little kids playing dodge ball. There were a dozen of them in the charge of a young woman and when the game ended she began to organize them for refreshments. She wanted two of them to go to the refreshment counter for ice cream but was having trouble getting volunteers. I quickly offered to help, for here was a chance to convert perhaps a dollar's worth of tickets into cash. She started to paw around in her change purse for the money but I said I'd get it when I came back with the cones. I collared one of the small boys to come with me to help carry the stuff and was off. I walked up to the counter, gave the girl the order, and plunked down the tickets.

The girl headed off toward the ice cream containers and as she did so she called, "Mr. White! Mr. White, will you come here a minute, please."

A tall, thin man came around a partition in the rear, the girl said something to him, and he came to the counter. He smiled blandly and asked, "Are these your tickets, son?"

I nodded and he asked, "And where did you get them?"

I turned in the direction of the ticket seller's cage in the corner. The cage was there, but the cashier was out. Instead a sign hung on it which read, "Closed, please pay at counter when served".

The jig was up, but panic seized me too tightly to run.

Mr. White reached over the counter, took a firm grasp of my arm, and led me through a little gate to the back of the area. He sat me down beside an old table that also served as a desk.

"Now," he said, very gently but very firmly, "how would you like to tell me where you got the tickets."

Strangely enough, in all our conversations about the tickets Harvey and I had never given any thought to what we would say if we were asked that question. When the first tickets were accepted without hesitation it never occurred to us that any of the subsequent tenderings would be questioned. I started to tell the man that I had found the tickets, but my throat choked up and I started to cry a little. The man waited and then he said, "Look, son, nothing is likely to happen to you if you tell me the truth. The worst trouble you can get into is if you try to lie to me."

I blurted out the whole story, which he listened to with growing astonishment, and, as it turned out, a great deal of relief. He asked me my name and I told him and where I lived and all about me. While I waited he telephoned the Cornish Baths and the attendant there confirmed all the facts that I had given him. Then he sat just looking at me for a long time.

"I could turn you over to the police," he said. "And you deserve to be turned over to the police and get a good hiding because what you have been doing is stealing just as much as if you had stolen money out of our till. But I'm not going to because you've told me the truth and by coming here today you have prevented me from doing a terrible injustice to the girls who work here."

He let me sit there while he made several other telephone calls to report to various people that the Kildonan Park mystery was solved.

"It is so simple you'll never believe it," he said. "Some kids have been gathering up tickets lying around the Cornish Baths and turning them in for refreshments . . . Sure . . . They use the same tickets we do . . . No, the boy says they don't collect them. There's just a box the public throws them into as they pass through the gate . . . Well, I've got one of the boys here and he told me everything and I've confirmed his story with Cornish . . . You see now why our cash always balanced with the ticket numbers but our stock never balanced . . . No, we never checked the numbers on the tickets we took in at the counter . . . We just dropped them in a box and burned them . . . Well sure, if we had checked we'd have seen the serial numbers were different from ours . . . No, we just never thought . . . Well, it's a relief to know none of our girls were involved . . . Well, after all is said and done I don't know as how you can really blame the kids, at that . . . Sure it will happen again if you don't change the system at Cornish and Pritchard . . . Well, you could put the receptacle inside the cage where nobody could get at them . . . "

I was beginning to think he had forgotten me as each phone call led to another and each was longer than the last. At last he came back to me. He fixed me with his sternest look.

"I ought to give you the spanking of your life," he said. "When I think of how close I came to accusing an innocent girl of stealing . . . " his voice trailed off in a splutter. He got out a pencil and paper and again asked me my name and where I lived. I told him. Then he asked for my father's name, and where he worked. I told him, and I thought Mr. White would explode.

"Your father works for the city and you'd actually steal all this ice cream and candy from your father's own employer?" To a conscientious public parks employee I had clearly committed the crowning infamy. But his new-found anger had little effect. I was already too worried about what my father could do and what my mother would say to carry any more grief. Besides, if I didn't soon get to a bathroom there would be an unspeakable disaster.

"Please," I blurted out, "can I go to the bathroom?"

My request shocked him into silence, ending the tongue-lashing I was getting.

His permission came with a wave of his arm in voiceless resignation. I rushed off and when I came out of the toilet he was back on the telephone. I tiptoed out of the pavilion and went home. For a week I lived in fear that Mr. White would locate my father and tell him what I had done. If he did, and I think he did not, my father never mentioned it to me. I sneaked most of the ten dollars that was left into my mother's purse during the next weeks and spent the balance on a Martell-Hooper hockey stick, which somebody pinched on me before the season was half over.

CHAPTER FOURTEEN

———

And I Have Forgotten Your Name

O n the couple of dozen teachers I ran through in my journey through the Winnipeg schools I never had one whom I actively disliked, nor one of whom I could say I was overly fond. They encompassed the whole range of personalities, of course, from the completely permissive to martinets. We had a history teacher in Room 35½ in Kelvin school who plodded his weary way through Gibbon's *The Decline and Fall* while some of his pupils scuffled in the aisles and others slept on folded arms. And we had a teacher in Grade Eight at Alexandra school who'd hand out a hundred lines at recess if a pupil looked sideways and who felt that the twelve times table could be taught by jabbing it into the thicker skulls with the butt end of a piece of blackboard chalk.

"Eel-even times twe-lve is a hundred and thirty-two!" she would intone and keep time by jabbing with each syllable.

Of all my teachers, and there must have been a score or more of them, I can recall scarcely half a dozen. And the curious thing about them all was their lack of memorable given names. I can remember Miss Horn, Miss Yuill, Miss Lawrie, Captain Wilkinson, Mr. Florence, and Miss Flanagan. But if I ever knew any of their Christian names they are gone from my memory and none of these memory gaps have anything to do with their competence as teachers, or the age at which I encountered them.

Miss Horn was our Grade One teacher at Machray school. The year I started in her class the room we occupied was either part of a new addition or had recently been done over. As far as I can recall, Machray was the only school I ever attended in which each room was connected with the principal's office by telephone. Miss Horn was almost a dwarf in height and, as the telephone was hung on the wall at a level for a person of average height, she could barely reach the receiver and could not make herself heard unless she stood on a chair.

Miss Horn was even shorter than many of her pupils, particularly the older Ukrainian and Polish immigrant boys, who came late into the public school system at the age of eight or nine. In a room made up of boys ranging in age from six to nine, and in weight from fifty to eighty pounds, Miss Horn had a king-sized discipline problem. The older immigrant children took a long time to discover that it was against the rules to talk in school. They thought nothing of starting an out-loud conversation about some aspect of a lesson or what to do at recess. Miss Horn had a small silver-plated bell on her desk which she would ring frantically for attention. When she got it she would explain with a set speech we must have heard a hundred times that it was forbidden for pupils to discuss the lesson with each other, that pupils might only speak after raising their hands to obtain permission. The recitation of her little speech seemed an essential preliminary to whatever action she proposed to take.

Miss Horn had a very hard time with the older beginners who understood little English. When excited, she spoke so quickly that even those of us whose mother tongue was English got left behind. It never seemed to occur to her that her pupils were not understanding much she was saying. In addition, a good deal of confusion was created as pupils adjacent to the object of Miss Horn's attention rushed to interpret her words to the newcomer. It seemed to be a behavioural law of the North End that when any one child began to interpret a conversation for another all the others within earshot would join in and bedlam would ensue. Pupils with a more advanced knowledge of English were often paired off with recent arrivals to explain the lessons. For Miss Horn, this system was filled with frustration. While the room was silently proceeding with a lesson, except for the whispered interpretations, a small arm would shoot up.

"Miss Horn, Miss Horn," the arm-waver would explain, "Sophie ain't explaining it right to Annie! You said to do it this way but that ain't the way Sophie is telling Annie how to do it."

So Miss Horn would have to launch a court of inquiry in which all the pupils in the seats around joined. Once in a long while the uproar would get so out of hand that the telephone would ring. Then Miss Horn would drag her chair over to the wall telephone and climb on it and answer the phone. We naturally watched in silence.

"There now," she'd say after hanging up, "they can hear your voices clear up to the principal's office. If they hear any more voices you will all be kept in at recess and the boys will get the strap!"

The strap was applied rather liberally to our roommates at Machray school, though I cannot remember ever getting it myself. When Miss Horn lost patience and decided to send one of her recalcitrants up to the principal's office for punishment, a complicated procedure was followed. When she ordered the pupil to go to the office she was often faced with defiance. The pupil just sat and refused to budge. The next move was for Miss Horn to drag her chair over to the phone and call for help. Down would come a couple of burly eighth-graders who would descend on the culprit, extract him roughly from his seat, and drag him bodily from the room. When he returned sobbing some minutes later Miss Horn's problems with that particular pupil were solved for the next couple of weeks. Whoever applied the strap at Machray school never spared the muscle.

My memory of the teachers I had after Miss Horn is a complete blank for almost four years. From two years at Isbister school I recall only some schoolyard fights and a near disaster when I was once a fire escape monitor. Winnipeg's two- and three-storey schools were all equipped with tube-shaped fire escapes down which we spiralled on the seat of our pants when we had fire drills. The monitor's task was to precede the other pupils down the chutes on a sack to clean away the accumulated dust from the last month. The steel doors on the escapes were kept closed by friction catches and were usually locked at night and unlocked in the morning by the janitor. As the first person down the chutes, the monitors hit the bottom doors with a crash that flung them open. One day at Isbister the janitor forgot to take the lock off the door. The boy monitoring with me insisted on going first. He went slithering down the polished metal chute at a fast clip and slammed into the door, which failed to open. He sprained his ankle, bruised his wrist, and got a large bump on his head when I came whizzing down a second later and slammed into him. Our howls and banging on the wall of the structure eventually attracted attention and we were freed.

I have near perfect recall of many of the physical things that happened to me when I was ten, and of all kinds of out-of-school fun and games. But the lone memory I have of the year I spent in Grade Four at Mulvey school was the day the principal, Mr. Beckett, caught a couple of us talking in line and sent us up for the strap. I got three or four whacks on the palm of each hand, which pained enough to bring tears and stung for half the afternoon. That is the total impression that a year's attendance at the school made upon me. Only when I got to Fort Rouge school at the age of eleven did I encounter a teacher whose personality left an indelible impression.

Miss Yuill was probably well into her forties when I came within her orbit. She ran the school and taught Grades Five and Six in the east room on the second floor of this four-roomed school, and she taught with a kind of flair no other teacher had. She was a tall, homely, brown-haired woman, a good-natured disciplinarian who kept the school strap in the drawer of her desk. When any of the other teachers wanted a pupil punished they had to do the job themselves. The strapping routine at Fort Rouge school was one I never encountered anywhere else. Miss Yuill's teachers

were required to send the culprit up to her room to get the
strap and take it to the office over the stair well where the
punishment was inflicted. When the knock came at the door,
the pupil in the front seat closest to the door always answered
it. Then she'd sing out, "Russell Kelly is here for the strap,
Miss Yuill."

Miss Yuill would fix him with a mock malevolent stare and
then question him about his behaviour. The boy stood in
front of our class and whimpered through the process of
self-incrimination, a process that made him increasingly fearful of the punishment to come.

"Well, Russell," she would say at last, "I imagine that if you
were the teacher you'd agree a strapping was certainly called
for, wouldn't you?" Russell would nod his head and take the
strap into the office to await his punishment. Miss Yuill would
choke back a smile, shake her head, and get back to work.

She believed in drill, drill, and more drill, but she varied
her drills with periods of relaxation in which she put on
spelling bees and quiz contests between chosen teams. If we
were doing well, an entire afternoon might be taken up with
history, grammar, or arithmetic quiz contests. If we fell behind in our work she would cancel all the contests, which we
enjoyed immensely, until we caught up. We were required, as
memory training, to commit chunks of Shakespeare to memory along with selections of poetry from our readers and to
recite them to the class. One day one of the girls said she hated
Shakespeare because he did not rhyme and was therefore
impossible to memorize. Miss Yuill thought about that and
then picked up her book and began to read aloud from
Cassius' polemic, which she had given us to memorize.

> *"Why, man, he doth bestride the narrow world*
> *Like a Colossus, and we petty men*
> *Walk under his huge legs and peep about*
> *To find ourselves dishonourable graves.*
> *Men at some times are masters of their fates:*
> *The fault, dear Brutus, is not in our stars,*
> *But in ourselves, that we are underlings.'"*

It sounded a lot more like poetry when she read it than it did for us. "Try to put yourself in Cassius' place as you read it and memorize it," she said. "He is trying to convince one of Caesar's oldest friends to join in his assassination plot by making him feel inferior and jealous of Caesar. Once you do that it has to come out as poetry even though it does not rhyme."

Something in the girl's objection stayed with Miss Yuill, however, and some days later she announced a new project. We were to find three new verses of any kind and memorize them for a test the following week. We could make our own choice—from our readers, from the newspaper, from anything we had at home or wherever else we might find material. Rummaging around in the old boxes of books my father had brought from Rennie, I found enough material to make me the poetry-memorizing champion of Fort Rouge school. I discovered such easy-to-memorize classics as "The Rubáiyát of Omar Khayyam", Gray's "Elegy", "Horatius at the Bridge", "Invictus", "The Village Blacksmith", and "Abou Ben Adhem". I had a trick memory when it came to poetry, for I could go over a verse two or three times and lodge it permanently in my memory cells. There was only one qualification— it had to rhyme, for my brain could not absorb blank verse. For some weeks I lived for the hours at school when I'd be called upon to recite the poetry I had learned. Unhappily the invitations became fewer and fewer. Getting my classmates through their recitations was always a chore for Miss Yuill, since few of them could complete their assignment without her helpful verbal nudging. With me, her problem was in getting me stopped. It was nothing for me to rattle off half a dozen verses of "Horatius" or the "Elegy" when half that many were required. With so many pupils to test, Miss Yuill had little time for show-offs and gradually phased me completely out of the exercise. But I went on memorizing poetry until I was into high school, even occasionally trying to compose it, with horrendous results.

Miss Yuill understood boys better than any maiden lady I

ever knew. Each year in early June she'd collect all the boys around her at noon or recess and warn them about going swimming off the *Sir John A. Macdonald*, the old barge sunk near the shore of the Red River a quarter of a mile from the school. The current in the river was very dangerous, she warned, the old hulk was very slippery, and a boy who lost his footing could drown before he could be rescued. The truant officer was keeping watch on the river bank and any of us who played hookey or went swimming at noon would be severely punished. As the hot weather came she knew the water would become irresistible, yet she was determined to protect us from the lurking danger. Came the first hot day, we went swimming at noon. Ordinarily we simply lined up outside the front door when the bell rang and marched into school on signal. On this day Miss Yuill decided she wanted us in straight lines. She went down our line, pushing a boy in here and pulling another out there. Only then did we get orders to move. When we were settled in our seats she wrote two names on the blackboard, mine and Jim Hamilton's. She called us to the front of the room, handed Jim Hamilton the strap from her desk, and motioned us to stand near the door.

"Now I want all the boys who were swimming with James Gray and James Hamilton to stand up." Nobody stood. "Very well, I will give you just one more chance. Then I'll write a note to your parents and notify the truant officer, who will call on your parents. I think," she said as a clincher, "that I have all your names on this slip of paper." She held up the paper as three of our swimming companions rushed to get to their feet. We all feared the strap, and with reason, but we feared the truant officer more, and parental wrath most of all. It didn't take us too long to figure out how Miss Yuill had discovered we had been swimming. She had spotted our damp hair and fresh-washed faces as we stood in line, and her straightening of the line was just a ruse to give our clothing and skin closer scrutiny, and to look for silt in our ears and mud on our shoes. None of us went swimming again that year until school was over for the summer.

The next fall we devoted days to trying to devise a plan to con Miss Yuill into signing some false entry forms for our soccer team. There were almost enough boys in Grades Five and Six to man a junior soccer team for the school league. The difficulty was that the weight limit for juniors was eighty-five pounds and three of our best players—Bill Alsip, Jack Brockest, and Jim Hamilton—were all well over ninety pounds. Without the three we simply could not field a team. So inevitably we concluded that we would have to tamper with the scales in the school office so that they would weigh about ten pounds light. None of us, however, had the foggiest notion of how scales were adjusted to achieve that result. We decided to go down to a friendly butcher who had a shop on River Avenue near Clark Street and ask him how to adjust a scale to give short weight.

If the butcher had had a meat cleaver in his hand when we popped that question we would all have been beheaded. As it was he hit Bill Alsip with a swipe of his arm and came around the end of the corner of the counter, with mayhem in his eye and a string of abuse flowing from his lips, and chased us from the store. Clearly he thought we were putting him on and in the process implying that he was schooled in the art of adjusting scales to give short weight. Certainly we had touched a tender nerve.

"It's bad enough having every customer who comes in accusing you of short weight without a bunch of smart aleck kids . . . " We got out of earshot on the double. We pursued the matter of adjusting scales with our fathers, who explained that a pair of large adjusting nuts at the top of the scale could be turned one way to make the scale weigh heavy and the other way to make it weigh light. Miss Yuill, however, could discover it was out of balance by throwing it back to zero. We thought of inserting chips of some kind between the base and the plate on which we stood. We thought of sticking some gum behind the horizontal bar of the scale, where Miss Yuill could not see it. We went down to the "Y" and fooled around with a scale for a couple of hours. We could find no simple way of fouling it up. In the end we settled for subterfuge. We would do something to get Miss Yuill back into her classroom halfway through the weigh-in. When she was gone we could insert false weights on the roster for the three heavies and Miss Yuill was unlikely to discover the mistake. One of the first boys weighed went back into the room and dropped a bottle of ink on the floor. It provided the necessary diversion and the plan worked perfectly. Miss Yuill never caught on, and signed our roster and sent it to the School Board.

After our first two games we had visions of getting into the city championships. We beat Gladstone easily and Riverview as well. Jack Brockest's height and reach made him almost unbeatable in goal and Bill Alsip and Jim Hamilton were just too strong for the boys trying to check our forward line. We were three goals up on La Vérendrye at half-time when a couple of much older boys, brothers apparently of La Vérendrye team members, came over to where we were lying on the grass sucking lemons. They focussed on our heavy-weights and demanded, "Where do you guys get off playing for a junior team! You must weigh at least a hundred pounds," one of them said pointing to Bill. There ensued a long "yes-you-do, no-I-don't" argument and then the questioners insisted that Bill and Jim go into the school with them and weigh themselves on La Vérendrye scales. Our fellows refused. Suddenly the big boys seized Alsip by the arms and hustled him into the school while the rest of us engaged in a pushing and shoving match. We could tell the jig was up when Bill came out and with a crestfallen shrug said he was ten pounds overweight. There was then no point in denying the other two were overweight, and no point in going on with the game with three men dropped from our team. Over the weekend somebody from La Vérendrye got in touch with Miss Yuill. When we got up to leave for morning recess on Monday she ordered all members of the football team to stay in. Miss Yuill sat at her desk, her lips compressed, nervously tapping her pencil, and staring from one of us to another. For what seemed an eternity the squeals of the girls in the schoolyard drifted into the room, where the silence was deafening. We sat with eyes downcast except when we sneaked glances at Miss Yuill or at each other.

"I want the boy who filled in the false figures on the entry form to stand up," she said at last. Two boys got to their feet. Miss Yuill started to speak several times and stopped. At last she got up and left the room and went out into the schoolyard until recess was over. When she came back the boy forgers were still standing where she had left them. Normally a dozen boys left alone in the room would have been shouting and arguing the minute she left. None of us said a word. We just sat there sweating remorse and being thoroughly ashamed. When recess was over Miss Yuill wrote all our names on the board and announced to class, "These boys are forbidden to take part in any playground activity for the balance of this year. I am appointing each of the rest of you monitors to see that this order is carried out to the letter."

Miss Yuill started to say something more but changed her mind. If she had given us all a thorough strapping the effect would have been ephemeral compared with this punishment.

For the next two weeks we stood around on the school walks before school and at recess watching the other kids playing. Each time we were reminded that we were a bunch of incredibly stupid guys to think we could have gotten away with the fraudulent weights. But after two weeks Miss Yuill decided we had suffered enough, rubbed the names off the board, and commuted our sentences. In the meantime the football team completed its schedule without the overweights and never won another game, or even came close to winning. For the rest of my attendance at Fort Rouge, I seldom looked at Miss Yuill without being reminded of the attempted weight fraud, and feeling guilty all over again.

Unlike other teachers, she seldom needed tattlers to inform her of unacceptable developments in her school. She had a genius for looking over her classroom and picking out the culprits. There was, for example, the time when we thought we had played the best ever Hallowe'en trick. The furnace at the Fort Rouge school burned full-length cordwood. The wood was delivered to the school in early fall and stacked in a pile five or six feet high and fifteen or twenty feet long. Each morning the janitor would throw enough wood for the day down a chute into the boiler room in the basement. We decided to barricade the front door of the school by transferring the wood from the pile beside the school into the twelve-foot front entrance alcove. The cordwood was heavy and it took two of us to lift many of the logs. Halfway through we got tired of the project and abandoned it in favour of ringing doorbells and tick-tacking windows. The next morning we all got to school early to see Miss Yuill's reaction. She saw at a glance that the school doors couldn't be opened without moving the wood. Not being able to get into the school for the bell to call us, she mounted the corner of the step, clapped her hands, and assembled us in lines.

"Well," she said, without a trace of anger, "it's plain to see that we had some Hallowe'en elves around last night. So as we can't get into the school I guess we will all take the morning off." We let out a spontaneous cheer at the suggestion of a half-holiday, but Miss Yuill squelched us. "All of us, that is, except the elves who piled the wood in the doorway. They will stay and remove the wood and put it all back neatly on the pile." Then, with uncanny accuracy, she tolled off the names of the half-dozen of us who had been involved in the prank. She missed only one of the boys. The wood was much heavier to remove and re-stack than it had been the night before.

During my public school days there was a drastic shortage of schools, even though there were between forty and fifty pupils in almost every class. Inevitably there was a good deal of switching of pupils from school to school. Thus I was once taken out of the Grade Three class at Isbister for a couple of months and transferred to John M. King, which was a little farther west on Ellice Avenue than Isbister was to the east of our home. When I passed out of Grade Six I also passed out of Fort Rouge school. Grade Seven was taught at Gladstone school on Osborne Street and for a month or so I went there. When the enrolment at Gladstone exceeded the supply of seats I was transferred to the Alexandra school, where I completed Grades Seven and Eight. By the time I got to Kelvin High School the huge three-storey building was so overcrowded that a temporary classroom was set up in an alcove at the top of the third-floor stairs. It was Room 35½ and my year at Kelvin was spent in this room.

Our principal at Alexandra school was a sports buff first and an educator second. Captain Wilkinson regarded any boy who did not aspire to excel in every sport he played as downright girlish. Alexandra was a melting-pot school, economically. Half its pupils came from the wealthy district between Broadway and Assiniboine, the other half from the rooming houses that surrounded the T. Eaton complex. The rich kids could afford to buy regular speed-skating outfits and the Alexandra team, led by Randy Swail, regularly battled for the city speed-skating championships. Immediately after Christmas Captain Wilkinson put his skating team into practice and arranged for its members to get afternoons off to go skating at the Kennedy rink. Naturally every boy who could skate at all wanted to try out for the team. But there was no way in which those on hockey skates could keep up with the boys who had speed skates, and it was only the rich kids like Randy Swail who could afford them. So the rest of us rationalized our disappointment by choosing to regard the speed skaters as sissified teacher's pets. Captain Wilkinson also tried to revive lacrosse at Alexandra. He turned up at all the inter-school soccer matches to coach our team and fancied himself as a baseball coach as well. Anybody who demonstrated athletic ability of any kind had Captain Wilkinson on his side.

At no time did that attitude extend to Marjorie Manson, however, despite the fact that she was a better ball player than most boys. Marjorie, or Maizie as she decided she wanted to be called, was the school sex-pot. She was one of the two or three girls in Grade Seven who used lipstick. Nobody thought much of that in Miss Lawrie's room. But when we moved on to Grade Eight and Miss Henderson, flaming youth collided head-on with puritan morality and the shock waves broke over our room periodically for the rest of the year. When Maizie turned up for the first day in Grade Eight she was involved almost immediately in an uproar with Miss Henderson. After we were all in our places the teacher had us go through an exercise designed to fix our identity in her mind. In turn we were asked to stand up, give our name, say where we lived and say something about our parents and where they came from. When it was Maizie's turn she stood up and had scarcely begun when she was interrupted by Miss Henderson.

"My name is Maizie Manson, I live in the Devon Court, and my father . . . "

"Yes, and you have enough rouge and lipstick on your face to ice a cake," Miss Henderson broke in. "Before you go any farther, young lady, I want you to march right out to the toilet and wash that stuff off your face. Under no circumstance will I permit any pupil in this room to attend class rouged and lipsticked like some painted hussy! I expect the young ladies of Grade Eight to be ladylike both in deportment and in appearance."

Maizie's shocked embarrassment reddened the back of her neck and she half collapsed into her seat, obviously on the verge of tears. But Miss Henderson had up a full head of steam. She interpreted Maizie's collapse as a sit-down strike and stormed down the aisle to her seat.

"I'll have you know, young lady, when I give an order in this room I expect you to obey it. Now you just go and do what I told you."

Maizie, who had probably been through the rouge and lipstick controversy at home on many occasions, sat her ground. She listened to Miss Henderson, bit her lips, and refused to budge. Miss Henderson lost her temper, grabbed the girl by the arm, jerked her erect, and marched her out of the room and down the hall to the girls' room. She came back quivering with anger, but got the introduction routine started again. When Maizie had not come back by the time that was completed Miss Henderson went to investigate. She was a woman of perhaps fifty, almost six feet tall, string straight and rake thin. She never walked anywhere. She strode, like an army of sergeants, with her heels pounding. She always wore a blouse and a skirt which tended to work loose and twist side to front when she moved around. The unstable skirt gave her endless trouble locating the front pocket where she kept her handkerchief. This she found most provoking because she had a habit of reaching for the handkerchief when she was annoyed, and the shifted pocket nettled her further. All this we discovered as time passed. The one thing that impressed us all that first morning was Miss Henderson's super-sober mien, which told us we were in for a tough, no-nonsense year.

Eventually Maizie came back *sans* rouge and lipstick, but with her spirit unbowed. She sat a couple of rows away from me and later in the morning I heard her whisper to her girl chum who sat in the next row, "The trouble with that old scarecrow is that she's just jealous because she hasn't got a shape like I have."

Unhappily for Maizie, the whisper carried to where Miss Henderson was standing, unbeknownst to Maizie, a couple of seats behind her. The teacher slammed the book in her hand down on the desk beside her.

"What did you say, young lady?" she demanded. Then she clamped a steel-like grip on Maizie's arm and again lifted her from her seat and pushed her down to the front of the class. "Now then, young lady, perhaps you would like to repeat what you said so that the rest of the class can hear."

Maizie just stood there with her head down. Miss Henderson, however, was a very determined woman. She kept baiting the girl until Maizie at last blurted out, "I said you were an old scarecrow and you were jealous of my shape." Then she broke into tears. Miss Henderson motioned her to follow and they went off to see Captain Wilkinson. Maizie got the strap and was sent home.

It was a chastened, clean-faced Maizie who took her seat in the afternoon. From then on she gave Miss Henderson little trouble, yet she never accepted the right of the teacher to order her personal appearance. As time passed she eased into the use of make-up again. First it was a touch of rouge only. Then she added lipstick. Then a little more rouge. We all seemed to notice it except Miss Henderson until one day during a speed-adding drill. Maizie was standing running down a column of figures aloud when Miss Henderson interrupted her.

"Go to the washroom and wash your face, Marjorie!" That was all she said. This time there was no resistance. Maizie did as she was told. For the rest of the term the face-washing order was repeated every couple of weeks. Each time Maizie would begin all over and gradually build up the make-up until Miss Henderson exerted her authority. On balance over the year, Maizie earned at least a draw with the sternest disciplinarian I ever had.

Miss Henderson was a believer in direct action, while Mr. Williams, who taught forging at Kelvin school, liked to make his point indirectly. Kelvin was a technical as well as an academic high school, and two shop courses were mandatory for all the boys. There was a machine shop, and rooms with a forge and wood-turning, cabinet-making, and mechanical-drafting equipment. The forge room was a completely equipped blacksmith shop. It contained at least a half-dozen charcoal-fired forges, anvils galore, and hammers and tongs in infinite variety. On our first day in the class Mr. Williams had us assemble around a forge in the centre of the room.

"How many of you have ever seen a forge before?" he asked. A good half of us raised our hands. "All right, I want all those who raised their hands to move back a little and let those who have never seen a forge come to the front. Now I want you all to pay very close attention because what I am going to tell you in the next two minutes will be the most important lesson you learn in forging. This is a forge. The black stuff is powdered charcoal. This is a power bellows. When I turn this handle it creates a draft which causes the charcoal to glow and burst into flame. We use the heat so created to change the character of iron temporarily so that we can shape it to our needs. Now watch very carefully what I am doing. I use this tool called a tongs to pick up this piece of iron and place it into the hot part of the charcoal. Notice I did not touch the iron with my hands. That is the first rule you must learn. Never under any condition, *never, never* pick up iron with your bare hands because it can give you a very bad burn even when it looks cold to the eye."

He turned the bellows handle, whipped up the heat, and, when the iron was hot, removed it and pounded it into a different shape on the anvil as we all watched. Then he tossed the iron back onto the forge some distance from the hot coals.

"By the time you are through with forging you will know a good deal about the various types of iron we can use and you will have made several things of which you will be quite proud. But I want to emphasize one thing above all else. You *never* pick up a piece of iron with your bare hands when you can use a pair of tongs. You will get to be quite dexterous with them after a while." He picked up the piece of iron he had worked on, tossed it in the air, and caught it with the tongs.

Then he held the iron out to a boy in the front row. The

boy reacted automatically, reached out with his hand, and took the piece of iron. He let out a howl and dropped the iron to the floor. Mr. Williams grabbed his hand and held up the burned fingers.

"Now do you see what happens when you don't listen to what I have been telling you and pick up a piece of iron with your hands." The pink marks that would soon be blisters were becoming discernible. He took the boy over to a medicine chest, sloshed a gooey mixture on his hand, bound it with tape, and sent him home.

I can seldom watch steak sizzling on a charcoal barbecue without remembering Mr. Williams and the lesson of the tongs. It wasn't even my fingers that got burned, but it was a lesson none of us ever forgot.

CHAPTER FIFTEEN

Who Did Pay the Gadarene Pigman for His Swine?

There is an aphorism, possibly in Loyola somewhere, which goes something like this: "Give me a child until he is six and he will be mine forever." The reference is to the inculcation of religion, and if it has any validity as an educational principle I would assume that the reverse should also be true. That is, unless instruction began in infancy there is small chance of its taking effect. Certainly that happened in our family. If my mother and father were ever inside a church it was either before my birth or long after I left home. There was one occasion when the school board sent around a questionnaire connected with a census of some sort. Miss Yuill distributed the forms and our class spent a few minutes one morning filling them in. I left the question of religion blank and when Miss Yuill checked over the papers she noticed it and called it to my attention and assumed the non-answer was an oversight.

"I don't know what it means," I said.

"Oh come, James, of course you do. What church do you go to?"

"I don't go to any church," I replied.

"Well, I never. I wonder what your parents are thinking of. All children should go to church." Miss Yuill was scandalized. "Well, when you go home at noon ask your mother and I'll complete the form." Then as she was putting the papers away she came back to the subject. "James, religion is the gospel of creation. You must surely know the story of how God made the world, and Adam and Eve and Heaven and Hell and the salvation of man through the crucifixion of Jesus Christ. And Christmas, surely you know the Christmas story!"

I nodded that I was aware of all this, particularly about Christmas, but what this made me on the questionnaire I had not the foggiest notion. We had never received a word of religious instruction in the home, unless stern warnings about what was right and what was wrong could be included in that category. My father had a thing about telling lies and from the way he reacted when he caught us in small fibs one might have thought we had committed an indictable offence. Yet, as with most alcoholics, he was himself given to telling the most palpable untruths when on a drinking spree. In any event, we never said prayers at my mother's knee, a ritual followed by our younger cousins. When I approached my father with Miss Yuill's question he said he didn't put much stock in any religion, so to tell the teacher to take her choice or leave it blank. I gave up on him and tried my mother. But she couldn't recall whether she had gone to a Presbyterian or Methodist church in Carman when she lived with the Simpsons as a girl.

"If your teacher won't settle for nothing tell her we're Protestants and that will satisfy her, I'm sure," my father suggested in the end.

Though they never went to church, no one would ever have suspected it from my parents' conformity to the current mores. Sunday was the day when we got cleaned up, and played no games on the street or in the schoolyards. Only if we went on picnics to the parks or skating on the Kennedy rink were we allowed to enjoy physical activity of any kind. When we did go to the parks we still wore our Sunday-best clothes. Sunday was a day of rest and rest was enforced by law, by custom, and by strict parental directive. Aside from the street railway and railroad employees, policemen, and firemen, almost nobody worked on Sunday in Winnipeg.

I was going on twelve when I received my first exposure

to formal religion. Most of our chums in the Bryce Street neighbourhood went to the Augustine church Sunday school. When we moved there they invited me to go along with them. At first I demurred because school of any kind was not something I thought attractive for Sunday. But they argued that Augustine had a wonderful gymnasium in the basement where they played indoor baseball and basketball two nights a week, and in winter had a hockey team that played other church teams. My mother was all for my going to Sunday school and taking Walter along. My father was lukewarm to the project but said he didn't think there would be much harm in my going. For the next two or three years I was a participator in the life of Augustine church. I never missed a gym night, I played hockey for the church team, and I was a fairly regular Sunday school attender and sometimes went to church.

As time went on my father took a bit more than a passing interest in what I was learning at Sunday school. It seemed to me then that he had a very imperfect understanding of what Sunday school was all about because he was hipped on what we called morality.

"Well, my boy," he'd ask, "what did you learn today that is going to make a better boy out of you tomorrow?" My answer would usually be nothing much, I guessed. We were studying the story of Joseph in Egypt, or how Joshua had fought the battle of Jericho or David had defeated Goliath.

My father shrugged off these stories as being of little consequence. "Let me know when you get to studying the Ten Commandments," he said. "I'd like to see what they teach you then because everyone should have a code to live by and the Ten Commandments are as good as any, I guess. But you've got to know the why of it all. It isn't enough for me or your Sunday school teacher or God to say 'Don't lie!' or 'Don't steal!' or 'Don't kill!' It isn't wrong for you to lie because some preacher tells you God forbids you to lie; it's wrong because liars can't tell the truth. Once you start lying you can't stop and then the time must come when you absolutely need somebody to believe you and they won't believe you and that could ruin your life. Then you'll have nobody to blame but yourself." He went on and on.

Unhappily for my father, our Sunday school never got around to morality. Our teacher was very strong on miracles. We skipped through the Old Testament from one miracle to the next and went through the New Testament the same way. It was the miracle business that eventually nudged me into becoming a Sunday school drop-out. Meanwhile I enjoyed the fun and games of the gymnasium so much that I wanted to take out some insurance against my father getting so provoked at what the Sunday school was neglecting that he'd pull us out of Augustine. So from time to time I'd ask our Sunday school superintendent when we would get to study the Ten Commandments because my father thought they were important. I never really understood his answer, so I never tried to pass it along to my father.

Christians, he said, didn't really have to *study* the Ten Commandments. Christians who believed in the saving grace of Jesus Christ *knew* why the Ten Commandments were the will of God which had to be obeyed. To break the Ten Commandments was sin and the wages of sin was eternal damnation. We could avoid that penalty by accepting Jesus Christ as our saviour and the Ten Commandments as the law of God which he had ordered mankind to obey. This frightened more than enlightened because it got me to worrying about the petty thieving we had all done; and whether the penalty that would be imposed on us when God got around to us was greater than that which he would impose on the contractors who stole millions from the government and who were then in the news. But if the church lost me in the metaphysics of Christianity, I lost it among the Gadarene swine.

Our teacher, who was also our hockey and basketball coach, had completed his reading of a chapter in St. Luke that dealt with the miracles worked by Jesus on one of his journeys. He concluded with the story of the Gadarene swine—how Jesus had driven the demons out of a cave-dwelling lunatic into a herd of swine, which promptly tore over a seashore cliff and were drowned in the sea. The teacher then asked us to comment on the story. Instead of a comment I had a question and it sparked the most irreverent discussion ever held in an Augustine Sunday school.

"I wonder who paid the poor guy for his herd of pigs?" I asked. Perhaps, as a newspaper carrier whose customers often decamped without paying, I had become too money-minded. But it did seem to me that the swine man had been given a raw deal.

The teacher reacted angrily. "This is no time for jokes, Jimmie; this was one of the great journeys of mercy which Jesus took through the Holy Land, healing the sick of body and mind." But I had started something that could not be stopped. One by one the other boys chirped up with questions.

"But why didn't Jesus just heal the man with the demons like he restored the sight to other people and not kill all the pigs?" one asked.

"The Jews don't eat pork so what was the herd of swine doing in Palestine in the first place?" another wondered aloud.

"What happened to the poor guy who owned the swine? Boy, if it had been my swine I'd sure have been looking for somebody to punch," another said.

To our teacher, our questioning must have seemed doubly blasphemous, for we seemed to be sitting in judgment on the miracles of Jesus and questioning the verities of the Bible to boot. Nevertheless he took a stab at answering the last question first. The swineherd, he said, had run back to his village to spread the story of what had happened and had aroused the anger of his people against Jesus. At this point we got such a triple-barrelled discussion going that it disturbed the rest of the Sunday school. The superintendent came to our door and sternly demanded a return to decorum. When he was gone our teacher read the riot act to us. Either we were going to cut out the horseplay and bring the proper attitude toward our study of the Bible or we would have another teacher. He was a deeply committed member of the church and was almost in tears when he completed his dressing-down. I should, I suppose, have felt very contrite at having stirred up so much trouble, but I didn't. My sympathy stuck with the owner of the swine and the more I thought about it, the worse it seemed to me that he had been treated. At supper I mentioned the episode to my father.

"Do they still believe in devils and demons in the Augustine church?" was his only comment. I frankly didn't know the answer except to say that the story was in the Bible so I guess it had to be true. My father just grunted.

Our Sunday school class never did get around to morality, as I have said, and neither did any of the sermons I attended. This was more than passing strange because our society could have used some basic instruction in moral principles. The morality that existed in Winnipeg could hardly have differed much from that of generations before. Biblical injunctions against adultery to the contrary, segregated brothels existed with extra-legal sanction. Despite the expansion of the MacFarlane-Annabella streets red-light district, Winnipeg was conceded to be inadequately served with whore houses when the Minto Armouries got into operation after the outbreak of the war. So approval was given to the establishment of two king-sized bawdy houses on Thomas Street, later re-named Minto Street, to serve the needs of the Canadian troops. Here and there signs were appearing that humanity was trying to curb the worst excesses of business and commerce. But headway was slow, and it was to take an orgy of thievery and fraud in the 1920s to provide a push forward. Certainly the era of my boyhood was the age of *caveat emptor* in Winnipeg. The conditions were right for sermons on morality, and had the churches so desired they had captive audiences on which to work. The deadly Winnipeg Sunday being what it was, going to church was at least an escape from boredom, and most of the kids went to Sunday school and their parents to church.

Whatever moral principles we emerged with from our

childhood were acquired neither by religious instruction in the home nor by absorption in church. Rather they were imbedded in us, as it were, by our experiences in life in the community in which we lived. Like everybody else, we were on the receiving end of so much fraud, so many deceitful and dishonest practices, that we developed a negative sort of golden rule—don't do things to other people you wouldn't like done to yourself. We didn't like being short-changed, or being short-weighted, or being lied to as paper boys, or being falsely accused in school. As for being envious of our neighbours, it was simply a waste of time for a family as poor as we were.

In those days a prime requisite of every Winnipeg kitchen was a set of scales on which to weigh every package of groceries and meat as it came from the store. It was not uncommon, when she had bought something for cash, for my mother to return to the store with two or three items that had weighed short on her scales. And likely as not the weights would be exactly right when the grocer put them on his own scales. There simply were not enough inspectors in Winnipeg to keep all the scales honest. When my mother was getting her groceries on credit, which she did most of the time, short weight seemed to be so common that in the end she stopped checking. As she said, it was pretty difficult to confront the merchant with short weight when she hadn't yet paid for the goods. Though they were continually before the courts for short loads, the fuel dealers nevertheless persistently short-weighted. The hoariest excuse known to the courts was that somebody had stolen coal from a wagon while the driver was in a house making a delivery. In addition to short weight there was adulteration of just about everything. During the war particularly, substitution of cheap filler in bulk foods became almost universal.

The business morals of Main Street were pretty well the pre-war morals of Winnipeg, with the exception perhaps of a couple of large department stores. In order to compete with the saloons, poolrooms, and Free Admission Parlours for the money in the pockets of people arriving by train from the country, most of the other stores employed "pullers" to drag the customers in from the streets. Somebody would get the money in the shoppers' pockets by nightfall and if the merchants did not use desperate efforts it would wind up in the bars, the poolrooms, or the whore houses.

Any country family that stopped to look at something in a window was doomed. The "puller" would come out and sweet-talk them into the store, from which they might emerge with a package containing two left shoes, a suit which had an unmatching vest, or sometimes even a coat with pants that did not match. The first pair of boots I ever bought for myself turned out, when I got them home, to be two sizes too small. I had a small foot but was still growing, so when I went off with my paper money to buy the boots my mother warned me half a dozen times to "get them big enough to grow into". I took about a size six, so just to be on the safe side I got a pair of size sevens. When I got them home I discovered that I had been given a pair of inferior-quality size-four boots.

I rushed back to the store to get the mistake rectified only to discover there had been no mistake, I had never been in the store, and the store never handled the boots I claimed to have bought there. And all this from the merchant who had sold them to me barely two hours before. To add insult to injury, the pair I thought I had bought were back in the window with the price tag precisely where it had been when I had spotted them there and had them taken out and fitted to my feet. My brother Walter fell heir to my new boots, and he didn't even need a pair.

It was not only the Main Street merchants, or even the merchants generally, who functioned with an elastic code of ethics. The drug industry lived off human gullibility. Drugstore shelves were loaded from floor to ceiling with patent medicines which were infinite in variety and unalloyed in their worthlessness. New brands of patent medicines bloomed and died like the detergents and soaps a half-century later. Launched with half-page newspaper advertisements,

peppered with testimonials from housewives with every ail-
ment from back-ache to acne, they mainly contained alcohol,
flavouring, and a laxative. My mother searched endlessly for
a tonic that would help her migraine but all she ever got from
the standard directions "two tablespoons before meals and at
bedtime" was an improved appetite she never needed. Advertising was only then in its infancy and "truth in advertising"
was still two generations away.

Businessmen, however, had no monopoly on downright
thievery. Cash registers were sold on the pitch that they could
prevent employees from mixing their employer's money in
with their own. Yet as soon as one avenue of thievery was
closed another was opened, as I discovered one winter when
I got a Saturday job at Jerry Robinson's department store
during the Christmas rush. I was assistant parcel wrapper. My
job was to take the sales bill from the clerk, attach it to the
article sold, and wrap the parcel. When a rush developed at
the bargain tables the clerks might take two or three sales at
a time and dump the goods on the wrapping counter while
they rang up the sales in the cash register. Waiting for the sales
slips created a backlog of wrapping, so the clerks instructed
me to wrap the goods without waiting for them. On the last
Saturday before Christmas we were closing up when the
floor-walker came and herded us all up to the company's
office on the second floor. There were three clerks, the
regular parcel boy, and myself. To my horror the floor-walker
began his questioning with me.

"You," he said, "were told always to place the bill on the
goods before wrapping, were you not?" I nodded my head
and he went on. "Well, why were you not doing so?" I
explained that the clerks told me when I got behind in the
wrapping to forget about the bills, which they would give to
the customers.

He then turned on the clerks and accused them all of
systematic theft. He had been watching them all day. Sometimes they had sold four items and only rang in three.
Sometimes they sold two and only rang in one. He had also

seen them slip money into their pockets. The room began to explode as the floor-walker made his first accusation. The clerks shouted angry denials of pilfering.

"All right," he shouted back at them, taking his place by the door, "we'll see who's lying. Empty your pockets, all of you!" That started another argument but in the end they approached the manager's desk and did as they were told. One of them had crumpled bills in both his coat and trouser pockets. When one of them emptied only his trouser pockets, the floor-walker nudged him and told him to empty out the breast pocket of his coat as well. He had several bills and some change pushed down behind his handkerchief. The money made small piles on the manager's desk and he picked it up, counted it, scribbled a figure on each pile of bills, and put them in his desk drawer. This set off another chorus of protests from the clerks, who demanded their money back.

At this point the floor-walker noticed me and told me I could go home. I never knew what happened to the clerks, and I felt very sorry for them when I was telling the story to my mother and father. Neither had the slightest sympathy for them.

"They deserve to go to jail, if that is what will happen, and I hope this is a lesson to *you*," my mother said. "Anybody who gets caught stealing pays for it many times over. Now they'll lose their jobs and go to jail for Christmas and what will their families do then? You don't only hurt yourself when you steal, you hurt everybody around you as well."

Yet while nothing ever shook my mother's faith that honesty was the best policy, our society continually demonstrated that it honoured her precepts more in the breach than in practice. At all levels of government, corruption was a way of life in which cabinet ministers often got as rich as contractors on government jobs, and even minor civil service jobs were filled from patronage lists. My father got his menial City Hall job only through influence exerted by a couple of aldermen for whom he had done some electioneering. And it so happened that when I eventually settled into a permanent job, thievery was almost a way of life among the friends I made in the Winnipeg Grain Exchange. In addition to the physical movement of prairie wheat into export markets, the Grain Exchange then functioned as Canada's most celebrated gambling hell. Its corridors were lined with brokerage offices in which the gambling public could bet from $1 to $10,000 on the rise or fall of the grain market. Only it was not called gambling or betting. It was called purchase and sale of wheat or coarse grain futures. By putting up as little as $50 the speculators could buy 1,000 bushels of wheat "on margin". If the market went up they could sell the wheat for a profit, if it went down they could sell it at a loss. If they wanted to carry it overnight they could buy protection against total loss for $1 per 1,000 bushels in the "privilege" market after the close of the regular market. This was called buying "bids" or "offers" or "puts" or "calls". The brokerage offices which did this business were known jocularly as the "bucket shops" after the stock brokerages where the brokers ran swindles on their customers. In the grain brokerage offices, as I learned from the young friends I soon made, "bucketing" was unknown. The brokers lived very well indeed on the ¼-cent-per-bushel commission they earned each time they bought or sold grain for their customers. In an active market an option broker usually handled a minimum of 100,000 bushels a day, which would yield $250 in commissions.

The thievery took place between the order desk and the customer. In an active market there was no way for an individual customer to know which of the sales that ran through on the ticker was his. While his order was being processed, the market might have moved from $1.25 a bushel to $1.25¼. If the purchase was made for him at $1.25, the order clerk might confirm the customer's order at $1.25⅛ or even $1.25¼ if he was feeling greedy. The difference on a 5,000-bushel order would be $6.25 or $12.50 depending on the confirmation price. So in effect the order clerk was stealing that amount from the customer. To get it out required a confederate in another brokerage office to put through two "wash sales". I had half a dozen somewhat older friends among the order clerks who made more money scalping their customers than they got in salary. They proceeded at once to demonstrate the truth of one of my mother's precepts—"easy come, easy go". After the market closed they would adjourn to a St. Boniface bootlegger's and spend most of their profits on beer. Unhappily for them, when the fluctuations of the market died down, their opportunities for continued scalping disappeared, although their taste for beer and high living remained. Some of them pressed their luck in the quiet markets, got caught, and were fired. That was the end of them in the Grain Exchange, for once caught they could seldom get another job there. But they did not all get caught. Some of them used their early scalping profits to launch into business for themselves. And some, perhaps most, of the option clerks were reasonably honest and never tried to scalp their customers.

I never got into any of the categories because my job was with a vessel broker who acted as agent for Great Lakes grain boats. In our business there was no way for anybody to steal anything; so, completely removed from temptation, my growing up was a period of impeccable rectitude, despite my lack of religious instruction, fear of the wrath of God, or commitment to any of the denominational establishments. But all this was to come later, a couple of years later, after I dropped out of high school; a dropping out that was all the more wrenching because of its suddenness.

During the Augustine Sunday school period I had had my first stirrings of ambition and took a first tentative look into the future. Most of the boys in my group looked forward with some eagerness to leaving school when they passed out of Grade Eight. The doors of business and industry were wide open to boys with a Grade Eight standing who were eager to work their way to the top. Leaving school at this age by no means condemned the leavers to a lifetime of toil in a menial occupation. It often meant getting a head start in the race for promotion and pay over those who stayed longer in school. On our Augustine hockey team only one of the boys, a lawyer's son, was counting on going on to high school and college. The rest of us talked about the best trade a boy could get into. My own inclination was toward the construction industry, which had piqued my imagination when my father worked on various big projects. The other boys were more interested in the railways or jobs in stores and offices.

Instead of leaving school at the end of Grade Eight, however, I stayed on for another year. Jobs of all kinds were exceedingly scarce in 1921, since the re-establishment of the returning war veterans was still going on. The price of newspapers had risen twice since I first became a carrier so that I was earning between five and six dollars a week with my morning papers. I also had occasional Saturday jobs and grocery delivery jobs after school. I was earning almost as much going to school as I might have in steady employment, so I kept on at school.

In high school that year the teacher who taught mechanical drawing said I had a talent for drafting and should consider future employment in some branch of engineering. Perhaps, he suggested, I should think of enrolling in civil engineering when I graduated from high school. My father encouraged me in that suggestion. The engineers were not only the big bosses on all the construction projects, they earned big money into the bargain. During the second half of my year in Grade Nine I spent more time trying to understand the engineering texts I borrowed from the library than on my assigned studies. It seemed to be taken for granted that I would go on working my way through high school, which would lead to a career in engineering.

After the races were over the next summer I got a steady job delivering groceries, and I counted on going back to Kelvin in the fall. That notion was shattered on the Labour Day weekend of 1922. My father had started drinking again on paydays some time during the winter but somehow had managed to hold his job. Late in the summer, however, things reached a crisis and he was given notice that he was through at the end of August. Fearful, no doubt, of my mother's reaction, he kept the news secret until she called him for work the day after Labour Day. We were all having breakfast in preparation for returning to school when my father came into the kitchen in his night-shirt. He dropped himself into his chair, rubbed his hand across his face a couple of times, and said, "I'm not going to work. I lost my job."

It seemed to take forever for the enormity of the news to break through to my mother. She just sat and stared and stared and stared at him. Then she got up, took off her apron, and fled out the front door and down the street. My brothers left the table and ran after her, crying, "Mommy, Mommy." Instead of completing my plans for school I picked up my paper bag and went off to the grocer's to see if I could keep my summer job until I could find something better to do. It was an automatic response on my part, taken without emotion as though I had never really believed I would be going back to school. A week later I managed to get a seven-dollar-a-week job with an engraver and six weeks later got a ten-dollar-a-week job as an office boy in the Winnipeg Grain Exchange. In the days that followed, my mother spoke occasionally of my going back to school when my father again got a steady job. But when he did go back to work there was so large a financial backlog to make up that the subject was never raised, and my engineering career gradually withered away. And for me it went without a sigh of regret. The Grain Exchange in 1922 was the wildest and most exciting place in Canada in which a boy could begin his business career. The tumult and shouting in the Wheat Pit could be heard clear down to the Red River and I was soon wandering on and off the trading floor as if I had been born to the place.

The growing-up process ended a year later on my seventeenth birthday, not with my loss of innocence but with the acquisition of my first suit of "store-boughten" clothes with long pants. That was how the boys were separated from the men in those days. You became a man when you wore your first pair of long pants to your permanent job. I wore them onto the Grain Exchange trading floor that morning with an aura of red-necked self-consciousness as my boyhood disappeared behind me without a thought, a tear of regret, or a wave of good-bye.